SHEFFIELD HALLAM UNIVERSITY
LEARNING & IT SERVICES
ADSETTS CENTRE CITY CAMPUS
SHEFFIELD S1 1WB

MATHEMA +
NOTICING

D0322236

SHEFFIELD HALLAM UNIVERSITY
LEARNING CENTRE
WITHDRAWN FROM STOCK

In everyday language, *noticing* is a term used to indicate the act of observing or recognizing something, and people engage in this activity regularly as they navigate a visually complex world. Recently, however, there has been a groundswell of interest by researchers in the particular type of noticing done by teachers—how teachers pay attention to and make sense of what happens in the complexity of instructional situations. This is the first book to examine research on mathematics teacher noticing. In the midst of all that is happening in a classroom, where do mathematics teachers look, what do they see, and what sense do they make of it?

Mathematics Teacher Noticing explores issues related to teacher noticing in four main sections. The first introductory section provides an overview of the construct of noticing and how it is addressed in each of the chapters. The second section focuses on historical, theoretical, and methodological perspectives on teacher noticing. The third section focuses on studies of mathematics teacher noticing in the context of teaching and learning. The concluding section highlights the consequential nature of noticing and suggests links to other constructs integral to teaching. This groundbreaking collection represents a major advance in the study of mathematics teacher noticing and showcases a range of methodologies for further study. By collecting the work of leaders in the field of noticing in one volume, the authors present the current state of research and provide ideas for how future work could further the field.

Miriam Gamoran Sherin is an Associate Professor of Learning Sciences in the School of Education and Social Policy at Northwestern University.

Victoria R. Jacobs is an Associate Professor of Mathematics Education in the School of Teacher Education and a member of the Center for Research in Mathematics and Science Education at San Diego State University.

Randolph A. Philipp is a Professor of Mathematics Education in the School of Teacher Education and a member of the Center for Research in Mathematics and Science Education at San Diego State University.

Studies in Mathematical Thinking and Learning
Alan H. Schoenfeld, Series Editor

Artzt/Armour-Thomas/Curcio *Becoming a Reflective Mathematics Teacher: A Guide for Observation and Self-Assessment, Second Edition*

Baroody/Dowker (Eds.) *The Development of Arithmetic Concepts and Skills: Constructing Adaptive Expertise*

Boaler *Experiencing School Mathematics: Traditional and Reform Approaches to Teaching and Their Impact on Student Learning*

Carpenter/Fennema/Romberg (Eds.) *Rational Numbers: An Integration of Research*

Chazan/Callis/Lehman (Eds.) *Embracing Reason: Egalitarian Ideals and the Teaching of High School Mathematics*

Cobb/Bauersfeld (Eds.) *The Emergence of Mathematical Meaning: Interaction in Classroom Cultures*

Cohen *Teachers' Professional Development and the Elementary Mathematics Classroom: Bringing Understandings to Light*

Clements/Sarama *Learning and Teaching Early Math: The Learning Trajectories Approach*

Clements/Sarama/DiBiase (Eds.) *Engaging Young Children in Mathematics: Standards for Early Childhood Mathematics Education*

English (Ed.) *Mathematical and Analogical Reasoning of Young Learners*

English (Ed.) *Mathematical Reasoning: Analogies, Metaphors, and Images*

Fennema/Nelson (Eds.) *Mathematics Teachers in Transition*

Fennema/Romberg (Eds.) *Mathematics Classrooms That Promote Understanding*

Fernandez/Yoshida *Lesson Study: A Japanese Approach to Improving Mathematics Teaching and Learning*

Greer/Mukhopadhyay/Powell/Nelson-Barber (Eds.) *Culturally Responsive Mathematics Education*

aput/Carraher/Blanton (Eds.) *Algebra in the Early Grades*

MATHEMATICS TEACHER NOTICING

Seeing Through Teachers' Eyes

Edited by Miriam Gamoran Sherin,
Victoria R. Jacobs and Randolph A. Philipp

Routledge
Taylor & Francis Group

NEW YORK AND LONDON

First published 2011
by Routledge
270 Madison Avenue, New York, NY 10016

Simultaneously published in the UK
by Routledge
2 Park Square, Milton Park, Abingdon, Oxon OX14 4RN

Routledge is an imprint of the Taylor & Francis Group, an informa business

© 2011 Taylor & Francis

The right of the editors to be identified as the authors of the editorial material,
and of the authors for their individual chapters has been asserted by them
in accordance with sections 77 and 78 of the Copyright, Designs and Patents Act 1988.

Typeset in Bembo by Swales & Willis Ltd, Exeter, Devon
Printed and bound in the United States of America on acid-free paper by
Walsworth Publishing Company, Marceline, MO

All rights reserved. No part of this book may be reprinted or
reproduced or utilised in any form or by any electronic,
mechanical, or other means, now known or hereafter
invented, including photocopying and recording, or in any
information storage or retrieval system, without permission in
writing from the publishers.

Trademark Notice: Product or corporate names may be
trademarks or registered trademarks, and are used only for
identification and explanation without intent to infringe.

Library of Congress Cataloging in Publication Data
Mathematics teacher noticing : seeing through teachers' eyes/edited by
Miriam Gamoran Sherin, Victoria R. Jacobs, Randolph A. Philipp.
    p. cm.—(Studies in mathematical thinking and learning)
    1. Mathematics—Study and teaching (Elementary) 2. Mathematics—
Study and teaching (Middle school) I. Sherin, Miriam Gamoran.
II. Jacobs, Victoria R. III. Philipp, Randolph A.
    QA135.6.M3854 2011
    510.71—dc22
    2010042837

ISBN 13: 978–0–415–87862–3 (hbk)
ISBN 13: 978–0–415–87863–0 (pbk)
ISBN 13: 978–0–203–83271–4 (ebk)

SUSTAINABLE
FORESTRY
INITIATIVE
Certified Chain of Custody
Promoting Sustainable
Forest Management
www.sfiprogram.org
NSF-SFI-COC-C0004285
The SFI label applies to the text stock.

SHEFFIELD HALLAM UNIVERSITY
WL
510.7
MA
ADSETTS LEARNING CENTRE

372.7
MA

Tell me to what you pay attention and I will tell you who you are.
José Ortega y Gasset

Dedicated to our parents, Judith and Hillel Gamoran, Sandy Schiele, and Lottie and Walter Philipp, our first teachers, who shaped who we are by teaching us to what to attend.

CONTENTS

FIGURES

TABLES

LIST OF CONTRIBUTORS

Deborah Loewenberg Ball (dball@umich.edu) is an experienced elementary school teacher and the William H. Payne Collegiate Professor and Dean of the School of Education at the University of Michigan. She studies instructional practice and how it can be developed and measured. With her colleagues, she has developed the construct of "mathematical knowledge for teaching" and designed ways to measure it. She has authored or co-authored over 150 publications and has served on national and international commissions and panels focused on the improvement of instruction and teacher education. Ball is a member of the National Academy of Education.

Cathy Carroll (ccarroll@wested.org) is a Senior Research Associate in the Mathematics, Science, and Technology Program at WestEd, where she is involved in several mathematics education projects. She is co-Principal Investigator of the National Science Foundation-funded Researching Mathematics Leader Learning project and the Institute of Education Sciences-funded Linear Functions for Teaching Efficacy Study. She is co-author of *Learning to Lead Mathematics Professional Development* and *Making Mathematics Accessible to English Learners*. Her primary work involves designing and facilitating mathematics leadership development programs. She also designs and facilitates professional development for K–12 mathematics teachers.

Adam A. Colestock (a-colestock@northwestern.edu) is a graduate student in the Learning Sciences program in the School of Education and Social Policy at Northwestern University. He received a B.A. in Mathematics from Williams College and has worked as a middle school technology coordinator and sixth grade math teacher. As both a mathematics teacher and researcher, he is interested in understanding the work that teachers do in order to provide students with meaningful opportunities for learning mathematics. In particular, his dissertation work focuses on investigating how teachers are attending to, interpreting, and responding to students' mathematical thinking while teaching.

Rebekah Elliott (elliottr@science.oregonstate.edu) is an Assistant Professor of Mathematics Education in the College of Science at Oregon State University. She is Co-Principal Investigator of the National Science Foundation-funded Researching Mathematics Leader Learning project. Her teaching and research focus on learning to teach mathematics with students and teachers and on teacher and professional educator learning.

Frederick Erickson (ferickson@gseis.ucla.edu) is the George F. Kneller Professor of Anthropology of Education and Professor of Applied Linguistics at the University of California, Los Angeles. He has been a pioneer in the use of qualitative research methods in the study of teaching and in the development of video-based methods for the study of social interaction as a learning environment. An elected Fellow of the National Academy of Education, he is also a Fellow of the American Educational Research Association (AERA). His book *Talk and Social Theory* received an Outstanding Book Award from AERA in 2005.

Lynn T. Goldsmith (lgoldsmith@edc.org) is a Principal Research Scientist at Education Development Center, Inc. in Newton, Massachusetts. Her interest in mathematics education grew from research focusing on the development of mathematically talented students. She now investigates issues related to mathematics education from a variety of perspectives: the development of teachers' noticing, the role of the facilitator in promoting teacher learning during professional development, teachers' understanding of formative assessment practices, the relation between students' intensive study of visual arts on their mathematical reasoning, and the support curriculum materials provide for both teaching and learning.

Victoria R. Jacobs (vjacobs@mail.sdsu.edu) is an Associate Professor of Mathematics Education in the School of Teacher Education and a member of the Center for Research in Mathematics and Science Education at San Diego State University. Her research interests focus on children's mathematical thinking and how to support teachers in using children's thinking as the foundation for instructional decisions. Her professional development work embraces these same ideas and often involves long-term collaborative relationships with teachers and school districts.

Elham Kazemi (ekazemi@u.washington.edu) is an Associate Professor of Mathematics Education in the College of Education at the University of

Washington. She is Co-Principal Investigator of the National Science Foundation-funded Researching Mathematics Leader Learning project and the Spencer Foundation-funded Learning in, from, and for Teaching Practice. Her interests include designing and studying programs for prospective and practicing mathematics teachers.

Megan Kelley-Petersen (meg199@u.washington.edu) is a postdoctoral scholar in Mathematics Education in the College of Education at the University of Washington. She is a former classroom teacher and mathematics coach. Her research interests are focused on supporting teachers to develop and sustain ambitious instruction in elementary mathematics. She is a graduate research assistant for the National Science Foundation-funded Researching Mathematics Leader Learning project.

Lisa L. C. Lamb (lisa.lamb@sdsu.edu) is an Associate Professor of Mathematics Education in the School of Teacher Education and a member of the Center for Research in Mathematics and Science Education at San Diego State University. Her research interests focus on teacher inquiry and, most recently, understanding and supporting children's conceptions of integers.

Kristin Lesseig (lesseigk@onid.orst.edu) is a doctoral candidate at Oregon State University. Driven by classroom teaching experiences, her interest is in providing opportunities for both preservice and in-service teachers to develop mathematical understandings necessary for teaching. She is a graduate research assistant for the National Science Foundation-funded Researching Mathematics Leader Learning project.

Kathleen Lynch (kathleen_lynch@gse.harvard.edu) is a research assistant at the Graduate School of Education at Harvard University. She is a graduate of Harvard College and the Harvard Graduate School of Education. Prior to beginning graduate school, she taught mathematics at the middle and high school levels. Her interests include mathematics education and policy.

John Mason (j.h.mason@open.ac.uk) has taught mathematics for more than 50 years, first as tutor, then as teaching assistant, and then as lecturer. His best-known book is *Thinking Mathematically*, after 27 years appearing in a second edition. His book *Researching Your Own Practice: The Discipline of Noticing* summarizes 20 years of seeking to provide a well-founded method for teachers and people in other caring professions for moving from professional development to research, whether for themselves or for publication. He has published materials for teachers at all levels, primary through tertiary, as well as for Open University courses and for publication in academic journals.

Kevin F. Miller (kevinmil@umich.edu) is a Professor in the Departments of Psychology and Educational Studies, and the Combined Program in Education and Psychology at the University of Michigan. His research focuses on cognitive processes related to teaching and learning in classroom contexts.

Judith Mumme (jmumme@wested.org) is a Senior Project Director at WestEd. She is Principal Investigator of the Researching Mathematics Leader Learning project, funded by the National Science Foundation (NSF). She served as the Principal Investigator of several other NSF-funded projects involving mathematics professional development. She is co-author of *Learning to Lead Mathematics Professional Development* (video-based leadership materials for K–12) and *Learning and Teaching Linear Functions* (video-based professional development curriculum for middle grade teachers).

Natasha Perova (nperova@gmail.com) is a research assistant at the Graduate School of Education at Harvard University. She currently conducts research on students' learning of algebra and is also interested in science and engineering education at the high school and undergraduate levels.

Randolph A. Philipp (rphilipp@mail.sdsu.edu) is a Professor of Mathematics Education in the School of Teacher Education and a member of the Center for Research in Mathematics and Science Education at San Diego State University. His research interests include mathematics teachers' beliefs and content knowledge, studying the effects on prospective and practicing teachers of integrating mathematics content and students' mathematical thinking, mapping a trajectory for the evolution of elementary school teachers engaged in sustained professional development, and, most recently, studying students' integer sense.

Rosemary S. Russ (r-russ@northwestern.edu) is a Research Assistant Professor of Learning Sciences in the School of Education and Social Policy at Northwestern University. Her research examines K–16 science and mathematics learning evident in classrooms and clinical interviews to understand student and teacher epistemology and cognition. She studies these settings as discourse interactions and draws on methodological traditions from qualitative education research, cognitive science, and conversation analysis. She has co-authored several book chapters on student and teacher cognition, and recent articles appear in *Science Education* and *Issues in Teacher Education*. She is a 2010 National Academy of Education/Spencer Postdoctoral Fellow.

Rossella Santagata (r.santagata@uci.edu) is an Assistant Professor of Education in the Education Department at the University of California, Irvine. Her research focuses on the design and study of professional development experiences for mathematics teachers at both preservice and in-service levels. Specifically, she is interested in investigating the use of digital video and multimedia technologies to engage teachers in learning about effective practices. Recent articles summarizing her research appear in the *Journal of Teacher Education* and the *Journal of Mathematics Teacher Education*.

Bonnie P. Schappelle (bschappe@sunstroke.sdsu.edu) is a Research Associate at the Center for Research in Mathematics and Science Education at San Diego State University. Her research interests include the relationship between teachers' beliefs and content knowledge and their effects on the teachers' productive dispositions.

Deborah Schifter (dschifter@edc.org) is a Principal Research Scientist at the Educational Development Center. She has worked as an applied mathematician, has taught elementary, secondary, and college level mathematics, and, since 1985, has been a mathematics teacher educator and educational researcher. Among the books she has authored or edited, she produced with Virginia Bastable and Susan Jo Russell a professional development curriculum series for elementary and middle grade teachers called *Developing Mathematical Ideas*. The series consists of seven modules addressing themes of the base-10 structure of number, operations on whole and rational numbers, geometry, measurement, data, algebra, and functions.

Alan H. Schoenfeld (alans@berkeley.edu) is the Elizabeth and Edward Conner Professor of Education and Affiliated Professor of Mathematics at the University of California, Berkeley. He studies thinking, learning, and teaching.

Nanette Seago (nseago@wested.org) currently serves as Principal Investigator for the Learning and Teaching Geometry: Videocases for Mathematics Professional Development project (National Science Foundation, NSF) and Co-Principal Investigator for Linear Functions for Teaching: An Efficacy Study of Learning and Teaching Linear Functions (Institute of Education Sciences). Additionally, she has served as Co-Principal Investigator for three NSF projects: Turning to the Evidence: What Teachers Learn by Using Classroom Records and Artifacts in Mathematics Instruction; Developing Facilitators of Practice-Based Professional Development; and the Learning and Teaching Linear Functions: Video Cases for Mathematics Professional Development project. She is lead author of Learning and Teaching Linear Functions: Video Cases for Mathematics Professional Development, 6–10.

Bruce Sherin (bsherin@northwestern.edu) is an Associate Professor of Learning Sciences in the School of Education and Social Policy at Northwestern University. His research focuses primarily on conceptual change in science, particularly as it occurs within novel technology-based learning environments. In recent research, he is investigating the use of techniques from computational linguistics for the analysis of natural language data. In addition, he is exploring the use of novel technologies for the study of teacher cognition.

Miriam Gamoran Sherin (msherin@northwestern.edu) is an Associate Professor of Learning Sciences in the School of Education and Social Policy at Northwestern University. Her interests include mathematics teaching and learning, teacher cognition, and the role of video in supporting teacher learning. She recently served as Principal Investigator on the National Science Foundation grant Using Video to Study Teacher Learning. Recent articles appear in the *Journal of Teacher Education*, *Teaching and Teacher Education*, and the *Journal of Mathematics Teacher Education*. In April 2003, she received the Kappa Delta Pi/American Educational Research Association Division K Award for early career achievements in research on teaching and teacher education.

Jon R. Star (jon_star@harvard.edu) is the Nancy Pforzheimer Aronson Assistant Professor in Human Development and Education at the Graduate School of Education at Harvard University. He is an educational psychologist who studies children's learning of mathematics in middle and high school, particularly algebra. In addition, Star is interested in the preservice preparation of middle and secondary mathematics teachers. Prior to his graduate studies, he spent six years teaching middle and high school mathematics.

Elizabeth A. van Es (evanes@uci.edu) is an Assistant Professor in the Department of Education at the University of California, Irvine. Her research focuses on teacher thinking and learning and designs for preservice teacher education and professional development. Specifically, she investigates teacher "noticing"—what stands out to teachers when they observe and analyze teaching and how they interpret these events. She is interested in understanding how video can be used to help teachers learn to "notice" and how teachers' noticing develops over time, in their preservice teacher education program through their induction into teaching.

Foreword

Deborah Loewenberg Ball

To notice is to observe, realize, or attend to. We notice that the days are getting longer, that the color red looks terrific on a friend, or that the coffee tastes delicious. We also notice that we haven't heard from a colleague, or that someone seems a little down. Noticing is part of everyday life; it is what we do as we perceive and interpret our way through the day.

The authors of this book point out that teaching places intense demands on the noticing skills of its practitioners. Teachers, whose work it is to build connections between learners and content, to enable others to develop capability and skills, must notice a plethora of things in order to be successful. They must notice what a young person is thinking, and they must notice what is important about it. They must notice that a particular task interests a pupil and that a certain book fascinates him. They must notice when students are engaged, and when they are understanding. They must notice what makes an idea difficult and what a child already knows that offers a bridge to the difficult idea. And they must notice all of this, and more, in a fast-moving and complex environment overflowing with inputs.

Noticing is a natural part of human sense making. In our daily lives, we see and interpret based on our own orientations and goals. However, the noticing entailed by teaching is specialized to its purposes. In teaching, teachers must notice things that are central not to personal goals but to professional ones. That a small child has beautiful physical features is not relevant, but it is of interest that she has an affinity for words. Teaching does not require attentiveness to a child's food preferences, or the length of her hair, or the scent of his skin. Teaching does require skilled perception of a child's response to questions, patterns in his approach to counting a set of objects, how he forms the letter B, or the logic underlying a claim he makes. Because the noticing required in teaching is specialized, it is not a natural extension of being observant in everyday life.

In fact, noticing in teaching is not only specialized but often even unnatural. Some things that seem crucially important to the untrained observer are actually not so. Although a child fidgets with his pen, he may still be paying attention. Despite the fact that he starts his sentences over and speaks choppily, he may still be demonstrating robust reasoning. And messy writing and ragged papers do not necessarily represent sloppy thinking, nor neat papers strong understanding. Preferences and biases that inevitably shape everyday noticing are inappropriate in professional noticing. Learning to be aware of how seamlessly cultural experience infuses perception and interpretation is vital to developing the disciplined skills of noticing in teaching. Do you equate being quick with being smart or being reckless? Do you hear dialect as vibrant cultural language or as grammatically incorrect? Do you find narrative explanations ill structured or exemplary of rich exposition? Noticing is not purely neutral attention, but culturally shaped perception. Noticing skillfully in teaching requires the development of understanding and discipline to control what is otherwise a natural, but not entirely appropriate, skill.

Still more unnatural is the basic task of attending to someone else's thinking in a domain you know well. A paradox of expertise is that ideas that seem obvious are not so to the learner. Disciplinary knowledge, which teachers are responsible for helping students develop, is both an asset and a liability. Students' thinking will go unnoticed by someone who does not know the terrain (Ball & Bass, 2009). For example, when a student raises a fundamental question about a historical event based on examining a primary source, a historian will notice the insight that another might miss. But, in order to notice what learners think and know, concepts that are second nature must be felt as new and unfamiliar. Teachers must notice what a child does not say as well as what she does. For example, if a child says that plants need to be in the light, it does not mean that she understands photosynthesis. If a child explains that 1/7 means that you make a whole into seven equal parts and then "take one," the child may actually be attending to the 6/7 (after "taking one") and not the 1/7 (Philipp, Cabral, & Schappelle, 2005).

This book makes visible an aspect of the work of teaching that is often left unnoticed (Lewis, 2007). The chapters enable the reader to see noticing as a practice essential to attending to learners, to the domain for which the teacher is responsible, and to connections between learners and the domain. Each of these is itself a complex arena in which to notice. Teachers attend to and must notice important aspects of learners' thinking, experience, and resources. And they must learn to do that for many learners at one time, across significant divides of age, culture, and knowledge (Ball, 1997). Figuring out what students think, and what they mean, is complicated not only by these "gulfs" of human experience, but also by the influences of contexts as well as teachers' desires and assumptions regarding their students' learning. Teachers also have to notice the domain they are teaching, with eyes and ears trained to perceive the content both from the perspective of the expert (to know what there is to know and learn to do) and from the fresh perspective of the learner (to see the familiar as strange).

Content knowledge for teaching is a specialized form of knowing a terrain that supports the ability to take this complex bifocal view (Ball & Bass, 2003, 2009; Ball, Thames, & Phelps, 2008):

> Students in a grade 1 class were measuring their handprints as part of an exploration of the notion of area. They traced the outline of their hands on graph paper, and then counted the number of square cells contained inside the hand outline (Figure F.1).

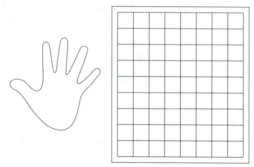

FIGURE F.1　Measuring handprints with graph paper

> One child suggested that they get the graph paper used by older pupils because the squares were much smaller and they would be able to get a closer count of the area of their handprints (Figure F.2).

FIGURE F.2　Graph paper with a smaller grid

> The teacher, who happened to have recently studied integral calculus, paused and regarded the child. She heard the comment as reflecting a surprising intuitive grasp of the fundamental idea that finer mesh affords more accurate measurement.

Ball & Bass, 2009, p. 11

In this example, the teacher notices the child's idea through the lens of the content. Without the perspective of major ideas in calculus, the pupil's suggestion might have either remained unnoticed or been valued only for generic reasons of creativity or imagination. Hearing the mathematics in a child's idea is a basic task of noticing in teaching, dependent on particular ways of knowing math, of hearing students, and dispositions to connect the two.

Noticing connections—both actual and possible—requires an in-the-moment agility that must be both imaginative and disciplined. Consider this example in which a teacher is managing a whole class discussion, geared by her finely tuned ability to notice:

> Lynne listened for the rhythm of the discussion to time her entrance into it. She used her experience with leading discussions to know when her comments would move the discussion forward rather than bringing it to a halt. . . . She noticed how each child was participating and how each child's participation fit into the larger discussion or activity. In this leaf discussion, the contributions included both actions—the students placed their leaves in groups and moved them around—and words, so that Lynne followed students' gestures as well as their vocal contributions.
>
> Schultz, 2003, p. 56

In this brief snapshot of a teacher's work, Schultz captures a tiny slice of the intensity of the practice of noticing. The teacher notices very specific things about many students, and integrates what she notices with her prior organization of the purpose of the activity—to learn to characterize and classify leaves—as she decides what to do and when to do it. Having thought carefully about the activity and its goals and noticed what there was for students to do and learn, she is enabled to attend closely to the students' thinking, using multiple sources of evidence, and to hold in mind and consider alternative moves and their timing. The rhythms of noticing and acting require not only substantial usable knowledge and skill, but also high levels of coordination.

But teacher noticing is not an unqualified virtue. Teacher noticing is not inherently good. Just as knowing mathematics in conventional, even highly accomplished, ways is not always good for the work of teaching, neither is being highly and sensitively observant. Classrooms are buzzing settings, and the surrounding environments and children's outside-of-school experiences only further fill the space in which teachers must notice. As several authors discuss, key is what to attend to and how to interpret it. What may "naturally" attract notice may be either unimportant to teaching or culturally biased. Noticing and interpreting from everyday perspectives, however finely tuned, may distract or distort teaching. Moreover, not noticing may be at times as important as noticing. When Sean, a boy in my third grade class, stretched his feet out on his desk, another teacher became preoccupied with getting him to put his feet down and thus missed both his and his classmates' discussion of an important mathematical point. Another boy, Jason, was so disorganized and messy that several of his teachers thought him academically weak and referred him for special services. Systematic "overlooking" or suspension of "natural" noticing is as important a component of the practice of teacher noticing as is the detailed ability to see and hear as a professional. Teacher noticing is appropriately discriminating and selective.

This fascinating book opens the door to the construct of teacher noticing. The contributors offer a panoply of examples and ideas that deepen and extend appreciation of the concept and our ability to notice it in action.

To identify noticing as a central practice of the essential work of teaching is a fundamental contribution to the challenge of decomposing practice for the purpose of making it learnable (Grossman et al., 2009). This book opens and unpacks this construct, tracing its foundations and scope and displaying insights garnered from studies of teacher noticing. It offers both language and frameworks for making more precise the study of teaching practice and the resources needed for its skillful enactment.

References

Ball, D. L. (1997). What do students know? Facing challenges of distance, context, and desire in trying to hear children. In B. Biddle, T. Good, & I. Goodson (Eds.), *International handbook on teachers and teaching* (Vol. II, pp. 679–718). Dordrecht, Netherlands: Kluwer Press.

Ball, D. L., & Bass, H. (2003). Toward a practice-based theory of mathematical knowledge for teaching. In B. Davis & E. Simmt (Eds.), *Proceedings of the 2002 Annual Meeting of the Canadian Mathematics Education Study Group* (pp. 3–14). Edmonton, AB: CMESG/GCEDM.

Ball, D. L., & Bass, H. (2009). With an eye on the mathematical horizon: Knowing mathematics for teaching to learners' mathematical futures. In M. Neubrand (Ed.), Beiträge zum Mathematikunterricht 2009: Vorträge auf der 43. Tagung für Didaktik der Mathematik vom 2. – 6. März 2009 in Oldenburg (Bände 1 und 2, pp. 11–29). Münster: WTM-Verlag.

Ball, D. L., Thames, M. H., & Phelps, G. (2008). Content knowledge for teaching: What makes it special? *Journal of Teacher Education, 59*(5), 389–407.

Grossman, P., Compton, C., Igra, D., Ronfeldt, M., Shahan, E., & Williamson, P. (2009). Teaching practice: A cross-professional perspective. *Teachers College Record, 111*(9).

Lewis, J. M. (2007). *Teaching as invisible work.* Unpublished doctoral dissertation, University of Michigan, Ann Arbor.

Philipp, R. A., Cabral, C., & Schappelle, B. P. (2005). *Integrating mathematics and pedagogy to illustrate children's reasoning.* Upper Saddle River, NJ: Pearson Education.

Schultz, K. (2003). *Listening: A framework for teaching across differences.* New York: Teachers College Press.

PREFACE

What is noticing and why does the field need a book addressing this construct? In everyday language, *noticing* is a term used to indicate the act of observing or recognizing something, and everyone engages in this activity regularly as they navigate a visually complex world. Recently, however, there has been a groundswell of interest by researchers in a particular type of noticing—the noticing done by professionals. Groups of individuals who hold similar goals and experiences often display similar patterns of noticing and, in fact, learning to notice in specific ways can be considered part of developing expertise in a profession. In this book, we focus on the noticing of one of these groups of professionals: mathematics teachers.

This book grew out of our belief that noticing is a critical component of mathematics teaching expertise and thus a better understanding of noticing could become a tool for improving mathematics teaching and learning. We began with a small conference held at Northwestern University in January 2008, with support from the Spencer Foundation. The conference involved presentations and video-analysis sessions designed to promote discussion of the processes through which teacher noticing occurs, its development over time, and the state of recent research on teacher noticing. Many of the participants were inspired by similar work, namely the classic studies by Goodwin (1994), Mason's (2002) captivating book on the discipline of noticing, and the research on expertise in which noticing seems to play a large role (for a summary, see National Research Council [NRC], 2000). Nonetheless, there were also substantial differences in the ways that noticing was conceptualized and studied by participants at the conference, and it was this range that we try to capture in the book.

Most of the chapter authors conceptualize noticing as attending to and making sense of particular events in classrooms or other instructional settings, but what constitutes making sense varies from author to author, with some exclusively focusing on teachers' interpretation of events while others also include consideration of teachers' instructional responses. In addition, authors vary on whether they are interested in the variety of what teachers notice or in teachers' expertise when noticing through a particular lens (e.g., students' mathematical thinking or specific mathematical ideas). Other variations in the conceptualization of noticing reflect consideration of the individual versus social nature of noticing, attention to what is not noticed (as well as what is noticed), and recognition that noticing can be a deliberate, conscious process or not.

The book also showcases a range of methodologies for studying noticing. First, the authors targeted the noticing of different groups of mathematics teachers including prospective teachers, practicing teachers (ranging from elementary to secondary levels), and leaders of teacher leaders. Second, the authors studied teachers' noticing related to a variety of instructional settings including classroom discussions, one-on-one conversations, and examination of written student work. Sometimes these instructional settings were presented on video and at other times they involved live interactions. Finally, the authors captured teachers' noticing in two main ways: by collecting video recordings of discussions or by requesting written responses to prompts.

We have organized the book into four sections: I) an introductory section that provides an overview of the construct of noticing and how it is addressed in each of the chapters; II) a section on the foundations of teacher noticing that focuses on the historical, theoretical, and methodological perspectives on teacher noticing; III) a section that focuses on studies of mathematics teacher noticing in the context of teaching and learning; and IV) a concluding section that highlights the consequential nature of noticing and suggests links to other constructs integral to teaching. Our intended audience is researchers and professional developers as well as anyone else who is interested in noticing as a theoretical construct or as a tool for improving instruction. By collecting the work on noticing in one volume, we hope to help readers understand the current state of research on noticing and to provide ideas for how future work could further the field. We note that the work on noticing already has links to several current efforts in mathematics education, including research on decomposing practice so that it can be productively discussed and practiced (see, e.g., Ball, Sleep, Boerst, & Bass, 2009), research that conceptualizes teaching as adaptive and responsive in that teachers make decisions on the basis of the ongoing nature of a lesson (National Council of Teachers of Mathematics, 2000; NRC, 2001), and research that emphasizes the promise of helping teachers learn from their own teaching (see, e.g., Hiebert, Morris, Berk, & Jansen, 2007). Thus readers are encouraged to consider not only the power of exploring noticing as its own field of study but also the benefits of conceptualizing noticing as a critical component of other research efforts.

As we have talked about noticing in different circles, we have come to realize that noticing resonates with, and even captures the imagination of, people across the spectrum, including researchers, teacher educators, teachers, and administrators. Perhaps part of the appeal of noticing lies in its simultaneous simplicity and complexity. On the one hand, everyone notices every day. On the other hand, as the chapters in this book illustrate, learning to notice productively in an instructional setting is an important teaching skill, but one that is complicated and challenging to learn. We have found the study of noticing to be fascinating and productive, and we hope that this book will similarly intrigue readers and assist them in their own efforts to improve mathematics teaching and learning.

Victoria Jacobs, Randolph Philipp, Miriam Sherin

References

Ball, D. L., Sleep, L., Boerst, T. A., & Bass, H. (2009). Combining the development of practice and the practice of development in teacher education. *The Elementary School Journal, 109*, 458–474.

Goodwin, C. (1994). Professional vision. *American Anthropologist, 96*, 606–633.

Hiebert, J., Morris, A. K., Berk, D., & Jansen, A. (2007). Preparing teachers to learn from teaching. *Journal of Teacher Education, 58*, 47–61.

Mason, J. (2002). *Researching your own practice: The discipline of noticing.* London: RoutledgeFalmer.

National Council of Teachers of Mathematics. (2000). *Principles and standards for school mathematics.* Reston, VA: Author.

National Research Council (Eds.). (2000). *How people learn: Brain, mind, experience, and school.* Washington, DC: National Academy Press.

National Research Council (Eds.). (2001). *Adding it up: Helping children learn mathematics.* Washington, DC: National Academy Press.

ACKNOWLEDGMENTS

This book was a collaborative effort that was made possible by the contributions and dedication of many. We thank the Spencer Foundation (200800110) and the National Science Foundation (ESI0455785) for their financial support of the work involved in creating this book.

The project began with a two-day conference at which attendees thoughtfully shared and discussed their ideas. This conference would not have been possible without support from the Spencer Foundation and Dean Penelope Peterson. From this conference came many of the core ideas presented in the book, and we are indebted to the authors not only for writing (and rewriting) chapters but also for substantially furthering our thinking about noticing. We especially note the role played by Alan H. Schoenfeld, who wrote the concluding chapter and serves as editor for the Studies in Mathematical Thinking and Learning series. From the beginning, Alan recognized the potential of a book on mathematics teacher noticing, and we are grateful for his valuable feedback and encouragement throughout the process. Our thanks also to Catherine Bernard, editor at Taylor & Francis, for shepherding this project and providing needed advice and support along the way, as well as to the anonymous reviewers for their thoughtful comments and suggestions. We thank those who provided editorial assistance: Georgette Enriquez of Taylor & Francis, Candace Cabral, and Katherine Linsenmeier.

We also recognize the many colleagues and friends who have supported the creation of this book and have pushed our thinking about noticing over the years. In particular, we acknowledge Hilda Borko, Tom Carpenter, Megan Franke, Adam Gamoran, Rogers Hall, Lisa Lamb, Bonnie Schappelle, Jim Stigler, and Elizabeth van Es. We offer special appreciation to Bruce Sherin for his unwavering professional and personal support and to Margaret Benedict-Philipp for her indefatigable personal support and for noticing what is most important. Finally, we thank the many teachers with whom we have worked over the years and from whom we have learned so much about teacher noticing. Only by observing and talking with them have we been able to appreciate the complexity of teacher noticing and its importance in effective mathematics teaching.

SECTION I
Introduction

1

SITUATING THE STUDY OF TEACHER NOTICING[1]

Miriam Gamoran Sherin, Victoria R. Jacobs, and Randolph A. Philipp

Theoretical constructs are the cornerstones on which the advancement of any field rests. Constructs are not valued simply in terms of whether they are right or wrong; instead, they are valued by their usefulness to the field. Occasionally a construct emerges that transforms the field by enabling researchers to reconceptualize their endeavors and to shift, sometimes in subtle ways, the focus of their attention. Such constructs may not be entirely novel. They may be consistent with previous ideas and yet bring to light new research questions and new methodological approaches. Pedagogical content knowledge is one such example. Pedagogical content knowledge appeared quite suddenly with the publication by Lee Shulman (1987) of "Knowledge and Teaching: Foundations of the New Reform." However, the core insight behind pedagogical content knowledge goes back at least 100 years (Dewey, 1902, 1904/1964). The idea that teachers might possess knowledge about teaching that is specific to subject matter cannot have been entirely foreign to researchers reading Shulman's article. Nonetheless, Shulman's introduction of this construct significantly changed the field, and, although the introduction of pedagogical content knowledge faced obstacles, the change was dramatic enough to drive decades of research on teaching and to influence the preparation of a generation of teachers.

This book is dedicated to another construct in teaching that we call *teacher noticing*. Perhaps it is an accident, or perhaps the time is just right, but, across institutions, researchers in teacher education have begun to describe their work as being about teacher noticing. Those researching teacher noticing ask what are, in some respects, primal questions of teaching: Where do teachers look, what do they see, and what sense do they make of what they see? Although these questions are relevant to teaching in any domain, this book is focused on noticing as a component of teaching expertise in mathematics.

The idea that noticing is a component of expertise is well documented. Experts in a variety of domains are able to recognize meaningful patterns in their areas of expertise (National Research Council [NRC], 2000). For example, expert chess players are better able than novice players to identify established chess moves, and radiology experts reading an x-ray call upon a combination of perceptual processing followed by extended qualitative reasoning (Lesgold et al., 1988). But the situation in teaching is arguably more complex. The chess expert is faced with a static display of arrangements of a small number of pieces, which are always the same; a radiologist looks at what is essentially a picture. A teacher, in contrast, faces a much more varied and amorphous set of phenomena that are constantly in motion, and hence the processes of teacher noticing must, in some respects, be more complex.

We believe that the importance of noticing, as a theoretical construct for understanding teaching, extends well beyond any brief definition that we might give of this construct. Consider, again, pedagogical content knowledge. The introduction of this construct moved the field forward not solely because of the notion of pedagogical content knowledge itself—that teachers possess subject-specific pedagogical knowledge. Just as importantly, pedagogical content knowledge brought with it a particular stance toward teaching and toward what teaching involves, and it drew our attention to distinctions that heretofore did not exist.

The same is true, we believe, of teacher noticing. A focus on teacher noticing is associated with a particular stance toward teaching, and it is a stance that draws our attention to phenomena that have received relatively little attention. At the heart of this stance is an image of the teacher-in-action as a teacher in a maelstrom, confronted with a "blooming, buzzing confusion of sensory data" (B. Sherin & Star, this volume, chapter 5). Embracing this stance toward teaching opens the door to new research paradigms and methodologies, and, though it is too early to determine how influential teacher noticing will be, we think that the groundswell of interest raises the possibility that teacher noticing may emerge as another transformative idea in teacher education.

This image of teacher noticing is, of course, not completely novel. In fact, Walter Doyle, writing in 1977, asserted that the "most salient features of the classroom" for teachers are its "(a) multidimensionality; (b) simultaneity; and (c) unpredictability" (p. 52). Given the prevalence of new technologies today, including inexpensive and ubiquitous digital video that can capture teachers in action, conducting a program of research that is dedicated to understanding how teachers negotiate these "most salient" features of teaching now seems particularly feasible.

What Is Teacher Noticing?

We recognize that the term *noticing* is used in everyday language to refer to general observations that one makes. Here we use the phrase *teacher noticing* to encompass the processes through which teachers manage the "blooming, buzzing confusion of sensory data" with which they are faced, that is, the ongoing information with which they are presented during instruction. Note that, in describing teacher noticing in this way, we intend to imply that teacher noticing is not at all a passive process. Teachers do not merely sit back and try to make sense of what is going on in a classroom or other instructional setting. Instead, teachers are actors in the instructional scene that they are observing.

Across the chapters in this book, the authors adopt somewhat diverse conceptualizations of noticing. In general, however, the authors discuss teacher noticing as involving two main processes (or a subset of those processes):

- *Attending to particular events in an instructional setting.* To manage the complexity of the classroom, teachers must pay attention to some things and not to others. In other words, they must choose where to focus their attention and for how long and where their attention is *not* needed and, again, for how long. Some chapter authors focus on the range of things to which teachers do (and do not) attend whereas others focus on whether teachers attend to particular things of interest (e.g., students' mathematical thinking).
- *Making sense of events in an instructional setting.* For those features to which teachers do attend, they are not simply passive observers. Instead teachers necessarily interpret what they see, relating observed events to abstract categories and characterizing what they see in terms of familiar instructional episodes. The chapter authors offer different conceptualizations of what this reasoning encompasses and, in particular, whether it includes consideration of teachers' instructional responses.

These two aspects of noticing are interrelated and cyclical. Teachers select and ignore on the basis of their sense making; the way they respond shapes subsequent instructional events, resulting in a new and varied set of experiences from which teachers attend and make sense.

To be clear, we do not see teacher noticing as something that can be grafted onto existing accounts of teaching, at least not in any simple manner. For example, it is not helpful to think of teacher noticing as simply another category of teacher knowledge. To some extent, this should be obvious just from the name. The word *noticing* names a process rather than a static category of knowledge. And this word choice points to what we believe is a real, consequential difference: The focus is on how, at a fine-grained level, the teacher interacts with the classroom world rather than solely on a teacher's reasoning.

Linking Teacher Noticing to Current Efforts in Mathematics Education

Thus far, we have emphasized the importance of studying teacher noticing because it is at the heart of managing the "most salient features of teaching" (Doyle, 1977,

p. 52). At the same time, however, we believe that recent interest in teacher noticing derives, in some measure, from the current zeitgeist in mathematics education and what the field currently takes to be important.

Here we highlight three areas of mathematics education research that support the idea that teacher noticing is likely to be an important and productive focus:

- *Adaptive and responsive teaching.* In contrast to a traditional style of instruction in which the structure of a mathematics lesson is determined by the teacher prior to instruction, reform recommendations promote mathematics teaching that is adaptive and responsive, so that teachers make decisions on the basis of the ongoing nature of a lesson (National Council of Teachers of Mathematics, 2000; NRC, 2001). In particular, teachers are expected to attend closely to the ideas that students raise in class and to how these ideas relate to the mathematical objectives of the ongoing lesson. This style of teaching is, by its very nature, heavily informed by teachers' noticing in the moment of instruction—what teachers see as the essential components of the unfolding lesson and the sense teachers make of those features. Thus, in this volume, authors explore one of the critical skills needed for the type of teaching envisioned in the reform movement.

- *Learning from teaching.* A promising approach to supporting the growth of prospective and practicing mathematics teachers is to help them learn from their own teaching (see, e.g., Franke, Carpenter, Fennema, Ansell, & Behrend, 1998; Hiebert, Morris, Berk, & Jansen, 2007). We believe that teacher noticing plays a central role in making teaching generative because the principles that a teacher extracts from an experience of teaching depend intimately on how the teacher perceives those events and what meaning the teacher attaches to them. For example, many of the chapters in this volume are focused on teachers' noticing of students' mathematical thinking, and research has shown that, when teachers learn how to learn from the thinking of students in their classrooms, teachers can continue learning throughout their careers (Franke, Carpenter, Levi, & Fennema, 2001). Thus, students' mathematical thinking can provide a coherent and constant source of professional development for teachers, but only if they learn to productively notice students' thinking in their classrooms.

- *Decomposing practice.* A movement gaining voice among mathematics educators calls for decomposing teaching into core activities that can be productively discussed and practiced (Ball & Cohen, 1999; Ball, Sleep, Boerst, & Bass, 2009; Grossman & McDonald, 2008; Lampert, 2001; Lampert, Beasley, Ghousseini, Kazemi, & Franke, 2010). The idea is that, by decomposing the complexity of mathematics teaching into specific activities, we can more feasibly and directly address key practices and develop a common language for discussing these practices. This volume contributes to these efforts by decomposing mathematics teaching in a way that makes it accessible while simultaneously preserving its interactive nature. In particular, we provide multiple examples of how a focus on mathematics teacher noticing—on teachers' seeing and sense making—can provide language for describing teaching, enhance our understanding of the complexity of teaching, and promote the development of teaching expertise.

An Overview of the Book

The chapters in this book represent a variety of perspectives and programs of research on mathematics teacher noticing. We have organized these perspectives into two broad sections preceded by this introductory section and followed by a concluding section.

Foundations of Teacher Noticing

Section II is an exploration of historical, theoretical, and methodological perspectives on teacher noticing. As a collection, the five chapters in the section situate current research on mathematics teacher noticing within prior studies of teaching as well as within studies of noticing outside of teaching. The chapters also highlight key characteristics of teacher noticing and features of past and present studies of teacher noticing. In chapter 2, Erickson offers a historical account of research on teacher noticing. He describes a program of research on teacher noticing that began in the early 1980s and draws connections between studies of teacher thinking and teacher noticing. On the basis of extensive observations of teachers, Erickson proposes that teacher noticing is an active process that draws heavily on a teacher's prior experiences and is opportunistic in that teachers notice in order to take action. In chapter 3, Mason discusses roots of attention to noticing and uses his own experience as the context through which to explore the development of attention to noticing. Mason writes about the *discipline of noticing* and emphasizes the need to train oneself to "notice in-the-moment," that is, to be able to act with fresh intent rather than simply out of habit.

Miller, the author of chapter 4, considers how research in domains other than teaching can inform research on teacher noticing. In particular, he characterizes *situation awareness*, the sort of "skilled viewing" that is required of experts in complex domains such as sports and aviation, and emphasizes that expert noticing is distinguished not only by that to which experts attend but also by that to which they choose not to attend.

The authors of chapter 5, B. Sherin and Star, review a number of ways that researchers typically study teacher noticing. They assert that different approaches to this task do not represent solely methodological differences but instead reflect different conceptions of teacher noticing on the part of researchers. B. Sherin and Star recommend that researchers attend closely to these different conceptions as research on teacher noticing moves forward.

In the final chapter of the section, chapter 6, M. Sherin, Russ, and Colestock explore methodological issues in the study of teacher noticing. They highlight the difficulty in accessing teachers' in-the-moment noticing and describe how new technology in the form of teacher-wearable cameras may help to mediate this challenge.

Studies of Mathematics Teacher Noticing

Section III presents studies of mathematics teacher noticing in the context of teaching and learning. Across the seven chapters in the section, the noticing of both prospective and practicing teachers is explored. In addition, teacher noticing is investigated as it takes place during instruction and in professional development. A theme running through most chapters in the section concerns the *development* of teacher noticing—how noticing expertise changes over the course of a particular intervention with teachers or over the career paths of teachers.

In chapter 7, Jacobs, Lamb, Philipp, and Schappelle investigate a specialized type of mathematics teacher noticing, *professional noticing of children's mathematical thinking*. The authors use a cross-sectional design to study the development of this expertise among prospective teachers and practicing teachers who have been engaged in sustained professional development for different amounts of time.

The chapter 8 authors, Star, Lynch, and Perova, explore the noticing of prospective secondary mathematics teachers before and after a semester-long methods course designed to improve observational skills. Using video, the authors examine participants' abilities to notice features related to classroom environment, management, tasks, communication, and mathematical content.

The next three chapters (9, 10, and 11) share a focus on mathematics teacher noticing in the context of professional development work with practicing teachers.

In chapter 9, van Es presents a framework for studying the development of elementary school teachers' noticing of children's mathematical thinking. Drawing upon her framework, the author presents a developmental trajectory from basic to specialized noticing.

The author of chapter 10, Santagata, describes an approach for supporting the noticing of middle school mathematics teachers by promoting in-depth analyses of classroom lessons. Specifically, Santagata describes the testing and revision of an observational framework for teachers' reflection on lesson learning goals, the extent to which learning goals are achieved, and alternative instructional strategies.

In chapter 11, Goldsmith and Seago explore the development of teacher noticing when middle and high school teachers participate in professional development centered on written and video-based records of practice. The authors discuss shifts in three area of teachers' noticing: teachers' use of evidence, attention to students' thinking, and attention to mathematical content.

The authors of chapter 12, Kazemi, Elliott, Mumme, Carroll, Lesseig, and Kelley-Petersen, take a different approach to the study of noticing in professional development. Rather than explore a setting of teacher professional development, they examine professional development for leaders of teachers. Specifically, they reflect on their own noticing while they worked with leaders, helping the leaders learn to more effectively facilitate teachers' engagement with mathematical tasks in teacher professional development. Thus chapter 12 is a report on the noticing of "leaders of leaders."

In contrast to the previous focus on noticing in the context of professional development, the focus in chapter 13 by Schifter is on the noticing of an elementary school teacher as it is revealed during instruction—what the teacher *hears* in her students' questions and how the teacher recognizes the significance of their comments and the opportunities these comments afford the class. This study takes place in the context of instruction designed to support early algebraic reasoning for elementary school students.

Conclusion

To conclude the volume, Alan H. Schoenfeld argues for the consequential nature of teachers' noticing. He also discusses the need for further study of the connections between teachers' noticing and teachers' knowledge, goals, and orientations.

Variations in the Study of Teacher Noticing Across the Chapters

Earlier in this introduction, we explained that the authors in this volume draw on somewhat diverse conceptualizations of noticing. Although some authors (e.g., M. Sherin et al., chapter 6; Star et al., chapter 8) define noticing solely as that to which teachers attend, most authors consider noticing to involve two main processes (*attending* to particular events in an instructional setting and *making sense* of those events). However, authors differ on their conceptions of *making sense*. Specifically, some conceptualize making sense only as *interpreting* (e.g., van Es, chapter 9; Goldsmith & Seago, chapter 11) whereas others conceptualize making sense as both *interpreting* and *deciding how to respond* (e.g., Jacobs et al., chapter 7; Kazemi et al., chapter 12). Similarly, Erickson (chapter 2) notes that teachers generally notice instrumentally, that is, in order to take action in their teaching.

Another variation in how authors conceptualize noticing concerns whether they narrow their focus to a particular aspect of noticing, for example, noticing of students' mathematical thinking (e.g., Jacobs et al., chapter 7; van Es, chapter 9) or of particular mathematical content (e.g., Schifter, chapter 13). This contrasts with the approach of other authors, who explore, more broadly, the range of events that teachers notice (e.g., M. Sherin et al., chapter 6; Star et al., chapter 8).

These variations in how noticing is conceptualized also have methodological implications. Indeed, there is quite a bit of variability in the methods employed in the research reported in this volume. For example, some authors choose to study individual teachers' noticing whereas others look at groups of teachers. Variations also occur among the media used to assess teachers' noticing, including written student work, video clips of instruction, and teachers' live classrooms. Among those who use video, researchers differ on how the video was selected (from the teachers' classrooms or from unknown classrooms), the length of video (entire class lessons or short clips), and whether or not the clips were edited. Researchers also vary in how they capture teachers' noticing, some by examining teachers' discussions and others by analyzing teachers' written responses to prompts. One innovative approach involved attaching cameras to teachers' foreheads in order to capture that to which teachers attend while they teach (M. Sherin et al., chapter 6).

Clearly, each of these different methodological approaches may be more or less consistent with a particular conception of noticing (see B. Sherin & Star, chapter 5, for further discussion of this issue). For example, Jacobs and colleagues (chapter 7) maintain that, because teachers are constantly making decisions, they need to attend to and interpret students' ideas in the service of deciding how to respond to those ideas. Thus, in studying "professional noticing of children's mathematical thinking," their data necessarily includes both teachers' descriptions of children's ideas and the reasoning teachers use when deciding how to respond to children. Star and colleagues (chapter 8), on the other hand, suggest that, before prospective teachers can make sense of classroom features, they must first learn to attend to pertinent features. Their data collection reflects this conceptualization of noticing, and therefore focuses exclusively on what teachers attend to.

Although we believe that the state of research on teacher noticing is too young to benefit from a single definition or methodological approach, we suggest that researchers will move the field forward by clarifying the conceptualizations they are using and by explicitly connecting these conceptualizations to the methodological commitments made in their studies. In doing so, we will further our understanding not only of mathematics teacher noticing but also of the affordances and constraints that are linked to various conceptualizations of noticing.

Key Considerations in the Study of Teacher Noticing

Because this is an edited volume, each chapter stands on its own as a piece of research, but our hope is that the book is more than the sum of its parts. Our goal here has been to give the reader the sense that a new subfield is forming within research on teaching. We would like this book to be read as beginning to map the boundaries of this new field. For that reason, we close this introduction by stating what we believe to be the core questions of this new field, and we encourage readers to consider these questions while reading each chapter:

1. *Is teacher noticing trainable?* A key set of questions has to do with the trainability of teacher noticing. For example, can we teach prospective teachers to notice, or can they learn this skill only through hours of experience teaching a class? Of particular interest are questions related to the use of video. In what ways can video be used as a tool for helping teachers gain expertise in noticing?

2. *What trajectories of development related to noticing expertise exist for prospective and practicing teachers?* There are many questions that have to do with the nature of the learning trajectories associated with teacher noticing. How does the noticing of expert teachers differ from that of novices? How long do novices need to acquire more expert noticing? Is the learning curve steep or shallow? What benchmarks exist to identify growth?

3. *How context specific is noticing expertise?* How unitary a skill is teacher noticing? If a mathematics teacher has expertise in noticing, will he or she have noticing expertise for all mathematical domains and instructional contexts? For example, do the teaching of algebra and the teaching of fractions require different noticing skills? Will a teacher who has expertise in noticing student thinking necessarily also have expertise in noticing classroom climate?

4. *How can researchers most productively study teacher noticing?* The study of teacher noticing poses particularly thorny methodological challenges. Noticing is a fleeting phenomenon in the midst of an often complex environment. Given these challenges, what techniques are most productive for us, as researchers, to gain access to teacher noticing? For example, what can we learn from studying teacher noticing in the act of teaching, and what can we learn from studying teacher noticing in university classes and professional development contexts?

5. *Why do we (or should we) study teacher noticing?* Finally, there are the ultimate questions of the real importance of teacher noticing. If teachers have more expertise in noticing, will they have more effective classrooms, ones in which students learn more?

We close by sharing that our own interest in teacher noticing grew out of our commitment to helping teachers improve their practices. Because teachers are bombarded with a "blooming, buzzing confusion of sensory data" (B. Sherin & Star, chapter 5), we believe that for teachers to consider all the ways to respond in a particular context is a hopeless task. Therefore, instead of trying to teach teachers how to deal with all possible contingencies, we focus on ways to help teachers better understand their learning environments so that they can make more informed instructional decisions. Through our research and professional development experiences, we have found that, when teachers are making this transformation, they are seeing and making sense differently of things that are happening in the classroom. In short, teachers' changing practices are accompanied by new and enhanced teacher noticing, and it is this idea that we try to capture and explore in the book.

Note

1   The writing of this chapter was supported in part by grants from the Spencer
Foundation (200800110) and the National Science Foundation (ESI0455785). The
opinions expressed in this chapter do not necessarily reflect the position, policy, or
endorsement of the supporting agencies. The authors wish to thank Bruce Sherin for
his thoughtful comments on an earlier version of this chapter.

References

Ball, D. L., & Cohen, D. K. (1999). Developing practice, developing practitioners:
Toward a practice-based theory of professional education. In L. Darling-Hammond
& G. Sykes (Eds.), *Teaching as the learning profession* (pp. 3–32). San Francisco:
Jossey-Bass.

Ball, D. L., Sleep, L., Boerst, T. A., & Bass, H. (2009). Combining the development of
practice and the practice of development in teacher education. *The Elementary School
Journal, 109*, 458–474.

Dewey, J. (1902). *The school and society: The child and the curriculum.* Chicago: University of
Chicago Press.

Dewey, J. (1964). *The relation of theory to practice in education.* New York: Random House.
(Original work published 1904)

Doyle, W. (1977). Learning the classroom environment: An ecological analysis. *Journal of
Teacher Education, 28*(6), 51–55.

Franke, M. L., Carpenter, T. P., Fennema, E., Ansell, E., & Behrend, J. (1998).
Understanding teachers' self-sustaining, generative change in the context of professional
development. *Teaching and Teacher Education, 14*, 67–80.

Franke, M. L., Carpenter, T. P., Levi, L., & Fennema, E. (2001). Capturing teachers'
generative change: A follow-up study of professional development in mathematics.
American Educational Research Journal, 38, 653–689.

Grossman, P., & McDonald, M. (2008). Back to the future: Directions for research
in teaching and teacher education. *American Educational Research Journal, 45*(1),
184–205.

Hiebert, J., Morris, A. K., Berk, D., & Jansen, A. (2007). Preparing teachers to learn from
teaching. *Journal of Teacher Education, 58*, 47–61.

Lampert, M. (2001). *Teaching problems and the problems of teaching.* New Haven, CT: Yale
University Press.

Lampert, M., Beasley, H., Ghousseini, H., Kazemi, E., & Franke, M. (2010). Using
designed instructional activities to enable novices to manage ambitious mathematics
teaching. In M. K. Stein & L. Kucan (Eds.), *Instructional Explanations in the Disciplines*
(pp. 129–141). New York: Springer.

Lesgold, A., Rubinson, H., Feltovich, P., Glaser, R., Klopfer, D., & Wang, Y. (1988).
Expertise in a complex skill: Diagnosing x-ray pictures. In M. T. H. Chi, R. Glaser, &
M. J. Farr (Eds.), *The nature of expertise* (pp. 311–342). Hillsdale, NJ: Erlbaum.

National Council of Teachers of Mathematics. (2000). *Principles and standards for school
mathematics.* Reston, VA: Author.

National Research Council (Eds.). (2000). *How people learn: Brain, mind, experience, and
school.* Washington, DC: National Academy Press.

National Research Council (Eds.). (2001). *Adding it up: Helping children learn mathematics*. Washington, DC: National Academy Press.

Sherin, B., & Star, J. R. (this volume, chapter 5). *Reflections on the study of teacher noticing*.

Shulman, L. S. (1987). Knowledge and teaching: Foundations of the new reform. *Harvard Educational Review, 57*(1), 1–22.

SECTION II

Foundations of Teacher Noticing

2

ON NOTICING TEACHER NOTICING[1]

Frederick Erickson

> To see what is in front of one's nose needs a constant struggle.
>
> George Orwell

Human noticing is active rather than passive. We "direct" our attention (i.e., to some objects rather than others) and we "pay" it (i.e., there are costs in attending to certain objects rather than to others). It follows that this is also the case for teacher noticing from within the everyday circumstances of practical action in the classroom.

This chapter presents perspectives and initial findings developed in an exploratory study of teacher noticing that I conducted in the early 1980s in early grades classrooms. The first section of the chapter presents background for the study and an overview of its design and conduct. The next section presents findings from the study, as a series of propositions accompanied by illustrative narrative examples. The examples show teacher noticing in a variety of subject areas, yet the processes of noticing that are discussed are all involved in the teaching of mathematics. Connections with mathematics instruction in particular are noted in a brief concluding statement at the end of the chapter.

An Early Study of Teacher Noticing

When in 1981 I began a study of teacher noticing very little research was being done on what teachers pay attention to while they teach. Study of that, and teaching about it, was becoming a lost art. This was not so in the early years of the twentieth century, when, under the influence of the child study movement (e.g., Stern, 1930) and the development of progressive pedagogy, beginning teachers were encouraged to watch closely the children they taught—in the heritage of Pestalozzi, Herbart, and Froebel—and to try to develop powers of acute observation. The supposition was that one needed to "learn" the children one was trying to teach.

Teachers and researchers associated with the Bank Street Laboratory for Educational Experiments made explicit some ways of directing careful pedagogical attention to indications of children's interests and thinking processes, as evidenced by the children's activity in block construction, drawing, speaking, and writing (see Biber, 1984; Johnson, 1933; Pratt, 1948; Stern & Cohen, 1958; see also the more recent overviews of those pedagogical perspectives in Antler, 1987; Shapiro & Nager, 2000).

John Dewey wrote an essay in 1904 titled "The Relation of Theory to Practice in Education" that was published in the third yearbook of the National Society for the Scientific Study of Education. He made a distinction between two types of attention behavior by children that teachers could recognize through observation: outer attention and inner attention. Outer attention was the surface appearance of attending—sitting up straight, looking where the child was supposed to be looking, sitting still, and not talking to one's neighbor. In other words, outer attention was "good deportment," and it was relatively easy to see. Inner attention, in contrast, was the genuine interest of the child, which might or might not be displayed to the teacher in the child's behavior (e.g., a child is looking out the window while the teacher or another child is talking. Is this evidence that the child is attending to what is being said, or is disattending?). Dewey said that it was of fundamental pedagogical importance to be able to distinguish between students' inner and outer attention and that it was a common error of novice teachers to mistake the former kind of attention for the latter kind. (See also the discussion in Scheffler, 1974, p. 90.)

An implication of this is that, over time, such misreadings of student behavior could become mis-educative for teachers. The longer they taught, unless they learned to subject to critical reflection their snap judgments based on the surface appearances of student behavior in the classroom, the more self-deceived they might become in their seeing. Mere years in the classroom did not have a straight-line relation to improvement in teaching practice—noticing in superficial ways was not pedagogical *experience*. Rather, pedagogical experience required reflection within action.

Here are Dewey's own words, in what reads now as a somewhat archaic style of discourse, with the male pronoun used generically in a manner we currently avoid. Yet as we read Dewey's text of more than a hundred years ago he seems so wise, and he reminds us of how much we have forgotten about how to pay attention to what and how teachers notice. In the discussion of students' outer and inner attention that follows we can easily envision a contemporary classroom:

> As every teacher knows, children have an inner and an outer attention. The inner attention is the giving of the mind without reserve or qualification to

the subject at hand. As such, it is a fundamental condition of mental growth. To be able to keep track of this mental play, to recognize the signs of its presence or absence, to know how it is initiated and maintained, how to test it by results attained, and to test *apparent* results by it, is the supreme mark and criterion of a teacher . . .

External attention, on the other hand, is that given to the book or teacher as an independent object. It is manifested in certain conventional postures and physical attitudes rather than in the movement of thought. Children acquire great dexterity in exhibiting in conventional and expected ways the *form* of attention to school work, while reserving the inner play of their own thoughts, images, and emotions for subjects that are more important to them, but quite irrelevant [i.e., irrelevant to the teacher].

Now, the teacher who is plunged prematurely into the pressing and practical problem of keeping order in the classroom has almost of necessity to make supreme the matter of external attention. . . . The inherent tendency of the situation therefore is for him to acquire his technique in relation to the outward rather than the inner mode of attention.

Dewey (1904, pp. 13–14)

After World War II, as systematic research on teaching began to develop, behaviorist perspectives on learning led researchers to focus primarily on teachers' actions in the classroom rather than on what teachers might be thinking or perceiving as they taught. As the "cognitive revolution" in thinking about learning developed in the 1960s and early 1970s, research attention returned to the study of teacher thinking, and this was the central focus of the federally funded Institute for Research on Teaching at Michigan State University. I became a senior researcher there in 1978 and from 1982 to 1985 I undertook an intensive observational study of what early grades teachers paid attention to while they taught. The study was titled "Teachers' Practical Ways of Seeing and Making Sense" (TPWS). (The final report of the TPWS study, submitted September 30, 1986, is available from the ERIC online database, document no. ED 282 847, SP 028 872. This is listed in the references section of this chapter as Erickson et al., 1986.)

The study examined how different second grade public school teachers—two in suburban classrooms and three in inner city classrooms—observed and made practical sense of what happened in their classrooms daily. These were veteran teachers, all of whom had taught for at least ten years full time as we began to observe them. We also studied five teacher education students longitudinally—from the time just before they had begun their student teaching internships through the end of their first year of full-time teaching. We were thus able to compare the characteristic ways of seeing of inexperienced and experienced teachers.

We observed four of the veteran teachers in their classrooms for entire school years and one of them, an inner city teacher, for two successive years. In separate focus group interviews we also showed the veteran and beginning teachers video clips of instruction from a kindergarten–first grade classroom in a working-class suburban neighborhood in the Boston metropolitan area—a classroom in which I had been previously engaged in observation over the course of two years.

Since the TPWS study I have engaged in various collaborative action research projects with teachers who were trying to improve their teaching (see Erickson, 2006). In all these endeavors I have been paying attention both to what teachers notice while they teach and to what they notice while watching videotapes of other teachers' teaching. (N.B. As increasing research attention is given to teacher noticing we should make use of first-person accounts by teachers on their own teaching—what is now often called "teacher research." An excellent example of such reporting that focuses on literacy instruction in an elementary classroom is found in Ballenger, 1999. Lampert and Ball have published extensively on their teaching of mathematics at the fifth grade level; see especially Lampert, 2001; Lampert and Ball, 1998.)

What follows is a series of propositions about teacher noticing, based on my experiences in observing and working with early grades teachers. The patterns of noticing on which I will comment come from self-contained classrooms in which the teacher and students are present for an entire school day and the classroom teacher instructs students in all subjects. Much of what I will discuss below may also apply to middle school and high school classrooms in which a single subject is taught to a class for one instructional period, and then a new class enters for a subsequent period of instruction. (N.B. In qualitative research generalization is an empirical matter—judgments of external validity lie in the eye (and experience) of the reader. If you as a reader recognize in my descriptions processes you find also at work in settings you know, then you are determining that what I am saying below "generalizes" beyond the cases I am reporting.)

Findings from the Study, With Illustrative Examples

Among the teachers I studied:

1. noticing was very selective—it involved attending to some phenomena and disattending to others;
2. noticing was multidimensional—attending to subject matter, to deportment, and also to other objects of attention;
3. noticing was usually highly instrumental—tactically opportunistic and triage-like—what was attended to was that which required action by the teacher;
4. noticing was occasionally non-instrumental—appreciative rather than tactical—but this was atypical;
5. noticing patterns were highly influenced by the teacher's prior experience in teaching—experienced and novice teachers differed in what they noticed;
6. noticing was narratively interpretive—connecting disparate behavioral details within "story frames";

7. noticing interpretations differed markedly along lines of differing "pedagogical commitments" held by different teachers;
8. taken together, propositions 1–7 suggest that noticing was highly variable across individual teachers—this implies that differing teachers do not inhabit identical subjective worlds as they are engaged in the real-time conduct of noticing while they teach.

In the discussion that follows, each of the propositions will be restated and will be illustrated by specific examples.

Proposition 1

The teachers I studied noticed very selectively, that is, they "constructed" what they saw and heard, and their attention to some potential seeables and hearables was combined with disattending to other potential objects of attention.

Teachers in the midst of teaching must deal constantly with information overload. There is far too much potential information in a scene for a human information processor to attend to, in its entirety, and so selecting and simplification by perceptual "chunking" are necessary. Teacher attention was active, not passive—prehensive rather than apprehensive, constructing what was seen, as described in the psychology of visual perception of Gibson (1986).

Proposition 2

(In self-contained classrooms especially) the teachers I studied noticed multidimensionally; in particular they noticed both deportment and subject matter content in what they saw and heard students doing.

In spite of information overload there was tremendous variety in kinds in the differing objects of teacher attention. From my observation of a second grade suburban teacher in the TPWS study (as presented in Erickson, 2007b, pp. 195–196) the objects of her attention ranged from (a) a penciled-in answer on a math workbook (read upside down as the teacher walked past the child's desk), through (b) an expression of intense concentration on the face of a child while working on a writing assignment, through (c) an expression of grief on a child's face as the teacher tells the class that their pet hamster died over the weekend, to (d) a bee sting on a child's arm, gotten during recess, and (e) a bee sting on another child's arm, gotten during the same recess period.

What is obvious from this list is the multiplicity of the kinds of objects with potential assessment significance for the teacher—observations of indicia on many different dimensions, some having to do with subject matter learning and skill, some having to do with deportment and effort, some having to do with physical or emotional well-being. Moreover, not only is there diversity of kind in the objects of attention—there is also the diversity of significance of objects of attention that, from an outsider's perspective, might seem to be the "same" object. . . . For example, the [first and second bee stings were] phenomenally similar entities in that both bee stings were acquired during the recess period after lunch. Yet [the first bee sting] appeared on the forearm of a child whose cumulative folder contained a note warning of the danger of anaphylactic shock because of a severe allergy to bee stings. Accordingly, the teacher watched [the first bee sting] very closely throughout the afternoon—checking its color and swelling. [The second bee sting received more cursory attention from the teacher because there was no apparent risk of anaphylaxis.]

Erickson (2007b, p. 196)

Sometimes the variety in objects of teacher noticing can lead to misleading perceptions, as in Dewey's discussion of the problem of mistaking students' outer attention for inner attention. Especially as teachers notice what is happening in the classroom as a whole, from a "batch processing" perspective that is encouraged in contemporary teaching practice and in highly scripted instructional materials (i.e., teaching to the whole class as a unitary entity rather than to students as individuals) there is a tendency to use deportment evidence as a proxy for evidence of student understanding of and agreement with what the teacher is trying to teach (e.g., when students look busy in an activity the teacher assigned them to, or raise their hands enthusiastically when questioned as a whole group, or hand in work in an orderly way, a teacher may assume that the students understand what the teacher thinks has been taught, substantively). This can be a problem as teachers attempt to shift from a "batch processing approach"—providing instruction to the whole class without careful attention to whether or not individuals are actually learning what is being taught—to "teaching for understanding." It is easy to mistake the appearance of student attention and understanding for genuine attention and understanding. For some teachers the connection between observed deportment and presumed understanding is especially strong, for example for those teachers who believe that "order must be established before learning can take place."

Moreover, what teachers notice—about deportment or anything else—ends up affecting what students notice, as Dewey observed in his discussion of attention that was quoted above. Students constantly attend to their teachers' attending, in an ecosystem of mutual influence. For example, in a first grade mathematics lesson that I observed and videotaped in the fall of 1974, in the first classroom in which I did observational study, the following scene took place:

The teacher, Ms. Wright, was sitting on the carpet with her students, who were arranged in a circle. They were looking at painted wooden blocks in various shapes, colors, and sizes laid out in the center of the circle. Ms. Wright was using the blocks to illustrate the concepts of "set" and of "set property." The blocks were painted either green or yellow. Some were triangles, some were squares, and some were circles. Ms. Wright made a set of blocks whose members all shared the property of color—there were triangles, squares, and circles in the set but all the blocks were yellow. Ms. Wright looped a rope ring around the set of yellow blocks, encircling them. She then laid out a set of blocks that were yellow and green, but all of whose members were triangles—some large, some medium, some small, but all triangles. This second set was also enclosed by a rope ring.

The children had been talking with one another very animatedly as the sets were arranged on the floor, and they overlapped one another in talking—they were not speaking "one at a time."

Ms. Wright pointed to the set of triangles and said, "*These* blocks all have the property of what?" "SHAPE!" the students replied in chorus.

"And *these* blocks" (Ms. Wright pointed to the set of yellow blocks, as one child, Ricky, was repeatedly saying something unintelligible, in "motor-mouth" repetition) "all have the property of . . . Sh!" (addressed to Ricky, meaning "Be quiet").

"SHAPE!" the students said.

Into her question to the student group Ms. Wright had inserted a directive on deportment to an individual child, but her comment "Sh!" was heard by the rest of the students not as an interpolated comment to that child but as a clue to the right answer to the question that she had addressed to the student group. Apparently the students heard "Sh!" as the first sound in the word "Shape."

It took a couple of turns more before the teacher could get the group back on track. Then she was able to point again to the set of yellow blocks and say "*These* blocks all have the property of what?" "COLOR!" the students answered together.

The students were so attentive to the teacher that in simultaneous split-second judgments they over-interpreted what the teacher had said, reacting to the speech sound /SH/ ("Be quiet") as if it had been /SH/ ("The right answer starts with . . ."). Teaching can be thought of as a continuous stream of meaning making (A. S. Bolster, Jr., personal communication, August 4, 2009). Students can be seen to be making meaning interpretively *in the same time as their teachers*, at the speed of an eye blink. The stream of meaning making is thus a product of social ecology, mutual influence within real-time performance that is produced by the conjoint actions of teachers and students together.

Proposition 3

(In actual practice and while watching video segments) the selective attention of teachers I studied was tactically opportunistic and intuitively perceptive—the teachers I studied noticed

in the moment what they thought they needed to notice in order to take action in their teaching, often noticing by means of "quick scans" rather than by means of sustained attention.

In other words, teacher noticing was not armchair observation, normatively neutral and distanced description, held tentatively, but a "triage-like" exercise of successive foci of attention, shifting in bursts of attention from moment to moment. And this was noticing in order to act—to do something about what is noticed, often to do something right away. Recall, in the previous example, the teacher's noticing of Ricky's "motor-mouth" yammering. Recall the two bee stings mentioned in the first example. The first sting was more salient attentionally for Mrs. Smith than was the second one because the first child had a note in her file about potential danger of anaphylactic shock—something that Mrs. Smith might have had to act on rapidly.

This tendency *to attend to those things you think you need to take action on* gave the noticings of the teachers I studied an incorrigible character—they had to consider that they were seeing what was "really there" and usually, within the ongoing course of real-time performance of teaching, they did not question the presuppositions that constituted their construction of what they were seeing. The continual "now" of the conduct of practice does not allow time for armchair reflection. In this the teachers were no different from other practical social actors (see the references to ethnomethodology in point 6 below), but the taken-for-granted character of their habitual ways of noticing should not be overlooked—it is emphasized in the phenomenology of Schütz, Husserl, and Merleau-Ponty (particularly in the latter's *Phenomenology of perception*) and in the theory of practice of Bourdieu.

In a collaborative action project with teachers I was engaged in immediately after the TPWS study, one of the first grade teachers we worked with was very conscientious. If anything she was a bit too conscientious (she said that as she began working with us she felt that she was "100% responsible for everything that happened in my classroom"). After a few months of developing trust she asked us to videotape a particular activity in her classroom so that she could review the tape to study closely what certain children were doing while her attention was directed to a different group of children. We placed the camera in the back of the room, shooting forward toward the group of students whose activity the teacher wanted us to document. When the teacher viewed the videotape the first thing she remarked on was how different the room appeared on the tape from the way she experienced it in her teaching—the camera was looking toward the front of the room and at the backs of the children's necks, but she looked from the front to the back of the room and saw children's faces. She said with the force of a new and important revelation: "I never realized that there was more than one way to see my room—other than the way I did—and that someone could come into my room and see different things than I do!" After that watershed moment, how she thought about her teaching (and about "100% responsibility") began to change profoundly. She became willing to entertain for herself competing interpretations about what was going on—trying out ways of seeing her room differently—and she developed a wider range of approaches to teaching reading. (For further discussion of this project see Berkey et al., 1990 and Erickson, 2006.)

Proposition 4

Exceptions to the previous assertion did occur—in a minority of cases. Some teachers took an aesthetic pleasure in watching students do things that did not call for intervention by the teacher. But this was rare even for the teachers who did observe students in this way—the instrumental, triage-focused pattern was more typical.

Mrs. Smith, one of the suburban teachers in the TPWS study, and Mr. Fairley, an inner city teacher in the TPWS study, did watch students occasionally in simple appreciation for something the students were doing well—not attending to something they thought they needed to fix.

In the second week of January 1983, as I returned to visit Mrs. Smith's classroom after the Christmas recess, she said to me at the first opportunity we had to talk, "Mona's flying!" (Mona was the best reader and writer in the class.) Mrs. Smith said that in the time after Christmas she started looking for students to "take off" academically. She compared this with watching baby birds on a branch, as they were beginning to fly. As her students, one by one, began doing something more complex academically than they had been able to do in the fall, watching them in their beginning attempts was a source of delight to her, each year.

Proposition 5

The story frames and action category judgments that teachers brought to their noticing were profoundly influenced by their prior experience in teaching.

Experienced teachers noticed details of the moment in terms of connections that went beyond the moment at hand—especially in terms of annual cycles and unit-level cycles ("We've got to move on or we won't finish the unit by the end of next week." "I had a kid like this last year and it wasn't until spring break that she . . ."). Connections for teachers in self-contained classrooms also went beyond a single subject area ("Mary often makes computational mistakes in mathematics, but her spelling and punctuation are very accurate").

> Mrs. Meier, a suburban teacher who taught across the hall from Mrs. Smith, was deeply troubled by what was *not* happening in her room in the weeks right after the Christmas break. She said, "It's near the end of January and this class hasn't 'jelled' in reading yet."

That's the kind of noticing that comes from having had multiple years of teaching experience—knowing it's time to have "jelled" and knowing what "jelling" is, as a collective, classroom level phenomenon. In contrast to the veteran teachers in the TPWS study the teacher education students on their way to becoming full-time teachers had not yet developed a sense of the "yearliness" of what was happening in the classroom. They also made fewer interpretive connections in their noticing than did the experienced teachers.

The preservice teacher education students we first studied before their term of practice teaching, when shown video clips, would notice student behaviors accurately, but they made written notes on them and commented on them in fragmentary ways. After their student teaching, watching the same video clips they had been shown before, the student teachers noticed a wider range of aspects of what was going on in the room—not just isolable behaviors, but "putting things together" in a sense of the room as a whole. They did not, however, show a sense of "yearliness" and its implications for how to view the students and how to make sense of strategies of teachers—the time of the year in the clips they were watching. They did not just look at isolated kids and behaviors—they also commented on groups of students and on the room as a whole, but not in terms of where the events were in the course of a year. During their first year of full-time teaching, those same individuals were "putting even more together" in looking at individual children, group patterns, and the classroom as a whole, and they had some awareness that the time of year of the clip was important—but they did not show an awareness of a whole year (which makes sense—they had not experienced a whole year yet as a teacher).

The veteran teachers, in contrast, not only "put more together" in looking at individual children, groups, and the whole classroom but they did so with a full story-like understanding that included not only a sense of the whole year out of which the video clip had been taken (i.e., wondering about that, speculating about the present clip with a sense of "yearliness"—"Is this clip from September or January or April?") but also a sense of prior years (e.g., "I had a student like that three years ago, and . . ."). In addition the veteran teachers asked about institutional contextual matters—"Did this teacher have any choice in the reading series being used, or was that decided by the central administration?" There is a distinct sense that the clinically experienced teachers were trying to "put it all together" in much more comprehensive ways—much more narratively framed ways—than were the teacher education students the first time we interviewed them before they had had student teaching.

Proposition 6

Teacher noticing placed the behavioral details attended to (whether of molar or molecular grain size) interpretively within narrative frames—as pieces of a story.

This is already apparent in the discussion of developmental differences in noticing between beginning and veteran teachers. Just as Bartlett observed long ago (1932) and Bruner more recently (1991, 2002), behavioral details are "read" by veteran teachers interpretively as pieces in strips of social action within story lines—i.e., as the result of intentions by the actor/actors and as having consequences for the actions of others, with assumed antecedents and consequents in prior and subsequent action "beyond the screen"—earlier and later than what is apparent in the video segment itself. In other words, teachers as practical actors do what early ethnomethodology claimed that all practical actors do—they use what Garfinkel (1967) called (somewhat misleadingly) a "documentary method" to make sense of what they see before them. A behavioral detail is taken as an instance of something that points to a larger story beyond the behavioral detail itself. For example, we see a middle-aged man lying head down in the gutter alongside a sidewalk: Is this a "document" of the man's having had a heart attack, or of having passed out drunk, or is this a homeless person who is asleep? We react differently to the man depending on the story frame we use to interpret his behavior—behavior whose meaning is to some degree always ambiguous in the absence of our locating it interpretively in some narrative context. So, in the classroom with a child who hesitates when asked a question by a teacher, was the child not paying attention to the question, does the child not know the answer, or is the child shy? (See also the classic paper by Sacks, 1972 titled "Notes on Police Assessment of Moral Character" and the classic essay on meaning in context by Mishler, 1979.)

It was by means of narrative understanding that veteran teachers were able to do what clinically experienced physicians do—"put it all together" and combine discrete items of information with diagnostic significance into a coherent interpretive picture. Yet while story-like understanding connects separate aspects of classroom life in ways that support powerful insight, the power of storying can also lead to unwarranted inferences, as in the following example:

> Mrs. Tobin, a veteran inner city second grade teacher, believed strongly in the overall approach to teaching literacy that was presented in the highly scripted instructional materials for reading that had been adopted by the school district, even though she was somewhat concerned that the material in the stories in the new reading series that was being introduced that year was not at as high a level as that in the previous series. Still she used the new materials in a thorough way, figuring that with its unit-by-unit tests the new reading program would benefit the students.
>
> Mrs. Tobin saw her main responsibility as a teacher as making sure that all students completed the tasks presented for them in the published materials. This included the provision of printed worksheets on which students could practice discrete skills in reading, such as letter–sound correspondence, consonant blends, punctuation, and spelling. One of the students in the room was Renee, a light-skinned African-American girl who lived in the neighborhood near the school. She was doing adequately in reading—not outstandingly well, but pretty well. On a humid, hot morning in late October, Renee was bored. While Mrs. Tobin was sitting at a table

with a small group of students who were reading aloud to her, Renee sat at her desk and dawdled with the worksheet she had been given. She didn't get up from her seat or call out to other students; she just sat at her desk, "zoned out," and didn't complete the items on her worksheet. It came time for recess. Mrs. Tobin left the reading table and, as she announced recess, she noticed that Renee had not finished her seatwork. As the children lined up to leave the room Mrs. Tobin spoke harshly to Renee—she would have to "stay in" as the other children went out to the playground. Renee must finish the worksheet during recess time. As Mrs. Tobin spoke to her, Renee's eyes brimmed with tears and one of them ran down her cheek. She didn't say a word.

Mrs. Tobin and I walked side by side through the hall behind the double line of children from the class, on the way to the school door and the playground.

As we came out onto the steps leading down to the playground Mrs. Tobin said, "Sometimes I wonder why I bother with students like Renee. She'll probably be a hooker by the time she's 14."

Proposition 7

The story frames and action category judgments that veteran teachers brought to their noticing were profoundly influenced by what can be called their "pedagogical commitments." Those commitments differed from one teacher to the next, and many aspects of them were held outside reflective awareness.

By pedagogical commitments I mean what more commonly is called the teacher's "philosophy of practice"—basic ontological assumptions, both tacit and explicit, concerning manifold aspects of teaching and learning activity, for example the nature of learners (high, medium, or low in ability; tries hard or does not try hard), of subject matter (easy, difficult; inherently interesting, or boring but necessary), of social relations (threshold levels of disruption, concern for face threat), of how semiotic systems communicate meaning ("If I said it clearly [or wrote it on the board] they should understand it"). These pedagogical commitments include such assumptions as the following: learners can [or cannot] be trusted to persist at a certain kind of task and finish it without close supervision and extrinsic rewards; students will [or will not] listen carefully to what other students say in whole class discussion; "classroom order must be in place before learning can take place"; "providing interesting/appropriate subject matter eliminates the need for much of what is conventionally called 'classroom management'"; children "naturally" compete; children "naturally" cooperate; mastery of simple discrete skills must precede [or need not precede] more complex and holistic kinds of understanding; most children are capable of learning most of what is being taught them; one can expect that half the class will perform "below average"; you should teach to the middle of the class and that way most students will learn the most;

the language of mathematical symbols presents mathematical ideas more clearly than does talk or students' use of manipulatives; getting the right answer is what is most important; students' failing to learn what is taught is often a matter of moral failure on the part of the child and it also leads one to suspect the moral status of the child's parent(s); or memorizing the times tables is morally superior to using a hand calculator to multiply or divide—the assumption of "no pain, no gain."

Mrs. Tobin, the inner city teacher whose interaction with Renee was described in the immediately previous vignette, had a particular pedagogical commitment. She believed that the best thing to do for her students was to see to it that they spent time working seriously, using the texts, workbooks, and worksheets that were available. Accordingly she and her aide were especially vigilant about student behavior during seatwork, and she used some behavior modification techniques during reading groups. Her job was to see to it that students completed assigned work. If they did so, learning would take place. What was most salient for her, in noticing what was happening in her room, was whether or not students were persisting in "doing the work" provided in the published materials, and whether or not they completed those tasks. In contrast, Mrs. Gates had different pedagogical commitments. She also taught in the same urban school system as Mrs. Tobin. Mrs. Gates thought that her students, many of whom came from low income families and were of minority racial and language background, were often misperceived as having less ability than they actually had. They needed explicit teaching in survival skills and encouragement to try new things. She felt that the school district, with its extreme emphasis on monitoring students' stepwise acquisition of mandated skills, was not leaving time for enrichment in reading and math and for the teaching of survival skills such as those of test taking. Accordingly she devised games, contests, and various self-testing activities by which children could practice working under timed conditions and get quick feedback regarding the accuracy of their work. At the same time she provided diverse enrichment activities because she valued the kinds of knowledge and experience that were not measured by the tests. She did this especially in language arts, an area in which she was more confident as an instructor than in math and science. She worried about the children and about her teaching. She watched individual children closely as they were engaged in the special activities she created for them. She wondered if she was doing right in adding things that "they," the school district, did not emphasize. The third inner city teacher, Mr. Fairley, had pedagogical commitments that differed even more from those of the school district than did the pedagogical commitments of Mrs. Gates. He thought that teachers needed to know their students well. He sometimes spent time with his students outside school, to discover the children's interests and to reveal to them that he had interests and curiosity too. He believed that academic skills were necessary but that they followed from engagement in work that was interesting and intellectually substantive. Teachers should believe in their students' capacity and foster their curiosity. The district's skills-testing emphasis would have interfered with this, but since his students did well on the tests he went ahead teaching in the ways he thought were right.

One of the consequences for noticing by the teachers had to do with the immobile pencils of students. For Mrs. Tobin, the curriculum was not the problem especially—classroom management was. For her the immobile pencil of a child at seatwork was the kind of occasion that one needed to watch for and react to. Mr. Fairley and Mrs. Gates sometimes would notice and call to account a student who was holding an immobile pencil when it should have been moving, but they did not do this as consistently as Mrs. Tobin did. Mrs. Gates would be especially vigilant for the immobile pencil during one of the activities she had designed to simulate timed test situations.

Teaching in suburban classrooms, Mrs. Smith and Mrs. Meijer were often vigilant about the immobile pencils in their rooms. Students in their classrooms were doing more academically advanced work than were the children in the inner city classrooms, and the suburban children did their work more quietly. Yet both suburban teachers had heard the term "time on task" and used it during interviews describing children in their rooms. They were especially careful in looking at the students' worksheets, correcting them and getting them back to the students quickly.

Mr. Fairley spent the least time looking at worksheets, because he used them the least. He was the teacher most acutely focused on children's talk in discussion as indicating not only their understanding of right answers but their underlying reasoning. Mrs. Meijer and Mrs. Gates were also interested in children's thinking. Mrs. Meijer seemed to enjoy reasoning with students, and for a number of years she had taught in upper grades where that could happen in even more extended ways. Mrs. Gates was concerned that, in the interest of their own academic survival, her students understood the kinds of things the tests were driving at. Her interest in the "how" of children's thinking was thus more pragmatic than Mr. Fairley's may have been, with his deep belief in the value of knowledge and curiosity in their own right.

A cautionary note is in order lest these characterizations seem stereotypical. All the veteran teachers were observed noticing and reacting to all the kinds of classroom phenomena that have been mentioned in this chapter. It was not that Mr. Fairley was never concerned about an immobile pencil or that Mrs. Tobin was never concerned about the originality of a student's insight as well as the correctness of it as an answer to a question or that Mrs. Meijer never noticed and resonated with the feelings of her students while Mrs. Smith was constantly awash with sentiment. Rather, the teachers' ways of seeing varied in terms of relative emphasis on the various domains of what was potentially noticeable. This variation had to do with the various teachers' primary pedagogical commitments as well as with their temperaments, and it also varied across differing classroom situations (for further discussion, see Erickson, 2007a).

The power of the influence of pedagogical commitments upon veteran teachers' patterns of noticing is illustrated especially in the following example:

In the TPWS study the veteran teachers were gathered for a focus group interview in which they were asked to view video footage of the classroom of Ms. Wright, who taught students in a working-class suburban neighborhood near Boston, a neighborhood in which the residents were predominantly Italian-American. We showed various video clips from that classroom, including one from the mathematics lesson on sets that was discussed earlier in this chapter. In watching those clips all of the veteran teachers besides Mrs. Gates continually commented on how disorderly the classroom appeared to them. (Mrs. Gates, in a professional development course at the local university in the previous summer, had seen a number of tapes from Ms. Wright's room and had engaged with other veteran teachers in studying the tapes in detail—through that experience she had become convinced that Ms. Wright was a skilled and effective teacher.) Even Mr. Fairley reacted to the overall level of ambient noise in Ms. Wright's room, and Mrs. Tobin, Mrs. Smith, and Mrs. Meijer were very skeptical that learning could be taking place, because from their points of view "order" had not been firmly established first.

This conviction was so strong that, as the group watched a video clip of the first reading group held with first graders in September in Ms. Wright's room, all the veteran teachers but Mrs. Gates overlooked a crucial fact that was apparent in the clip. Recall that Ms. Wright taught a kindergarten–first grade class. This meant that at the beginning of each new school year the first graders were "old hands" from last year, when they had been kindergartners in Ms. Wright's room. In the video clip showing the first gathering of the year for the new first graders in a small group reading lesson there was banter and overlapping talk occurring among the children in the reading group, who were reading aloud in "round robin" fashion from their basal reading books. In the background was a constant buzz of ambient noise from the other students, who were engaged in multiple activities around the room as the reading group was meeting at the reading table. During the reading lesson, students—often kindergartners—repeatedly came to Ms. Wright and diverted her attention briefly with special requests. All that was what the veteran teachers noticed—overlapping talk, classroom buzz, interruptions of the teacher leading the reading group. What none of them noticed except for Mrs. Gates was that *all the children in the reading group were reading aloud from their books, fluently, and with apparent understanding—and this was happening on the first day of the new school year!* (In the 1970s and 1980s it was still unusual for kindergartners to be taught to read.)

The video clip stopped. The teachers watching it started to criticize Ms. Wright yet again for not having good classroom management skills, and then, quietly, Mrs. Gates asked them to consider what they had overlooked—the data on the tape pointing to the fact that the beginning first graders already knew how to read. What the children's reading aloud so fluently meant was that, during the previous year, when those children were kindergartners, they had learned to read very well—for kindergartners—well enough to be able to handle a new reading book at the beginning first grade level. There on the video clip was prima facie evidence that learning indeed had taken place in Ms. Wright's classroom, and that Ms. Wright must indeed have been doing something very effectively with those students during the previous year. But the "noise" of apparent disorder in the Boston area classroom (Ms. Wright herself complained that the students were constantly "interrupting") seems to have been so salient for the veteran teachers in the Midwest that they were unable to hear or see the "signal" content that was otherwise apparent on the video—clear behavioral evidence of students having learned to read before they entered first grade. In Dewey's terms, the video showed that these students had been devoting inner attention to learning to read, but the pedagogical commitments of the teachers led them to focus instead on noticing the absence of apparent outer attention.

Proposition 8

When the teachers I studied watched a single video segment or visited another teacher's classroom they did not all necessarily notice the same things in it. It follows that we cannot presume that every viewer of a video clip or visitor to a classroom inhabits the same subjective world as that of any other viewer or visitor. Rather they bring differing prior experience and differing pedagogical commitments to what they notice.

By way of summarizing what all the previous examples in this chapter have shown, I want to say that teachers and other viewers of classroom practice "made sense." Those to whom I have shown minimally edited classroom video footage (and those with whom I have visited in actual classrooms) were active and constructive rather than passively receptive in their noticing—they did not apprehend phenomena directly but saw and heard phenomenologically (as many have claimed that all other humans do, continually, including those doing social research—on this point again see Garfinkel, 1967). Consequently there is tremendous power in teachers' customarily practiced ways of noticing as they teach (and as they watch others teach)—a capacity for insight and for misperception as well.

Conclusion

The previous discussion has surveyed teacher noticing in general, as it appeared in various early grades classrooms and as illustrated by examples from teaching in differing subject areas. What about the noticings of mathematics teachers in particular? Does a teacher's pedagogical commitments concerning what counts most in math influence what the teacher will notice and emphasize in math instruction? Is math more about drill or more about sense making? Does the teacher attend more to the students' moving pencils or more to their moving thoughts—to the trajectories of the questions and conjectures that they display in words and in mathematical symbols? Does the teacher attend more to quiet in the room or to the play of ideas in mathematical dialog?

If we want to teach for student understanding, in mathematics or in any other subject area, I think we need to learn better ways of noticing student understanding and of noticing what Dewey called their "inner attention" to what we are trying to teach them (see Erickson, 2007b, for elaboration). As educators we also need to learn more about the what, how, and why of teacher noticing itself, whether that noticing be focused on student understanding or on the myriad other objects of attention that teachers need to be noticing from within the midst of the real-time conduct of their teaching. Moreover we need to learn more about the relativity of teacher noticing, its varieties in differing circumstances of pedagogical use and belief. The authors whose work is presented in this book have undertaken serious attempts to do this, taking a variety of perspectives and using differing methods. The chapters that appear here make major strides toward further insight concerning teacher noticing.

Note

1   I want to acknowledge former and current colleagues who have been especially help-ful in teaching me about teacher noticing: Courtney Cazden, Arthur S. Bolster, Jr., Martha Walsh, Sharon Feiman-Nemser, Constance Wardell, Judy Buchanan, Lisa Rosenthal-Schaeffer. I am grateful for their tutelage and also for review and discus-sion of this chapter with Bolster, who is Professor of Education, Emeritus, Harvard University. Defects in what this chapter says are my responsibility. I am grateful as well for editorial advice from Joanne Straceski.

Much of the data that are presented in this chapter come from a study supported by a contract from the United States Office of Educational Research and Improvement (OERI), awarded to the Institute for Research on Teaching at Michigan State University, Contract No. 400–81–0014. The support of OERI is acknowledged with thanks. My collaborators in that study were, in alphabetical order, David Boersema, Margaret Brown, Becky Kirschner, Brenda Lazarus, Catherine Pelissier, and Daisy Thomas. Thanks are also due to Magdalene Lampert for her advice that I revisit this study's final report and publish from it.

References

Antler, J. (1987). *Lucy Sprague Mitchell: The making of a modern woman.* New Haven, CT: Yale University Press.

Ballenger, C. (1999). *Teaching other people's children: Literacy and learning in a bilingual class-room.* New York: Teachers College Press.

Bartlett, F. (1932). *Remembering.* Cambridge, England: Cambridge University Press.

Berkey, R., Curtis, T., Minnick, F., Zietlow, K., Campbell, D., & Kirschner, B. (1990). Collaborating for reflective practice: Voices of teachers, administrators, and researchers. *Education and Urban Society, 22*(2), 204–232.

Biber, B. (1984). *Early education and psychological development*. New Haven, CT: Yale University Press.

Bruner, J. (1991). *Acts of meaning*. Cambridge, MA: Harvard University Press.

Bruner, J. (2002). *Making stories: Law, literature, life*. New York: Farrar, Straus and Giroux.

Dewey, J. (1904). The relation of theory to practice in education. In National Society for the Scientific Study of Education, *The relation of theory to practice in the education of teachers* (Vol. 3, Part 1). Bloomington, IL: Public School Publishing Co. (Reprinted in *Teacher education in America: A documentary history*, pp. 148–149, by M. L. Borrowman, Ed., 1965, New York: Teachers College Press)

Erickson, F. (2006). Studying side by side: Collaborative action ethnography in educational research. In G. Spindler & L. Hammond (Eds.), *New horizons for ethnography in education* (pp. 235–257). Mahwah, NJ: Erlbaum.

Erickson, F. (2007a). Ways of seeing video: Toward a phenomenology of viewing minimally edited footage. In R. Goldman, B. Barron, R. Pea, & S. Derry (Eds.), *Video research in the learning sciences* (pp. 145–155). Mahwah, NJ: Erlbaum.

Erickson, F. (2007b). Some thoughts on "proximal" formative assessment of student learning. In P. Moss (Ed.), *Evidence and decision making in education* (102nd Yearbook of the National Society for the Study of Education, pp. 186–216). Chicago: NSSE.

Erickson, F., with Boersema, D., Brown, M., Kirschner, B., Lazarus, B., Pelissier, C., & Thomas, D. (1986). *Teachers' practical ways of seeing and making sense: A final report*. East Lansing, MI: Institute for Research on Teaching/Washington, DC: Office of Educational Research and Improvement. (Contract No. 400–81–0014)

Garfinkel, H. (1967). *Studies in ethnomethodology*. Englewood Cliffs, NJ: Prentice-Hall.

Gibson, J. (1986). *The ecological approach to visual perception*. Mahwah, NJ: Erlbaum.

Johnson, H. (1933). *The art of block building* (The Cooperating Schools Pamphlets, No. 1). New York: The John Day Company.

Lampert, M. (2001). *Teaching problems and the problems of teaching*. New Haven, CT: Yale University Press.

Lampert, M., & Ball, D. L. (1998). *Teaching, multimedia, and mathematics: Investigations of real practice*. New York: Teachers College Press.

Mishler, E. (1979). Meaning in context: Is there any other kind? *Harvard Educational Review, 49*, pp. 1–19.

Pratt, C. (1948). *I learn from children: An adventure in progressive education*. New York: Simon & Schuster.

Sacks, H. (1972). Notes on police assessment of moral character. In D. Sudnow (Ed.), *Studies in social interaction* (pp. 280–293). New York: Free Press.

Scheffler, I. (1974). *Reason and teaching*. Indianapolis, IN: Bobbs-Merrill.

Shapiro, E., & Nager, N. (2000). *Revisiting a progressive pedagogy: The developmental-interaction approach*. Albany, NY: SUNY Press.

Stern, V., & Cohen, D. H. (1958). *Observing and recording the behavior of young children*. New York: Teachers College Press.

Stern, W. (1930). *Psychology of early childhood up to the sixth year of age*. New York: Holt.

3

NOTICING

Roots and Branches

John Mason

Starting with the roots of the idea of *noticing* as a potentially intentional rather than haphazard act, I first outline aspects of what I call the *discipline of noticing* (Mason 1984, 2002). Central to this view is the idea that noticing is a collection of practices designed to sensitize oneself so as to notice opportunities in the future in which to act freshly rather than automatically out of habit.

I next consider ways in which noticing has produced insights and informed action in teaching, learning, and conducting professional development having to do with mathematics. Constructs such as attention and intention, awareness, and consciousness not only are researchable using the discipline of noticing and informative about how noticing actually works but also contribute to our appreciation of intricacies of learning and teaching mathematics.

Roots of the Discipline of Noticing

Noticing is a common enough word in English, with an etymology tracing back to the Latin words *notitia* (being known) and *notus* (known). Clearly one notices all the time: For example, we pin *notices* on a *noticeboard* to bring things to people's attention so that they will *notice* them. In fact, there is a great deal that we do not notice, either because we are not attuned or sensitized or because our attention is directed and occupied elsewhere. Sometimes people do not notice, do not realize that they need to pay attention to some feature in a situation, with the result that things go wrong. For example, mathematics students often ignore structural relationships indicated verbally in a word problem, so they try to manipulate the numbers to get an answer; older students often forget to check the conditions required by a theorem before trying to apply it to some situation.

My attention was first directed to noticing as an intentional act when I spent a year under the direction of J. G. Bennett during 1973–1974. Some 120 of us ran and maintained an old manor house while learning to observe ourselves and to work with one another. Among the lectures that we attended was one on noticing in which Bennett (1976) brought together various strands of the practical work lying at the heart of the program of study. Bennett's lecture was based on what he had gleaned from years of traveling in the Near, Middle and Far East, and especially from being taught by an Armenian, Georgi Gurdjieff. Gurdjieff had brought to the West what Ouspensky (1950) called *fragments of an unknown teaching*, centered on self-observation. Gurdjieff in turn seemed to have been influenced by various Middle Eastern teachers whose roots can probably be traced to the most ancient of writings such as the Rg Veda and the Upanishads, and hence into the mists of time.

My use of noticing in mathematics began with working on mathematical animations and posters in the company of a number of colleagues in the Association of Teachers of Mathematics in the United Kingdom, particularly with Dick Tahta (1981). We would look at a poster or watch a short animation and then reconstruct what we had noticed, gradually developing a descriptive story or *account of* what we had seen. Sometimes this story would then be verified or augmented during a second viewing. Only then would we begin to *account for* what we recalled seeing by explaining the story development mathematically.

In the 1980s, when my colleagues and I at the Open University were asked to prepare videotapes of best practice in secondary mathematics classrooms, I transferred this way of working on animation together with insights from noticing to develop ways of working with the tapes. We eschewed the notion of best practice, and we discovered early on that we needed a way to counteract such reactions to the tapes as "my low attainers are lower than those low attainers" and "I wouldn't let that teacher in my classroom." Instead of getting people to analyze practices observed on the tapes, we found it more effective to use the tapes as stimuli to get people to recall and then analyze related incidents from their own teaching. We initiated a practice in which people were asked either to reconstruct collectively what they thought they had seen, incident by incident, or to choose some salient moment and describe it to colleagues while reducing to a minimum all judgments and emotive terms, so that the moment could readily be recognized by everyone. Emphasis was on "what you saw that others may have seen and can recognize," that is, on behavioral rather than affective or emotive aspects. Then we emphasized the importance of people bringing to mind from their own experiences incidents that were similar in some way (Mason, 1988).

The effect of this practice was that people used what they saw on the video as a combination of metonymic triggers into, and metaphoric resonances with, their own past experiences. By describing their own incidents to others, briefly but vividly, and by negotiating the senses in which different incidents were similar or different, the participants developed a collective vocabulary and a rich web of interrelated shared incidents. This experience, in turn, provided a foundation for individuals to recognize in the moment when a similar incident began to emerge, enabling them to avoid the habitual and to act freshly. This is the essence of the discipline of noticing: arranging to alert oneself in the future so as to act freshly rather than automatically out of habit.

Often, some moments after a habit has been activated, I become aware of that fact: I notice an opportunity retrospectively, too late, rather than in the moment. By making use of this retrospective noticing to trigger the act of imagining myself noticing an opportunity to act differently (to respond rather than to react) in the future, I prospectively prepare myself to notice in the future. By continued disciplined use of reflection and reconstruction in the form of prospective imagining, the moment of noticing moves closer and closer to the moment of instigation of action (*spective*), eventually displacing the habitual reaction with a fresh response.

Methodological Remarks

One unusual feature of the discipline of noticing is the form and nature of its results. Because its use to research personal practice is fundamentally experiential, the results of enquiries using the discipline fully are task exercises through which others may be sensitized to notice something freshly for themselves, to become aware of useful distinctions and possible actions to be initiated in the future. In papers I usually offer tasks based on workshop tasks, where I tell people that what they get from the workshop will be what they notice happening inside them. Thus the data offered are immediate experiences and what they trigger or what resonates from past experience, making the discipline entirely self-consistent. The validity of a finding lies not in the verisimilitude of someone's report but in whether others find their future actions informed and their future noticing enriched.

In line with this perspective, the distinctions I offer in this chapter must be treated as conjectures to be tested in experience. It is essential to pause every so often and try to bring to mind either specific instances or at least a general flavour of what is being said, from your own experience. I take the unusual methodological stance that the data I offer are *not* descriptions of my own incidents but, rather, what comes to mind for readers from their own experiences when they encounter my descriptions. In parallel with what my colleagues and I learned about using videotape of classrooms, what is most powerful is not what is presented as stimulus but, rather, what comes to mind from one's own experience, triggered by or resonating with what is read.

The Discipline in a Nutshell

The discipline of noticing is a collection of techniques for (a) *pre-paring* to notice in the moment, that is, to have come to mind appropriately, and (b) *post-paring* by reflecting on the recent past to select what you want to notice or be sensitized to particularly, in order to *pare*, that is, to notice in the moment and so be enabled to act freshly rather than habitually.

In addition to selecting incidents and situations in which you wish you had had, and wish in the future to be able to have, the mindfulness to act differently (Bateson, 1994; Langer, 1997), you need to accumulate different desirable actions that you prefer to your habitual reactions. In other words, to replace reaction by (considered) response, you need to have an action come to mind just before your automatic reaction takes over. You need therefore a collection of alternative actions and an awareness of situations in which these actions would be preferable.

Alternative actions are accumulated through noticing other people doing them, reading about them, or noticing yourself doing them. For example, in a pedagogic strategy sometimes referred to as *jigsaw groups* (see Aronson, 1978), three roughly equal-sized groups are set to work on three related problems. Each group works initially on its own problem; after a period of work, triples are formed so that each problem has been worked on by someone in each triple. Members of triples can then compare and contrast their tasks and their approaches, thereby enriching the experience of all without each person's having to work separately on each task. Thinking to use this strategy requires careful preparation of the tasks so that, when the triples form, they learn from the variation in the three problems. One might consider the strategy but then be dissatisfied with the three problems; be overwhelmed by the organizational difficulties; or experience other obstacles, such as concern that students will not react well to a change of ways of working. One may be fully prepared but then literally forget to use the strategy until insufficient time is left in the lesson (possibly a form of displacement activity) or balk at using it at the last moment for other complex self-justifying reasons. Even more likely, having experienced or heard about the strategy, one may consider it a good idea yet not have it come to mind while preparing for lessons in which it might be useful, which can happen with any good idea, however attractive initially. The discipline of noticing can be used to enhance the possibility of having come to mind. Indeed, the mark of effective professional development is that participants can imagine themselves in the future acting responsively and freshly rather than habitually. The mark of improving research capacities for individuals lies in their being able to imagine themselves in the future acting (responding) more appropriately than before.

Branches of Noticing

In the remainder of the chapter, I offer a glimpse into ways in which use of the discipline of noticing has afforded insights not only into the teaching and learning of mathematics but also into the functioning of noticing itself (for what some others have done, see Davis & Lerman, 2009). No natural path through these sections exists, because each section draws upon and informs others. Noticing can be used to focus on fine detail while ignoring other aspects, but it can also be used to maintain the complexity of phenomena of teaching and learning. True to the discipline of noticing, what is being offered here is, at best, a collection of signposts indicating that others have been this way before and suggesting foci for further self-study.

Account of and Accounting for

When reporting an incident as part of professional development or research into practice it is usual to intermingle description with explanation, justification, and theorizing. Think, for example, how often people preface a report with some self-deprecating comment or emotive explanation for its inadequacies. This is part of the functioning of self-justification, the construction of narratives for the purpose of self-assertion and self-calming. Think, too, how often data that are offered (especially when derived from video of classrooms) use theoretical constructs in their very description. For example, reporting two nearly contiguous moments in a classroom video, someone spoke of (a) "the moment the teacher entered and dominated the two children" and (b) "the moment the teacher tried to get the students to present what they had been doing iconically." Identifying precisely which moment is intended is difficult because of the judgmental baggage in the term *dominate*, and, no matter how familiar people are with the notion of iconic (re)presentation (Bruner, 1966), the technical term was not what was observed but, rather, its use signals an interpretation by means of theory. These statements could be modified to (a) "the moment the teacher entered [the shot] and started talking, standing behind the two children who were slouched on the table" and (b) "the moment the teacher suggested that they use a diagram to record their thinking"; these statements are closer to what could be observed by others, but again the term *slouched* contains evaluative judgment. We still do not know what the teacher said, so we cannot consider what sense the children made of it. A further modification to the first statement became "the moment the teacher entered [the shot] and started talking, standing behind the two children who had their arms on the table, their heads resting on their arms, and who were looking up at the teacher." This more precise description is more easily identified by someone spinning through the video and more easily recognized, both by people who have seen the video and more generally as an incident within most teachers' experience.

Listening to people's accounts of what they saw in a mathematical animation and to accounts of lesson incidents quickly brought out the distinction between giving an *account of* and *accounting for* the account-of. The former must be as free of theorizing, emotional content, justification, and explanation as possible so that others can recognize the incident being described (even if they were not present, they may be able to enter a similar incident of their own). Useful accounts-of provide brief but vivid descriptions. Only after the incident has been identified does it make sense to start theorizing, explaining, and accounting for not only what was observed but why it struck the observer sufficiently to be identified or marked (see Tripp, 1993). Similar remarks apply to descriptions of moments in a mathematical animation or, indeed, moments during work on tasks.

Labels, Multiple Meanings, and Interpretations

When incidents have been described briefly but vividly, listeners can usually recall similar situations from their own experiences. By describing these experiences in turn, the group can negotiate what is similar and what is distinctive so that a rich collection of related incidents become part of the discourse of the group. Finding a descriptive label using words that might occur in similar incidents in the future can help associated actions come to mind when something similar is developing in the future (Mason, 1999). Idiosyncratic labels (such as learners' names) are much less effective than descriptive labels in coagulating multiple experiences under one label. Deferring theorizing and accounting for enriches the collection, for, once the situation is boxed up and interpreted, it loses a great deal of its force to promote informed non-habitual action in the future.

Part of the practice of self-observation is the search for multiple interpretations. Human beings are complex organisms. Settling quickly on a single interpretation of one's own or someone else's actions promotes simplicity, but in reducing complexity one lessens the richness and significance of the interpretation. Consequently, a valuable practice when accounting for incidents captured as data is to seek multiple, preferably conflicting, interpretations. Holding multiplicity opens possibilities, whereas classifying and explaining away close them. Interpretations held in tension have residual energy; when tensions are removed, energy escapes and stasis results. For example, when the learners had their heads down, they might have been off task, perhaps even dozing, but they might also have been thinking deeply. Their "looking up at the teacher" might be an indication of dread or fear of being caught, of hope that they would get scaffolding to their thinking, or of concern that their pleasure at struggling might be about to be taken away by a teacher giving them the answer or clues towards an answer. Holding these as possibilities instead of choosing among them invigorates future incidents when learners are acting similarly, whereas otherwise one might be tempted to make an incorrect assumption about what was going on.

Experiencing: Not Noticing, Barely Noticing, Marking, and Recording as Energy States

Experience is a curious phenomenon. Of the myriads of sensations with which we are bombarded each day, most are censored out by somatic processing (Norretranders, 1991/1998). The extent of this censoring varies. First, I may think that I am experiencing, yet later, when asked whether I noticed something, I may be entirely oblivious of what the person is referring to—an example of simple *not noticing*: Nothing about what is described is immediately accessible even though I thought that I was awake and present. Second, I may recognize what is being described, although I had otherwise forgotten it. This is *barely noticing*. Third, I may think to make a remark to someone about something I noticed, which I call *marking*. Finally, I may be so struck by the incident that I make some form of *recording* to enable me to re-enter the incident at a future date—the role of brief but vivid descriptions in an account-of.

In order to learn intentionally from experience, we must withdraw from action and reflect on or reconstruct that action and its effects (Simon & Tzur, 2004). But, despite the view expressed by William James (1890/1950) about the flow of consciousness, observation reveals that experience is recalled in fragments, and the sharper conjecture that "experience is fragmentary" has considerable justification (Mason, 1988; Tversky, Zacks, & Hard, 2008). Something attracts my attention. I am bright and alert. Then, over time, my alertness fades until there is another sudden attracting of attention. When I recall incidents, I alight on such a fragment, just as I am struck by some fragment of an animation or of a lesson, whether in real time or on video. Being a narrative animal (Bruner, 1990), I glue these fragments into a story that helps me make sense of my experience. This scenario applies equally to the carrying out of mathematical techniques; to constructing meaning for mathematical concepts; to learning from experience of doing exercises, working on problems, or exploring; and to creating meta-stories about why I am learning mathematics, my place in the class, and my sense of agency.

When recalling, reflecting on, or reconstructing some incident or event, one readily recalls what was marked. What can then be reconstructed through metonymic association and metaphoric resonance (eschewing deductive chains of "I must have . . .") can then gain in significance or richness so as to be marked or recorded as well. Intentional reflection and reconstruction enhance the possibility of being sufficiently awake at some future moment so as to be able to respond freshly rather than to react habitually to the situation while it develops. An increasingly popular term for this state, taken from ancient Buddhism, is *mindfulness* (Korthagen & Vasalos, 2010; Langer, 1997).

Energy Levels

Examples of noticing, marking, and recording are encountered in work with teachers. Like members of any caring profession, teachers notice all sorts of things while teaching. Some things are sufficiently striking to come to mind later when the teacher is reflecting and reconstructing, perhaps with colleagues, whether formally or informally. But getting teachers to write accounts, to make records of what they notice, is much more difficult, just as sustaining a diary or journal is difficult: Energy is required to overcome bodily, cognitive, and affective resistance ("Time is too short," "There are other things that take priority," "I can't be bothered," "I don't really have anything to record," "I can't decide what to record," and so on). The requisite energy can come from commitment to regular exchanges with colleagues, from personal discipline developed over time, or in association with some goal, such as pursuit of a higher degree, promotion, and the like. The discipline of noticing provides a structure within which to work on noticing intentionally. The energy required to maintain the discipline comes from the individual's nexus of social relationships, inner resources, and commitment.

Inner Witness/Monitor

Intentional self-observation through disciplined attempts to notice can gradually build what might be referred to as an *inner witness* or *monitor*. This idea can also be traced back to ancient writings such as the Rg Veda (see Figure 3.1). One interpretation is of an inner witness that looks on while the rest of the psyche is involved in action. The monitor does not comment, judge, or evaluate. It simply observes. Its presence gives the person an enriched sense of being present, mindful, and awake to what is happening that goes beyond simplistic notions of consciousness and awareness.

The importance of developing a mathematical inner witness cannot be overstated. To have come to mind such questions as "Why are we doing this . . . (example, calculation, etc.)?" and "Are you sure that is what you meant to say or do?" in the midst of action is essential when working on mathematical problems (Schoenfeld, 1985) and when making sense of written mathematics. Such a witness can arise spontaneously, but for most people it needs to be nurtured intentionally through disciplined use of reflection on and reconstruction of recent incidents. Awakening the witness/monitor is the central aim of the discipline of noticing.

Two birds, close-yoked companions
Both clasp the self same tree
One eats of the sweet fruit
The other looks on without eating.
(Bennett, 1964, p. 108)

FIGURE 3.1 The inner witness
Source: From *Energies: Material, vital, cosmic*, by J. G. Bennett, 1964, p. 108. Photo reprinted with permission from the photographer, Andrew Rix.

Awareness ≠ Consciousness ≠ Awareness + Consciousness

Gattegno (1987) used the word *awareness* to mean "that which enables action." Thus not all awareness is conscious, inasmuch as our bodies regularly act to alter breathing, heartbeat, hormone flow, and many other somatic functions. He then suggested that only awareness is educable, and this assertion has the property of acting like a protasis (an assertion of generality) for a syllogism (Mason, 1998b): People naturally draw on and interrogate their own experiences as a particular, which, when juxtaposed with the general protasis, generates a syllogistic action. The tension in holding back from drawing a conclusion can be put to good effect to stimulate noticing and the growth of an inner monitor.

For example, pointing is an action enabled by an awareness, which, when brought to the surface through becoming consciously aware of it, leads to the notion of one-to-one correspondence and counting; labeling is another kind of action enabled by awareness grounded in use of language. These awarenesses are associated with functioning in the worlds in which we act (the material world, the mental world, and the world of symbols; cf. Bruner, 1966).

Gattegno (1987) suggested further that mathematics as a discipline arises or is extended when someone becomes aware of an awareness, often by becoming aware of the action that has been enabled. Lakoff and Nunez (2000) reached similar conclusions that the origins of much of mathematics lies in bodily awareness, though they seem to be less clear about how this idea applies to more advanced concepts. At times, locating a specific bodily awareness underpinning concepts, for example ratio, linear independence, or function, is difficult, but locating the actions and consequently the enabling awarenesses that underpin these and other mathematical concepts is not. To aid clarity, I refer to these awarenesses as *awareness-in-action*, because they arise through becoming aware of actions, and so articulating and formalizing them (Mason, 1998a). Examples of awareness-in-action include familiarity with putting things into bags and taking them out as a basis for addition and subtraction as well as for sets (bags within bags) and many-folding as a basis for multiplicative reasoning (I am grateful to Brent Davis, private communication, May 17, 2007 for this etymological insight).

Awareness of awareness arises from noticing; the noticing occurs spontaneously during investigation but usually requires intentional acts as shifts of attention (Mason, 1989; Mason & Davis, 1989) initiated by a teacher. The core awarenesses on which the school mathematics curriculum is built have been elaborated and referred to with different labels by other authors coming from slightly different perspectives, but they all contribute to awareness of the transformations, shifts, or awarenesses that need to be developed in order to make sense of school mathematics. For example, Simon (2006) described *a conceptual advance* as "one that changes students' ability to think about and/or perceive particular mathematical relationships" (p. 362). Similarly, Cuoco, Goldenberg, and Mark (1996) discussed *mathematical propensities* that can be developed.

The study of misconceptions is closely related to awareness of awarenesses because misconceptions often arise from misapplied, incomplete, or inappropriate awarenesses. For example, "More means bigger," "When in doubt, assume linearity," and $0.3 \times 0.3 = 0.9$ are incomplete or inappropriate awarenesses arising from a use of natural powers on incomplete data together with pedagogical lapses (Tirosh & Tsamir, 2004).

Teaching is another matter. Clearly, one can be an expert mathematician without being particularly skilled in teaching mathematics. Different attributes are required of mathematicians and effective teachers. A major thrust in mathematics education currently is to try to articulate precisely the distinction between what effective mathematicians have come to mind and what effective teachers have come to mind in their professional activities. Applying to teaching Gattegno's insight about awareness suggests that, in order to become expert, you need to become aware of your awareness–in–action, which I call *awareness-in-discipline*, but which is really awareness of awareness of awareness.[1] This awareness-in-discipline is a distinct type of awareness, because to function effectively mathematically you need to have come to mind heuristics such as "Try working backwards," powers such as "Try specializing in order to regeneralize for yourself," and mathematical themes such as "doing and undoing" and "invariance in the midst of change." An effective teacher needs to become aware of these as awarenesses to be called upon, in order to construct tasks that bring them to learners' awareness and in order to draw attention to them when they are relevant. Whereas to a mathematician these awarenesses are integrated or internalized actions rarely worthy of explicit attention, to a teacher they are important foci of attention as prompts to learners in such a way that they internalize them for themselves. At first they are pointed out directly and explicitly; over time they are referred to less and less explicitly and more and more indirectly until learners integrate them into their own functioning. The labels *directed–prompted–spontaneous* have been used (Floyd, Burton, James, & Mason, 1981) as a reminder to teachers that scaffolding (Wood, Bruner, & Ross, 1976) is accomplished only when the scaffolding has faded away (Brown, Collins, & Duguid, 1989; Love & Mason, 1992). For more examples, see Mason (1999) and Mason and Johnston-Wilder (2004).

Because even more is required of a teacher educator, teaching people to be teachers of mathematics is a discipline in itself, just as teaching mathematics and doing mathematics are disciplines. Applying Gattegno's insight once more, in order to become an effective educator you need to become aware of your awareness-in-discipline, which, for reference purposes, I call *awareness-in-counsel* (Mason, 1998a). Awareness-in-counsel includes awareness of ways of working with people so that they become aware for themselves of actions they are taking, which in turn are designed to prompt learners to learn mathematics effectively. Each level of awareness is built up through noticing, whether spontaneously or intentionally.

In summary then:

- *Awareness* is what enables action.
- *Awareness of awareness* (*awareness-in-action*) is a formalization and hence institutionalization of awarenesses that enable action.
- *Awareness of awareness-in-action* (*awareness-in-discipline*) is what enables articulation and formalization of awarenesses-in-action and so is the basis for and informs teaching.
- *Awareness of awareness-in-discipline* (*awareness-in-counsel*) is the self-awareness required in order to be sensitive to what others require in order to build their own awareness-in-action and awareness-in-discipline.

Each type of awareness develops and is internalized through being sensitized to notice, for which the discipline of noticing can provide helpful techniques. Thus an awareness of fractions as actions on sets of objects, and an awareness that different objects or parts of objects can be considered to be *the unit* enable multiplication and addition of fractions to be carried out; awareness of this awareness enables fractions to be considered as objects; awareness of this awareness of awareness is necessary in order to teach others effectively about the arithmetic of fractions; awareness of awareness of awareness of awareness is needed in order to teach others how to teach the arithmetic of fractions.

Role and Structure of Attention

To notice requires attention to something; indeed attention *is* both observation and the medium through which observation takes place. As William James (1890/1950) proposed, this attending can be either spontaneously reactive or intentionally responsive. An act of attention can be fleeting or sustained. When our attending is sustained, we may be aware, in the sense of being consciously, explicitly aware, and form a sufficiently lasting sense impression so as to have this incident or something related to it come to mind in the future (marking). We may not, however, be consciously aware, yet our bodies may be sufficiently aware subconsciously to incorporate (literally) something, which may then influence future behavior. For example, a new colleague repeatedly used the phrase "bottom line," and soon other colleagues and I were using it, mostly unwittingly with only the slightest twinge of recognition; another colleague started using "at the end of the day" frequently, with the same effect. The interwoven strands of noticing, attention, awareness, and consciousness form the basis for effective and intentional teaching as well as for socio-psychological analysis of learning (Mason, 2008).

Noticing is a movement or shift of attention. If I am working in my office and someone passes by in the corridor, my attention is diverted or attracted by my peripheral vision, and I look up; if I am working on a mathematical problem and something else pops into my mind that I am supposed to do, I start doing that; if I am gazing at a mathematical diagram or at some algebraic manipulation and suddenly I notice a recurring expression or something familiar about some part, I start attending to that. Some of these reactions are desirable, whereas some are literally energy leaks, drawing my attention away from a focus and so diminishing concentration.

What is noticed, marked, or recorded is necessarily being attended to. Attention can be seen as the manifestation of will, of intention. However, in a very central sense, "we are where our attention is," or even "we are our attention" (Harding, 1961). Thus we have habits of speech such as "Give me your attention," "Thank you for your attention," and the more sarcastic "Are you with us?" The military command "Attention!" is presumably intended to startle people into a heightened state of wakefulness. These uses signal the centrality of attention in human experience. As James said,

> Every one knows what attention is. It is the taking possession by the mind, in clear and vivid form, of one out of what seem several simultaneously possible objects or trains of thought. Focalization, concentration, of consciousness are of its essence.
>
> James (1890/1950, pp. 404–405)

Attention is not a thing to be observed in others, but its influence can be inferred. Even when eye tracking is used, all we can observe is where the subject's eyes appear to be focused, but not whether the subject is actually attending to that focus or in what manner. This fact raises a question about ways in which we attend to things.

Attention has at least macro-, meso-, and micro-structures, and these can be in rapid flux or relatively stable. In its macro-structure, attention can vary (a) in the focus (what is attended to, singular or multiple), (b) in the locus (the source or basis of attention, which can be in various parts of the body or external to it), (c) in the strength or amplitude (from feeble to intense), and (d) in the scope or breadth (broad or narrow) (Mason, 1982, 1998a, 2009; Mason & Davis, 1989).

In its meso-structure, attention can be dominated by a particular collection of beliefs or perspectives. Adolescents, for example, are engaged in an enterprise of discovering themselves as social beings, both dependent upon and independent of surrounding adults. They are concerned primarily about locating themselves within their growing awareness of the social communities of which they are part, so work on getting them to make significant mathematical choices can both resonate with and contribute to that enterprise, whereas imposing tightly structured tasks may not. From quite a young age, children are fascinated by the notion of infinity: As Dick Tahta (private communication, June 12, 1985) pointed out, addressing the notion of infinity is an opportunity to show how mathematicians work on and control a topic that resonates deeply with children's growing recognition of mortality and yet their youthful sense of immortality. Within mathematics, children may, for example, be dominated by a sense of number as discrete, so that one needs to help them gain confidence with a parallel or encompassing continuous sense of quantity to develop flexibility (Watson, 2008). To them, justifications may have previously been empirical and ad hoc, so a shift to deduction from agreed properties needs to be developed, opening the way to axiomatic mathematical reasoning.

In terms of micro-structure, people can attend differently at different times (Mason, 1998a, 2009) in the following ways:

1. *Holding wholes* is attending by gazing at something without particularly discerning details. Examples include gazing at a diagram, at the ceiling, or at algebraic calculations, as well as holding a problem in mind and allowing the subconscious to work away at it (Hadamard, 1945).

2. *Discerning details* is picking out bits, discriminating this from that, decomposing or subdividing and so distinguishing and, hence, creating things.

3. *Recognizing relationships* is becoming aware of sameness and difference or other relationships among the discerned details in the situation. In mathematics this awareness includes functional relationships; operational relationships such as additive, multiplicative or exponential; geometrical relations such as similarity, congruence and symmetry; and more general relations.

4. *Perceiving properties* is becoming aware of particular relationships as instances of properties that could hold in other situations.

5. *Reasoning on the basis of agreed properties* is going beyond the assembling of things you think you know, intuit, or induce must be true in order to use previously justified properties as the basis for convincing yourself and others, leading to reasoning from definitions and axioms.

In mathematics, the shift from recognizing relationships to perceiving properties is often subtle but immediate for experts and yet an obstacle for students. When teacher and students are attending to different things, communication is unlikely to be efficient. Even when teacher and students are attending to the same things, they may be attending differently, and so communication may be, at best, restricted and incomplete, if it does not break down altogether. Teaching people to reason mathematically is well known as a pedagogical challenge, despite its apparently deeply rational nature. Those who make the transition easily are challenged to see any difficulty. For example, Henri Poincaré (1956/1960) reported being astonished that most people find mathematics difficult, despite its being the most rational of disciplines. However, as Swift (1726/1941) noted, human beings are not so much rational animals as animals capable of reason. Most of us need help in making the requisite shifts of attention.

These distinctions in the micro-structure of attention arose for me from considering neo-Pythagorean studies of number (Bennett, 1956–1966) but match well with studies by Pierre and Dina van Hiele in geometry (Usiskin, 1982), with one notable difference: Shifts among ways of attending are usually frequent, and not confined to levels of understanding.

Summary

The core of the discipline of noticing is a collection of techniques for (a) preparing to notice in the moment, that is, to have come to mind appropriately; (b) post-paring by reflecting on the recent past to select what one wants to notice or be sensitized to particularly; in order (c) to *pare*, that is, notice in the moment and so be enabled to act freshly rather than habitually. This core applies to both personal and professional development. In this chapter, I have presented a brief version of the discipline of noticing and how it arose for me and came to be articulated. I am aware of some of its roots but, of course, not all: Ideas travel quickly, subtly, and often below the visible surface both across and within cultures. I have also indicated ways in which noticing can be and has been used and how it interweaves with attention, awareness, and consciousness.

In addition, I have tried, despite writing *about* noticing, to insert examples and descriptions of observations and to write in such a way that might resonate with or trigger associations with readers' experiences so as to initiate actions that might lead to informed choices in the future, whether those choices are concerned with professional development, research, or personal development. Validity lies in what you find does or does not inform your future practice.

Note

1 I am not claiming that this is sufficient, only necessary. Effective teaching also depends on forming and maintaining appropriate relationships with and sensitivities to students, including patient tolerance of students not understanding new ideas immediately and the effort required to internalize and integrate mathematical ideas and procedures into self-initiated actions.

References

Aronson, E. (1978). *The jigsaw classroom*. Beverly Hills, CA: Sage.

Bateson, M. (1994). *Peripheral visions: Learning along the way*. New York: HarperCollins.

Bennett, J. G. (1956–1966). *The dramatic universe* (Vols. 1–4). London: Hodder & Stoughton.

Bennett, J. G. (1964). *Energies: Material, vital, cosmic*. Kingston upon Thames, England: Coombe Springs Press.

Bennett, J. G. (1976). *Noticing* (The Sherborne Theme Talks, Vol. 2). Sherborne, Glos., England: Coombe Springs Press.

Brown, S., Collins, A., & Duguid, P. (1989). Situated cognition and the culture of learning. *Educational Researcher, 18*(1), 32–41.

Bruner, J. (1966). *Towards a theory of instruction*. Cambridge, MA: Harvard University Press.

Bruner, J. (1990). *Acts of meaning*. Cambridge, MA: Harvard University Press.

Cuoco, A., Goldenberg, P., & Mark, J. (1996). Habits of mind: An organizing principle for mathematics curricula. *Journal of Mathematical Behavior, 15*, 375–402.

Davis, B., & Lerman, S. (2009). *Mathematical actions and structures of noticing: Studies on John Mason's contribution to mathematics education*. Rotterdam, The Netherlands: Sense.

Floyd, A., Burton, L., James, N., & Mason, J. (1981). *EM235: Developing mathematical thinking*. Milton Keynes, England: Open University Press.

Gattegno, C. (1987). *The science of education: Part I. Theoretical considerations*. New York: Educational Solutions.

Hadamard, J. (1945). *An essay on the psychology of invention in the mathematical field*. Princeton, NJ: Princeton University Press.

Harding, D. (1961). *On having no head: Zen and the re-discovery of the obvious*. London: Arkana (Penguin).

James, W. (1950). *Principles of psychology* (Vol. 1). New York: Dover. (Original work published 1890)

Korthagen, F., & Vasalos, A. (2010). Going to the core: Deepening reflection by connection. In N. Lyons (Ed.), *Handbook of reflection and reflective inquiry* (pp. 531–554). New York: Springer.

Lakoff, G., & Nunez, R. (2000). *Where mathematics comes from: How the embodied mind brings mathematics into being*. New York: Basic Books.

Langer, E. (1997). *The power of mindful learning*. Reading, MA: Addison-Wesley.

Love, E., & Mason, J. (1992). *Teaching mathematics: Action and awareness*. Milton Keynes, England: Open University Press.

Mason, J. (1982). Attention. *For the Learning of Mathematics, 2*(3), 21–23.

Mason, J. (1984). Towards one possible discipline for mathematics education. In H. Steiner (Ed.), *Theory of mathematics education* (pp. 42–55). Bielefeld, Germany: Institute for the Didactics of Mathematics, Bielefeld University.

Mason, J. (1988). Fragments: The implications for teachers, learners and media users/ researchers of personal construal and fragmentary recollection of aural and visual messages. *Instructional Science, 17*, 195–218.

Mason, J. (1989). Mathematical abstraction seen as a delicate shift of attention. *For the Learning of Mathematics, 9*(2), 2–8.

Mason, J. (1998a). Enabling teachers to be real teachers: Necessary levels of awareness and structure of attention. *Journal of Mathematics Teacher Education, 1*, 243–267.

Mason, J. (1998b). Protasis: A technique for promoting professional development. In C. Kanes, M. Goos, & E. Warren (Eds.), *Teaching mathematics in new times: Proceedings of the Twenty-first Annual Conference of the Mathematics Education Research Group of Australasia* (MERGA-21) (Vol. 1, pp. 334–341). Gold Coast, Queensland: Mathematics Education Research Group of Australasia.

Mason, J. (1999). The role of labels for experience in promoting learning from experience among teachers and students. In L. Burton (Ed.), *Learning mathematics: From hierarchies to networks* (pp. 187–208). London: Falmer.

Mason, J. (2002). *Researching your own practice: The discipline of noticing*. London: RoutledgeFalmer.

Mason, J. (2008). Being mathematical with and in front of learners: Attention, awareness, and attitude as sources of differences between teacher educators, teachers and learners. In T. Wood (Series Ed.) & B. Jaworski (Vol. Ed.), *International handbook of mathematics teacher education: Vol. 4. The mathematics teacher educator as a developing professional* (pp. 31–56). Rotterdam, The Netherlands: Sense.

Mason, J. (2009). Teaching as disciplined enquiry. *Teachers and teaching: Theory and practice,* *15*(2–3), 205–223.

Mason, J., & Davis, J. (1989). The inner teacher, the didactic tension, and shifts of attention. In G. Vergnaud, J. Rogalski, & M. Artigue (Eds.), *Proceedings of the 13th Psychology of Mathematics Education International Conference* (Vol. 2, pp. 274–281). Paris: Psychology of Mathematics Education.

Mason, J., & Johnston-Wilder, S. (2004). *Designing and using mathematical tasks.* Milton Keynes, England: Open University Press.

Norretranders, T. (1998). *The user illusion: Cutting consciousness down to size* (J. Sydenham, Trans.). London: Allen Lane. (Original work published 1991)

Ouspensky, P. (1950). *In search of the miraculous.* London: Routledge & Kegan Paul.

Poincaré, H. (1960). Mathematical creation: Lecture to the Psychology Society of Paris. In J. Newman (Ed.), *The World of Mathematics* (pp. 2041–2050). London: George Allen & Unwin. (Original work published 1956)

Schoenfeld, A. H. (1985). *Mathematical problem solving.* New York: Academic Press.

Simon, M. (2006). Key developmental understandings in mathematics: A direction for investigating and establishing learning goals. *Mathematical Thinking and Learning, 8,* 359–371.

Simon, M., & Tzur, R. (2004). Explicating the role of mathematical tasks in conceptual learning: An elaboration of the hypothetical learning trajectory. *Mathematical Thinking and Learning, 6,* 91–104.

Swift, J. (1941). Gulliver's travels. In H. J. Davis (Ed.), *The prose works of Jonathan Swift: Vol. 11. Gulliver's travels.* Oxford, England: Blackwell. (Original work published 1726)

Tahta, D. (1981). Some thoughts arising from the new Nicolet films. *Mathematics Teaching, 94,* 25–29.

Tirosh, D., & Tsamir, P. (2004). Commentary: What can mathematics education gain from the conceptual change approach? And what can the conceptual change approach gain from its application to mathematics education? *Learning and Instruction, 14,* 535–540.

Tripp, D. (1993). *Critical incidents in teaching: Developing professional judgement.* London: Routledge.

Tversky, B., Zacks, J., & Hard, B. (2008). The structure of experience. In T. Shipley & J. Zacks (Eds.), *Understanding events* (pp. 436–464). Oxford, England: Oxford University Press.

Usiskin, Z. (1982). *Van Hiele levels and achievement in secondary school geometry.* Chicago: University of Chicago Press.

Watson, A. (2008). *Necessary shifts in secondary mathematics.* Retrieved July 14, 2009, from http://www.education.ox.ac.uk/uploaded/Mathematical%20thinking%20in%20adolescence.ppt

Wood, D., Bruner, J., & Ross, G. (1976). The role of tutoring in problem solving. *Journal of Child Psychology and Psychiatry, 17,* 89–100.

4

SITUATION AWARENESS IN TEACHING

What Educators Can Learn From Video-Based Research in Other Fields[1]

Kevin F. Miller

In both popular conception (e.g., "she has eyes in the back of her head," Corey & Teague, 2001, p. 10) and theoretical models (Erickson, 1984; Sabers, Cushing, & Berliner, 1991), a hallmark of expert teachers is their ability to monitor the complex, chaotic environment of a classroom and home in on key features relevant to monitoring student understanding. For beginning teachers, a key worry is whether they will be able to monitor and manage a classroom of children (Sadler, 2006), and this should be no surprise. Communicating complex ideas and information clearly is difficult enough, without the added need to monitor student understanding and maintain student attention.

Teaching is an enormously complex activity, but it is not the only complex skill that humans acquire. The focus of this chapter is on considering what research in other domains can show us that will inform our understanding of how expert teachers watch a classroom and guide our efforts to promote the acquisition of that expertise. Researchers in domains ranging from athletics to piloting aircraft have developed models of what expert looking entails, how it is developed, and the role that video-based training can play in the development of skilled viewing. Research on expertise in classroom viewing and in other skills shows the importance of skilled viewing—termed *situation awareness* (Endsley, 1995)—as a key and learnable feature of expert performance in a range of complex skills.

The term *situation awareness* embodies a theory of noticing, one that is useful in thinking about the cognitive and perceptual work of teachers. One needs to perceive what is important in a given situation and to infer what it portends with respect to the goals of that situation. This requires one to notice meaningful features of the classroom situation and to figure out what the meaning of those features is in time to do something about it (respond to a disruption, identify student misunderstanding, etc.).

The research reviewed here will also identify two important clarifications of the concept of *noticing*. The first is that experts are often distinguished as much by what they *do not* notice as by what they do. Expert viewing is often exquisitely tuned to the requirements of expertise, and a skilled teacher may be someone who has (in part) learned to ignore features that are unimportant. In my own work in Chinese schools, I have been impressed with the amount of misbehavior that teachers of elementary school students simply ignore, avoiding disruptions in the flow of a lesson. A second aspect of noticing is that it need not necessarily be a conscious process. Experts often have difficulty identifying what it is that they noticed (Allen & Reber, 1999), and it seems likely that much of what experienced teachers notice does not involve conscious processes that take attention away from the myriad other cognitive processes in which they are engaged. The concept of noticing that underlies this chapter is most consistent with an old quote from the mathematician Whitehead:

> It is a profoundly erroneous truism, repeated by all copy-books and by eminent people when they are making speeches, that we should cultivate the habit of thinking about what we are doing. The precise opposite is the case. Civilization advances by extending the numbers of important operations which we can perform without thinking about them. Operations of thought are like cavalry charges in battle—they are strictly limited in number, they require fresh horses, and must only be made at decisive moments.
>
> Whitehead (1911/1992, pp. 41–42)

Teachers need to be aware of what is going on in their classrooms relevant to student learning. If the development of teachers' situation awareness parallels that in other fields, this awareness should involve learning to react to what is important (and ignore what is not) and may, with expertise, become an increasingly tacit process.

To understand and improve teacher situation awareness, researchers need to answer three sets of questions that will be the focus of this chapter. They are:

1. What is the nature of expert viewing? That is, what are the strategies and mechanisms that underlie situation awareness?
2. How is expert viewing acquired? What obstacles stand in the way of developing situation awareness?
3. What kinds of materials and pedagogical approaches will enable us to promote the acquisition of situation awareness?

What Is the Nature of Expert Viewing?

The idea that experts quickly see what is important in their domains of expertise dates to the earliest studies of expertise (de Groot, 1965), and a consistent finding is that expert looking processes are attuned to the demands of particular domains of expertise. Chase and Simon (1973) demonstrated that expert chess players could reconstruct chess positions after very brief exposures, but only for meaningful (as opposed to random) configurations of pieces. More recently researchers have identified the viewing processes that develop with expertise in particular domains, primarily athletics and aviation.

Key Concepts: Situation Awareness Versus Cognitive Tunneling

Although the nature of expert looking varies by domain, the cognitive consequence of expert viewing has, as previously mentioned, been termed *situation awareness* (Endsley, 1995, 2000). Endsley (2000) defined situation awareness as involving three factors: (a) perception of meaningful elements in an environment, (b) comprehension of their meaning, and (c) projection of their status in the near future.

The opposite of situation awareness is a phenomenon termed *cognitive tunneling* (Dirkin, 1983), in which novices narrow their attentional field while performing a complex task. A teacher who only attends to a small subset of students and a pilot whose attention is focused on just a few instruments are examples of professionals engaged in cognitive tunneling.

But it is not the case that experts attend to everything in their perceptual field. Because attention is always limited, situation awareness involves learning not to attend to some aspects of the world. The difference between experts and novices is that the selection of what to attend to is adaptively tuned to the demands of the situation. For example, skilled soccer goalies defending against a penalty kick attend to the kicker's posture but not to other misleading cues about where the ball will be kicked, such as movement or positioning of the kicker's hands or shoulders (Williams & Davids, 1998). For situations in which the shot is made with a stick, as in hockey, goalies were more successful when their final gaze was on the stick or the puck rather than on any part of the shooter (Panchuk & Vickers, 2006). Although hockey and soccer seem quite similar in the goalie's role (defending a net against an object shot by the opponent), the viewing patterns of skilled goalies in these two sports differ systematically as a function of which aspects of the opponent's body predict where the shot will go. The viewing patterns of experts are attuned to the relevant features of a domain and thus contribute to maintaining situation awareness, whereas the viewing patterns of novices show a less optimal selection from the complexity of the perceptual world.

Skilled Viewing in Other Domains

The nature of expert viewing has been described in detail in a number of cognitive domains. Expert athletes in sports such as tennis, soccer, and cricket can determine the ball's path much earlier than can their less skilled peers. Abernethy and Russell (1984) pioneered a dramatic paradigm for revealing this phenomenon; they asked athletes to wear glasses with shutters that enabled the researchers to occlude the athletes' vision at different points in the activity. In tasks such as returning a serve in tennis or goalkeeping in soccer (Savelsburgh, Williams, van der Kamp, & Ward, 2002), skilled athletes were able to respond correctly even if their vision had been occluded slightly before the racket or foot made contact with the ball. Less skilled players required more time before they could predict the ball's path, leaving them less time to get into position and prepare to respond.

Vickers and colleagues (Vickers, Rodrigues, & Edworthy, 2000) have described a phenomenon, which they termed the *quiet eye*, in athletes' gaze patterns. Compared with the gaze of a novice, the expert's gaze directed toward a critical object or location in the performance space occurs earlier, is longer in duration, and is more regular and predictable. The quiet eye concept relates to the selective nature of expert viewing; skilled athletes are notable both for what they *do not* look at (noncritical features such as a soccer player's shoulders) as well as what they *do* (critical features such as the player's hips).

The nature of expert viewing varies greatly as a function of the domain and the demands of the skill. As the quiet phenomenon suggests, expertise in some domains is associated with narrowing the attentional focus to key areas that provide clues to what an opponent is likely to do (e.g., Goulet, Bard, & Fleury, 1989 found that, compared with novices, skilled tennis players looked more at the shoulder and trunk of their opponent and less at the head). In other contexts, however, expertise is associated with broadening rather than narrowing of looking. In the context of soccer, Williams and Davids (1998) found that novices tended to focus their attention on the ball, making far fewer peripheral looks to other players than did experts. Thus, depending on the context and the cognitive demands of the activity, expertise can be associated with a narrowing of attention to the relevant features (as in returning a tennis serve or hitting a golf ball) or to a broader scanning of a complex perceptual field (as in playing soccer or basketball).

Of the two kinds of sports discussed, teaching a class is clearly more like soccer than tennis (although one could argue that individual tutoring is more like tennis than soccer). Teachers need to attend to a large group of individual students, who may vary in their attentiveness, understanding, and personal goals (and, unlike in sports, without distinctive uniforms to identify who is on your side).

The most detailed models of expert looking have come from studies of pilot performance. Commercial pilots need to monitor a plethora of instruments while also attending to the external environment and to adjust their intended flight plans to the exigencies they encounter. This need to monitor multiple sources of information and adjust a preexisting plan to changing circumstances is similar to the situations confronting teachers.

Beginning pilots often show clear signs of cognitive tunneling, attending to only a subset of instruments, or they show difficulty moving attention between the outside world and instrument displays (Wickens, 2002). Adding task complexity can cause even experts to focus on some object or task and completely miss other key pieces of information (Wickens & Long, 1995), but, in general, an experienced pilot shows systematic scanning patterns that enable him or her to maintain awareness of the status of the airplane while it moves through the world.

A converging line of research by Simons and his colleagues has demonstrated that viewers performing difficult tasks (such as counting passes in a basketball game) can ignore information as dramatic as having a gorilla enter the scene and beat its chest in the center of the visual field (Simons & Chabris, 1999). This phenomenon, termed *inattentional blindness*, provides another example of how visual attention can be limited in the context of performing a difficult task. Simons's demonstrations are useful instructionally because they effectively counteract a naive belief that observing complex events is easy and veridical.

Skilled Viewing by Teachers

According to existing studies of expert teachers, skilled teachers are likely to differ from novices in the following ways:

1. Skilled teachers should be able to maintain attention to student understanding at the same time they are enacting a lesson.
2. Skilled teachers should show more systematic scanning patterns of students, whereas novices should be more likely to focus on a smaller sample of students while ignoring others.
3. Skilled teachers should be quicker to identify situations (misbehavior, lack of understanding, disruptive activity) that require intervention.

Although research on situation awareness in teaching is less developed than in domains such as sports, existing research is consistent with these basic ideas.

Starting with work by Berliner (1986), research on variation in what teachers notice has revealed large differences as a function of experience. Clarridge and Berliner (1991) looked at the performance of teachers varying in experience in a simulated high school classroom in which students were asked to simulate different student roles. Lessons were videotaped, and the teachers were asked to comment on the videotaped lessons. Novice and expert teachers differed greatly in what was recalled. Experts were able to identify instances of student misbehavior and discuss their reasons for responding in particular ways. Most surprising to the researchers, novices often simply failed to notice or recall instances of misbehavior on the part of students.

Sabers, Cushing, and Berliner (1991) presented participants varying in teaching expertise with videos of classrooms divided across three computer monitors. Viewers commented on instructional techniques and classroom management strategies and were asked to indicate about which monitor display they were commenting. They were also asked about specific events that were shown on particular monitors. Compared with novices, experts were better able to categorize and evaluate student behavior, and they did a much better job of dividing their attention among the computer monitors. This finding supports the view (Doyle, 1986) that experienced teachers are better able to deal with the simultaneous, multidimensional nature of classroom events.

A similar pattern of differences with expertise in recall of classroom events was found by Gonzales and Carter (1996) in comparing experienced cooperating teachers with their student teachers across the course of a semester. For instances in which novices and experienced teachers recalled similar events, novices attributed instructional problems to classroom management issues, whereas experienced teachers also connected such problems to broader instructional decisions. Researchers studying single lessons (Allen & Casbergue, 1997; Borko & Livingston, 1989) have found similar differences between novice and expert teachers, with novices focusing narrowly on their intended lesson and experts commenting on student responses to instruction.

In a cross-cultural study, Zhou (2006) found a similar narrowing of attentional focus in beginning elementary school mathematics teachers in China. Compared with their U.S. peers, Chinese mathematics teachers begin with much stronger content knowledge and also better pedagogical content knowledge (Ma, 1999; Zhou, 2006). In many ways, expert and novice Chinese elementary school mathematics teachers look identical. For example, lesson planning and initial presentations of lessons by novice and experienced teachers look very similar. Nonetheless, differences emerge when students ask questions. Experienced teachers, on the one hand, simply ignore or postpone many tangential or irrelevant questions. Novice teachers, on the other hand, repeat all student questions (perhaps to buy themselves time to think of how to respond). Once they have thus put the question on the record, they need to respond to it, even if the question is something that will lead the discussion off track. Thus even in a context in which beginning teachers show high levels of both content and pedagogical content knowledge (Ma, 1999) and provide clear initial lesson presentations, novices still suffer in comparison to expert teachers when the classroom becomes less predictable.

With expertise, teachers are able to attend to a broader range of relevant aspects of the overall situation. In an extensive review of research on teaching expertise, Hogan, Rabinowitz, and Craven (2003) argued that the shift between novice and expert involves a shift in perspective, from attending primarily to a teacher's actions to learning to monitor both teacher and student activity. Instead of focusing on delivering a lesson correctly (an example of cognitive tunneling), experienced teachers can also notice the effects of their actions on student comprehension, enabling them both to make immediate modifications to the lesson and to later reflect on what aspects of a lesson were and were not effective.

Research on expert teaching indicates that teaching expertise follows the same course of development as other complex skills, with skill the result of extended experience that leads to experts being able to attend to a broader array of information and to quickly identify what is important in classroom situations.

How Is Expert Viewing Acquired?

Studies of expertise in teaching have tended to focus on years of experience as the criterion for distinguishing novices from experts, because the effects of practice are enormous. Chase and Simon (1973) noted that grandmasters in chess have spent approximately 10,000 hours in practicing, and Hayes (1985) proposed this as a general rule across domains. This assertion has a sobering implication for thinking about teaching. Ingersoll (2003) reported that 46% of American teachers leave the field by the end of (what would have been) their fifth year of experience. Because 10,000 hours of practice approximates five years of full-time work, this finding shows that only half of American teachers will ever achieve this level of competence. Although expertise requires many hours of sustained effort, clearly time alone is no panacea. Recent models of the development of expertise emphasize that *how* one spends practice can matter as much as how much time is devoted to an activity. Ericsson, Krampe, and Tesch-Römer (1993) studied the development of expert musicians and identified a phenomenon they called *deliberate practice*. Deliberate practice is neither performing the skill nor unplanned play within the domain. As defined by Ericsson and colleagues, deliberate practice requires (a) well-defined tasks at appropriate levels of difficulty, (b) informative feedback, and (c) opportunities for repetition and correction of error.

In current American schools, practicing teachers have few opportunities to engage in anything resembling deliberate practice. The task of teaching is often ill defined, and teachers have difficulty separating their contributions from other factors (development, family background, etc.) that affect children's learning. Informative feedback on effective teaching is often rare, in part because connections between achievement data and teaching are often not drawn (but see Boudet, City, & Murnane, 2005, for a model of how schools and teachers can make these connections). Finally, because of the nature of the school calendar, a year may pass before teachers have the opportunity to reteach a unit and improve it.

In an interview and diary study of teachers, Dunn and Shriner (1999) concluded that frequent and mindful engagement in planning, assessment, and other deliberate practices may account for who develops into an expert teacher. Japanese lesson–study methods (Stigler & Hiebert, 1999) can be conceived as an example of deliberate practice, providing teachers with an opportunity to vary the way a lesson is taught and connect that variation with student learning outcomes. A number of innovative efforts to provide practicing teachers with opportunities to engage in deliberate practice are currently underway (e.g., Lewis, 2002; Sherin & Han, 2004). Given the realities of American schools, however, as well as the attrition data mentioned previously, finding opportunities to incorporate deliberate practice in preservice teacher education should be a priority.

Video-based viewing tasks may have a special role to play in promoting deliberate practice in the development of teaching expertise. Videocases can provide multiple examples of particular issues that arise in teaching, with the opportunity to explore ways of responding to those situations. If such viewing is incorporated into practice teaching, then the conditions Ericsson lays out for deliberate practice could be achieved.

What Kinds of Materials and Pedagogical Approaches Will Permit Us to Promote the Development of Situation Awareness?

In the domain of sports, several researchers have studied the extent to which perceptual training can lead to increases in performance. Farrow, Chivers, Hardingham, and Sachse (1998) showed novice tennis players video of serves from the point of view of the person returning the serve. They were taught to identify cues that predicted where the ball would go, and they responded by swinging at the virtual serve. Participants in a control group had an equal length of training watching and analyzing professional tennis matches. Eight 15-minute training sessions led to significant improvement in the ability of the experimental-group participants to predict where serves would go. A later study by Williams, Ward, Knowles, and Smeeton (2002) extended the outcome variables to include returning serves in a real tennis game, finding that perceptual training had effects that extended to real-life tennis play. Using the quiet-eye concept described previously, Harle and Vickers (2001) showed that training basketball players in how to look before shooting led to increases in free-throw performance.

Pilot training involves extensive use of video-based simulations, often coupled with realistic simulated cockpits that incorporate movement and sound. The chief advantage of these simulations is that through them pilots gain experience with rare and dangerous flight situations in a safe context. These simulations have led to a dramatic drop in deaths among beginning pilots (Allerton, 2000) and have reduced the amount of actual flying time required to achieve a given level of flying skill (Lintern, Roscoe, Koonce, & Segal, 1990).

Studies in which novices have successfully been trained to see what experts notice have two key features that differentiate them from the current state of affairs in use of classroom video. First, they are based on an understanding of how experts watch so that novices can be instructed in how experts scan scenes or where they direct their attention. This knowledge base is limited for teacher education, but the chapters in this book collectively make an important contribution to remedying this critical lacuna. Second, they present the viewer with a perspective on the event that approximates what the performer might see. One interesting shortcoming of past video-based research on teaching (including my own past work) is that it has not captured the view that teachers see, a situation that might limit its utility in teacher education. The growing body of research on expert viewing in sports provides a model for how to develop the models we need in mathematics education.

The successful video-based training techniques used in sport presented viewers with tasks relevant to performance in the domain: for example, simulating returning a serve or identifying where a ball is likely to go. As Roschelle has noted, educators often treat video material as though its meaning were self-evident, a mistake encapsulated in this anecdote:

> A researcher attends a prestigious conference armed with a project video to show. After brief introductory remarks, the researcher says, "I am going to let the data speak for themselves." But contrary to his or her expectation, the audience sees events in the video that did not appear in the researcher's analysis. Soon the session is spinning out of control, with the researcher unable to inject his or her point of view into what is becoming a charged and confrontational atmosphere.
>
> Roschelle (2000, p. 723)

Because classroom situations are complex events, the issue of what one should notice is a nontrivial one. Work by our group (Miller, Zhou, Perry, Sims, & Fang, 2009) has shown that cultural obstacles may cause American viewers to focus on aspects of the classroom (particularly the personality of the teacher and students) that may be less useful than other aspects for learning how to become a teacher. We asked teachers and college students in China and the United States to watch a set of brief classroom mathematics vignettes and provide open-ended descriptions. American viewers (both teachers and students) tended to comment on aspects of teacher personality, whereas Chinese viewers were much more likely to comment on the content of the lesson and features of teaching that would affect student understanding.

Social psychologists, starting with Ross (1977), have used the term *fundamental attribution error* to describe the tendency to overestimate the role of personal or dispositional factors (compared with situational factors) in accounting for behavior. Westerners are more likely to emphasize personal attributes as the cause of behavior than are their East Asian counterparts (Morris & Peng, 1994). Thus the finding that our U.S. viewers were particularly prone to comment on personal dispositions of teachers was not surprising, but it may have important consequences for efforts to use videocases in teacher education. To the extent that viewers (a) focus on such personal attributes and (b) view them as stable traits, they may be less likely to notice aspects of the instructional approach that could be applied to improving instruction.

A key component of developing a pedagogy of classroom video will be the development of effective instructional tasks. What kinds of tasks are likely to be helpful for novice and prospective teachers watching classroom video? Kersting (2004) has shown that successful professional development (as measured by increased pedagogical content knowledge) was also associated with measurable changes in teacher commentary on video clips of classroom instruction. Specifically, the video-based training led to increases in teachers drawing causal inferences connecting observed student mistakes and teacher responses to outcomes in the classroom. Sherin and van Es (2005) developed a successful video-based professional development program focused on helping both preservice and practicing teachers to analyze instructional practice and identify the evidence underlying these inferences. In both cases, the experience resulted in positive changes both in what viewers noticed and in how they interpreted classroom events. Spiro and his colleagues (Spiro, Collins, & Ramchandran, 2007) have developed a paradigm to facilitate the comparison of multiple videocases at the same time and have shown that this activity can lead to rapid increases in college students' abilities to compare and categorize videotaped events; this technique may be useful for helping novices identify what is important in complex classroom events.

The Importance of Perspective

Traditional classroom video takes an observer perspective, in which a main focus is on watching the teacher. Investigators in the influential TIMSS video study (Stigler, Gonzales, Kawanaka, Knoll, & Serrano, 1999) explicitly instructed their videographers to "assume the perspective of an ideal student, then point the camera toward that which should be the focus of the ideal student at any given time" (p. 35).

Is the perspective depicted important? A simple study suggests that it may be. Neisser (1983) described the results of a study of mental practice on dart throwing: College students spent time imagining themselves throwing darts at a target. Participants were asked (a) to consistently imagine either hitting a bull's-eye or narrowly missing (success vs. failure) and (b) either to take the perspective of a dart thrower (the field perspective) or to imagine watching themselves throwing darts (the observer perspective). The success/failure manipulation had no significant effect on improvement, but the perspective manipulation did, with far more of the participants in the field-perspective condition improving compared to those in the observer perspective. Later work has shown that the field versus observer[2] perspective has a large effect on the nature and emotional effect of recollections of traumatic events (McIsaac & Eich, 2004); events recalled from a field perspective yielded richer accounts of affective reactions, somatic sensations, and psychological experience.

My colleagues and I have recently begun collecting teacher-perspective video using a mobile eye-tracking system (Applied Science Laboratories, n.d.) that incorporates two cameras, one that tracks the wearer's gaze direction and the other that captures the scene in front of the wearer. By superimposing these views, we are able to capture video from the teacher's perspective while also seeing where she is looking. Although we are in the early stages of developing models of how teachers manage their attention in the course of instruction, the perspective provided by a mobile eye-tracking system can provide important insights into the nature of teacher cognition. For example, we have several instances of teachers reading passages to their students, and the task of reading in this context looks very different from the conventional picture of reading (e.g., Rayner, 1998). Reading by an experienced teacher in front of a classroom of children involves an enormous amount of divided attention, with glances up from the document every few fixations. It thus has more in common with studies of driving while talking on a cell phone (Strayer & Johnson, 2001) than with ordinary reading.

In addition to its usefulness in developing models of teacher attention during instruction, teacher-perspective video may have a more direct role to play in teacher professional development. Video from this point of view is strikingly different from standard classroom video. Because of the motion of the teacher, the video shows a far more complex and dynamic scene than that captured by traditional video. Because teacher-perspective video is more similar to what a teacher sees when she watches a classroom, watching such video will likely help viewers to see what teachers need to see in a way that will facilitate transfer to situations in which they themselves are teaching. (See also Sherin, Russ, & Colestock, this volume, chapter 6) for another project involving teacher-perspective video.)

A second potential advantage of teacher-perspective video is that it may serve to diminish the American tendency to focus on teacher personality when viewing classroom video. Teacher-perspective video literally takes the teacher out of the picture and, by so doing, removes the various visual cues that we use to quickly size up another person (Ambady & Rosenthal, 1993).

Conclusions

A key aspect of successfully teaching a classroom of students is quickly perceiving student behavior and understanding what that behavior means in terms of student understanding and engagement. These activities are the central features that constitute situation awareness in teaching. Research in other fields, among them sports and flying, has shown that expert viewing is closely tied to the demands of specific situations (e.g., hockey goalies focus on different features than do soccer goalies) but that viewing complex video that shows the performer's perspective can aid in the development of skilled performance.

Classroom video and viewing tasks in education have tended to focus on observation of the teacher, a focus that differs systematically from what prospective teachers will see when they themselves teach. Video that shows, or at least approximates, the teacher's view of a classroom is likely to be far more powerful in helping viewers develop the ability to rapidly perceive what is taking place in a classroom of students.

Educators are far from developing standards for the production of teacher-perspective video, viewing tasks that will make effective use of such materials, and models of the viewing practices that underlie the situation awareness of skilled teachers. But no one can doubt that this situation awareness is a central part of the work of teaching, and research in other fields gives reason for optimism about the likelihood of developing effective materials to help teachers improve in monitoring and understanding the dynamics of student behavior in the context of classroom instruction.

Notes

1   This chapter is based upon work supported by the Institute of Educational Sciences under Grant No. F018207 and the National Science Foundation under Grant No. 0089293.
2   For clarity, I use the term *teacher perspective* when talking about the field perspective in the context of teaching, while continuing to use the term "observer perspective" for traditional representations that focus on the teacher rather than trying to show events from her perspective.

References

Abernethy, B., & Russell, D. G. (1984). Advance cue utilization by skilled cricket batsmen. *The Australian Journal of Science and Medicine in Sport, 16*, 2–10.

Allen, R., & Reber, A. S. (1999). Unconscious intelligence. In W. Bechtel & G. Graham (Eds.), *A companion to cognitive science* (pp. 314–323). Malden, MA: Blackwell.

Allen, R. M., & Casbergue, R. M. (1997). Evolution of novice through expert teachers' recall: Implications for effective reflection on practice. *Teaching and Teacher Education, 13*, 741–755.

Allerton, D. J. (2000). Flight simulation: Past, present and future. *Aeronautical Journal, 104*, 651–663.

Ambady, N., & Rosenthal, R. (1993). Half a minute: Predicting teacher evaluations from thin slices of nonverbal behavior and physical attractiveness. *Journal of Personality and Social Psychology, 64*, 431–441.

Applied Science Laboratories (n.d.). *Mobile eye*. Retrieved October 23, 2009, from http://www.a-s-l.com/site/Products/MobileEye/tabid/70/Default.aspx

Berliner, D. C. (1986). In pursuit of the expert pedagogue. *Educational Researcher, 15*(7), 5–13.

Borko, H., & Livingston, C. (1989). Cognition and improvisation: Differences in mathematics instruction by expert and novice teachers. *American Educational Research Journal, 26*, 473–498.

Boudet, K. P., City, E., & Murnane, R. (2005). *Data wise: A step-by-step guide to using assessment results to improve teaching and learning*. Cambridge, MA: Harvard Education Press.

Chase, W. G., & Simon, H. A. (1973). Perception in chess. *Cognitive Psychology, 4*, 55–81.

Clarridge, P. B., & Berliner, D. C. (1991). Perceptions of student behavior as a function of expertise. *Journal of Classroom Interaction, 26*, 1–8.

Corey, S., & Teague, M. (2001). *Horus's horrible day.* New York: Turtleback Books.

de Groot, A. D. (1965). *Thought and choice in chess.* The Hague, The Netherlands: Mouton.

Dirkin, G. R. (1983). Cognitive tunneling: Use of visual information under stress. *Perceptual and Motor Skills, 56,* 191–198.

Doyle, W. (1986). Classroom organization and management. In M. C. Wittrock (Ed.), *Handbook of research on teaching* (3rd ed., pp. 392–425). New York: Macmillan.

Dunn, T. G., & Shriner, C. (1999). Deliberate practice in teaching: What teachers do for self-improvement. *Teaching and Teacher Education, 15,* 631–651.

Endsley, M. R. (1995). Toward a theory of situation awareness in dynamic systems. *Human Factors, 37,* 32–64.

Endsley, M. R. (2000). Theoretical underpinnings of situation awareness. In M. R. Endsley & D. J. Garland (Eds.), *Situation awareness analysis and measurement* (pp. 1–21). Mahwah, NJ: Erlbaum.

Erickson, F. (1984, Summer). What difference does teaching experience make? *IRT Communication Quarterly, 3.*

Ericsson, K. A., Krampe, R. T., & Tesch-Römer, C. (1993). The role of deliberate practice in the acquisition of expert performance. *Psychological Review, 100,* 363–406.

Farrow, D., Chivers, P., Hardingham, C., & Sachse, S. (1998). The effect of video-based perceptual training on the tennis return of serve. *International Journal of Sport Psychology, 29,* 231–242.

Gonzalez, L. E., & Carter, K. (1996). Correspondence in cooperating teachers' and student teachers' interpretations of classroom events. *Teaching and Teacher Education, 12,* 39–47.

Goulet, C., Bard, M., & Fleury, C. (1989). Expertise differences in preparing to return a tennis serve: A visual information processing approach. *Journal of Sport and Exercise Psychology, 11,* 382–398.

Harle, S., & Vickers, J. N. (2001). Training quiet eye (QE) improves accuracy in the basketball free throw. *The Sport Psychologist, 15,* 289–305.

Hayes, J. R. (1985). Three problems in teaching general skills. In S. F. Chipman, J. W. Segal, & R. Glaser (Eds.), *Thinking and learning skills: Vol. 2. Research and open questions* (pp. 391–405). Hillsdale, NJ: Erlbaum.

Hogan, T., Rabinowitz, M., & Craven, J. A. (2003). Representation in teaching: Inferences from research of expert and novice teachers. *Educational Psychologist, 38,* 235–247.

Ingersoll, R. (2003). *Is there really a teacher shortage?* Consortium for Policy Research in Education, University of Pennsylvania. Retrieved September 8, 2010, from http://www.gse.upenn.edu/pdf/rmi/Shortage-RMI-09-2003.pdf

Kersting, N. (2004, April). *Assessing what teachers learn from professional development programs centered around classroom videos and the analysis of teaching: The importance of reliable and valid measures to understand program effectiveness.* Paper presented at the annual meeting of the American Educational Research Association, San Diego, CA.

Lewis, C. (2002). *Lesson study: A handbook of teacher-led instructional materials.* Philadelphia, PA: Research for Better Schools.

Lintern, G., Roscoe, S. N., Koonce, J. M., & Segal, L. (1990). Transfer of landing skills in beginning flight training. *Human Factors, 32,* 319–327.

Ma, L. (1999). *Knowing and teaching elementary mathematics.* Mahwah, NJ: Erlbaum.

McIsaac, H. K., & Eich, E. (2004). Vantage point in traumatic memory. *Psychological Science, 15,* 248–253.

Miller, K. F., Zhou, X., Perry, M., Sims, L., & Fang, G. (2009). *Do you see what I see? Influences of culture and expertise on attention to classroom video*. Unpublished manuscript, University of Michigan, Ann Arbor.

Morris, M. W., & Peng, K. (1994). Culture and cause: American and Chinese attributions for social and physical events. *Journal of Personality and Social Psychology, 67*, 949–971.

Neisser, U. (1983). Towards a skillful psychology. In D. Rogers & J. A. Sloboda (Eds.), *The acquisition of symbolic skills* (pp. 1–17). New York: Plenum Press.

Panchuk, D., & Vickers, J. N. (2006). Gaze behaviors of goaltenders under spatial-temporal constraints. *Human Movement Science, 25*(6), 733–752.

Rayner, K. (1998). Eye movements in reading and information processing: 20 years of research. *Psychological Bulletin, 124*, 372–422.

Roschelle, J. (2000). Choosing and using video equipment for data collection. In A. E. Kelly & R. A. Lesh (Eds.), *Handbook of research design in mathematics and science education* (pp. 709–729). Mahwah, NJ: Erlbaum.

Ross, L. (1977). The intuitive psychologist and his shortcomings: Distortions in the attribution process. In L. Berkowitz (Ed.), *Advances in experimental social psychology* (Vol. 10, pp. 173–220). New York: Academic Press.

Sabers, D. S., Cushing, K. S., & Berliner, D. C. (1991). Differences among teachers in a task characterized by simultaneity, multidimensionality, and immediacy. *American Educational Research Journal, 28*, 63–88.

Sadler, T. D. (2006). "I won't last three weeks": Preservice science teachers reflect on their student-teaching experiences. *Journal of Science Teacher Education, 17*(3), 217–241.

Savelsburgh, G. J. P., Williams, A. M., van der Kamp, J., & Ward, P. (2002). Visual search, anticipation and expertise in soccer goalkeepers. *Journal of Sport Sciences, 20*, 279–287.

Sherin, M. G., & Han, S. Y. (2004). Teacher learning in the context of a video club. *Teaching and Teacher Education, 20*, 163–183.

Sherin, M. G., Russ, R. S., & Colestock, A. A. (this volume, chapter 6). *Accessing mathematics teachers' in-the-moment noticing*.

Sherin, M. G., & van Es, E. A. (2005). Using video to support teachers' ability to notice classroom interactions. *Journal of Technology and Teacher Education, 13*, 475–491.

Simons, D. J., & Chabris, C. F. (1999). Gorillas in our midst: Sustained inattentional blindness for dynamic events. *Perception, 28*, 1059–1074.

Spiro, R. J., Collins, B. P., & Ramchandran, A. (2007). Reflections on a post-Gutenberg epistemology for video use in ill-structured domains: Fostering complex learning and cognitive flexibility. In R. Goldman, R. Pea, B. Barron, & S. J. Denny (Eds.), *Video research in the learning sciences* (pp. 93–100). Mahwah, NJ: Erlbaum.

Stigler, J. W., Gonzales, P., Kawanaka, T., Knoll, S., & Serrano, A. (1999). *The TIMSS videotape classroom study: Methods and findings from an exploratory research project on eighth-grade mathematics instruction in Germany, Japan, and the United States* (NCES 99-074). Washington, DC: National Center for Education Statistics.

Stigler, J. W., & Hiebert, J. (1999). *The teaching gap*. New York: Free Press.

Strayer, D. L., & Johnston, W. A. (2001). Driven to distraction: Dual-task studies of simulated driving and conversing on a cellular phone. *Psychological Science, 12*, 462–466.

Vickers, J. N., Rodrigues, S. T., & Edworthy, G. (2000). Quiet eye and accuracy in the dart throw. *International Journal of Sports Vision, 6*, 30–36.

Whitehead, A. N. (1992). *An introduction to mathematics*. New York: Oxford. (Original work published 1911)

Wickens, C. D. (2002). Situation awareness and workload in aviation. *Current Directions in Psychological Science, 11*, 128–133.

Wickens, C. D., & Long, J. (1995). Object versus space-based models of visual attention: Implications for the design of head-up displays. *Journal of Experimental Psychology: Applied, 1*, 179–193.

Williams, A. M., & Davids, K. (1998). Visual search strategy, selective attention and expertise in soccer. *Research Quarterly for Exercise and Sport, 69*, 111–128.

Williams, A. M., Ward, P., Knowles, J. M., & Smeeton, N. J. (2002). Perceptual skill in a real-world task: Training, instruction, and transfer in tennis. *Journal of Experimental Psychology: Applied, 8*, 259–270.

Zhou, X. (2006). *First year in front of the class: The development of beginning elementary school mathematics teachers in China*. Unpublished dissertation, University of Illinois at Urbana-Champaign, Urbana, IL.

5

REFLECTIONS ON THE STUDY OF TEACHER NOTICING

Bruce Sherin and Jon R. Star

Let us start by imagining that the engine of our 1982 Camry is finally breaking down. Further, let us imagine that we have decided that it is time that we learned to make some repairs ourselves. So we have set ourselves the goal of understanding a bit about how engines work—enough, perhaps, to fix some of the more serious problems that currently afflict our beloved Camry.

But engines are fairly complex machines. So, at least initially, it probably does not make sense for us to try to understand everything about an engine. Instead, we will narrow our focus in some manner. If we are trying to repair a particular problem with the engine, we will doubtless want to narrow our focus in a way that we think is likely to help us diagnose the problem.

We can imagine narrowing our focus in multiple ways in seeking to understand our engine. One way is to narrow our focus in time and look only at events that occur occasionally. For example, one obvious problem with our engine might be that it periodically backfires. Perhaps it does so two or three times whenever we take it out for a drive. Thus seeking to understand just when and why the engine backfires might be a productive way to narrow our focus. It would not be productive, however, if we cannot understand backfiring without understanding virtually everything about how an engine works.

We might, instead, decide to focus only on a subcomponent of the engine's machinery. For example, we might know that an engine must have some way of filtering the air that it takes in and mixes with fuel. In that case, we might look for this component—the air filter—and seek to understand its functioning, an especially helpful way to narrow our focus if we believe that this is where important problems with the engine lie.

A final approach we might take, instead of looking at occasional events (e.g., backfiring) or system subcomponents (e.g., the air filter), is to take a step back and examine some attribute of the engine system as a whole. For example, we might decide to measure the engine's fuel efficiency, its temperature, or the amount of noise it makes. Such steps narrow our attention, but they do not involve a focus on any subcomponent of an engine. Rather, each of these attributes emerges from interactions among components of the entire system.

Of course, we are not budding automobile mechanics, and we are not seeking to understand how an automobile engine functions. Rather, the machinery that we wish to understand is a teacher in action—a teacher who is thinking and acting while embedded in a classroom context. However, in at least some respects, we face a similar situation to the one we would face in trying to understand an engine. Like the functioning of an engine, teacher behavior and reasoning are complex. The cognitive tasks faced by mathematics teachers are numerous and varied. They must, for example, solve mathematics problems, make sense of student ideas, craft lesson plans, and draft assessments. Furthermore, any one of these categories of cognitive tasks potentially implicates substantial cognitive machinery. Note, for example, that for a teacher to make sense of an idea expressed by a student requires mathematics knowledge and understanding of typical difficulties, not to mention the ability to understand natural language. Given the breadth of this undertaking, we, like the automobile mechanic, must narrow our focus.

The chapters in this volume are concerned with one part of teacher thought and action, mathematics teacher noticing. In announcing our focus on noticing, our goal is presumably to offer one way to take on a manageable portion of the larger task of understanding teaching. But what exactly is teacher noticing and how does a focus on teacher noticing narrow the task of understanding how teachers teach? In the above paragraphs, we listed three general approaches that we might adopt in attempting to narrow our focus when we set out to study how an engine works: (a) a focus on infrequent events, (b) a focus on a subcomponent of the machinery, and (c) a focus on an emergent attribute of the larger system. In the rest of this chapter, we look, in turn, at each of these three approaches, and we argue that those attempting to understand teacher noticing have all, at least implicitly, employed one of these three approaches.

Furthermore, we try to show that this difference in approach is much more than a methodological difference. Rather, each approach is associated with a quite different understanding of what teacher noticing means. (We call these *notions of noticing*, mostly because of opportunities for alliteration afforded by this choice.) Thus, teacher noticing has had multiple distinct meanings in the research literature. One of our goals in this chapter is to articulate some of these distinct meanings.

Thus, in a sense, this chapter is not about what teachers notice; it is about what we, as researchers, attend to when we study teacher noticing. To return to our metaphor, this is not a chapter about how engines work. It is about what a mechanic (researcher) notices when looking at an engine (a teacher embedded in a classroom).

To anticipate our conclusions, we suggest that most discussions of teacher noticing, including those that appear in this volume, adopt Approach 2. Accordingly, our discussion of Approach 2 is somewhat longer than the others, and it is associated with two notions of noticing. In contrast, Approach 1 and Approach 3 are each associated with only one notion of noticing.

Approach 1: Focus on Infrequent Events

In this first approach, we seek to associate noticing with a class of events that occur only occasionally, like the backfiring of an engine. If these events do not take place frequently, perhaps only once or twice a class session, examining them would constitute a significant, and potentially very helpful, narrowing of our focus. An intuitively sensible way to apply this approach to teacher noticing is to associate noticing with cognitive events in which a teacher sees some phenomenon as standing out, perhaps because it is surprising or important. For example, a teacher might notice an episode of particularly impressive student thinking or might notice that a student who normally doesn't participate is, for the moment, highly engaged.

In this approach, we might call these events in which teachers see something that stands out *noticing events*, and we would focus only on them. Such noticing events might happen only rarely; they might even be nonexistent during highly routinized teaching. We can call this notion *noticing as recognizing noteworthy classroom phenomena*.

This notion of noticing seems, a priori, to be quite reasonable. However, for a few sensible reasons, the field has generally not adopted this notion. The problem is that this notion of noticing might be so narrow that it is of limited usefulness. For this approach to significantly narrow the task we face in understanding teacher thinking, noticing events must be defined in such a manner that they are relatively infrequent. One using this notion of noticing would thus likely ignore a wide range of more routine recognition events. This is perhaps a good thing; as we have said, narrowing our focus is essential. However, this routine noticing might be precisely what we researchers want to capture. When teachers acquire more expertise, they might find fewer surprises in the world and more that is routine. This ability to recognize and respond to classroom phenomena in a routine way might be at the core of what we want to understand.

Second, this type of approach to noticing relies on the assumption that in a special class of events, noticing events, something stands out for teachers beyond the norm. Furthermore, one taking this approach assumes that these events are distinguishable, in theory if not in practice. But drawing a line between noticing events and more routine recognition events, both in theory and in practice, seems difficult to us. This problem of drawing lines between noticing and other behaviors and cognitive processes will reappear throughout our discussion. It is endemic to the task we have set ourselves, which is to, in some manner, separate something called *noticing* from the larger task of understanding teaching.

Although this notion of noticing is not widely adopted, we believe that one can occasionally see its influence. For example, the work of John Frederiksen has been a frequent reference point. Frederiksen's primary concern was not with teacher noticing per se. Rather, he was interested in developing methods for researchers and teachers to score video portfolios of teaching. The technique he developed was based on the identification of callouts, which are "noteworthy episodes of teaching" (Frederiksen, 1992, p. 4) that scorers recognize in a video.[1] Presumably scorers would see and understand events in the video that are worthy of a callout. We believe that this notion of noticing as recognizing noteworthy phenomena can occasionally be seen in discussions of teacher noticing, even when it is not the primary notion adopted.

Approach 2: Focus on a Subcomponent of the Larger System

The second approach to narrowing one's focus is to choose a subcomponent or subprocess of the larger machinery (in a manner analogous to focusing on the air filter in an engine). As stated in the introduction, this approach is probably the default in the literature, and it thus deserves the most attention. In fact, we distinguish two notions of noticing that flow from this approach: noticing as the selection of noticed-things from sense data and noticing as the interface between automated and controlled processes in the mind of the teacher.

Noticing As the Selection of Noticed-Things From Sense Data

This first notion of noticing that flows from Approach 2 is based on a particular intuitive model of teacher reasoning, as it occurs in the context of classroom events:

1   *A teacher is bombarded with a "blooming, buzzing confusion" (James, 1890) of sensory data.* The teacher is standing or sitting in the classroom and can hear students talking, see things written on the blackboard, and so forth.

2   *The teacher attends to some elements of these sensory data.* In some manner, some elements are selected out of the blooming, buzzing confusion of sensory data. We call one of these selected elements a *noticed-thing* (NT). Note that the NTs do not need to be particularly noteworthy or important but are just the elements that are filtered out of the blooming, buzzing confusion at every moment, just as an engine's air filter constantly filters the air it takes in.

3   *The teacher interprets, makes sense of, or otherwise reasons with the NT.* After the teacher has selected an NT, it can play a role in further reasoning. This reasoning can take different forms depending on the precise nature of the intuitive model of noticing.

4   *The teacher takes some action based on an NT.* On the basis of the reasoning in Step 3, the teacher can take action. For example, the teacher might initiate a

process of Socratic questioning (if a student seems confused) or call the class to order (if the students are being disorderly). This action would in turn lead to some modification in the blooming, buzzing confusion of sensory data.

5   *The above process iterates.*

If as researchers we accept this intuitive model of teacher reasoning in the context of classroom phenomena, we can, if we choose, localize noticing to some subset of the steps in the model (and hence to some subcomponent of the machinery of teaching). If we wish to hew closely to the meaning of the word *notice* as it is used in everyday language, we should localize noticing to the first two steps of the intuitive model. In everyday language, the word *notice* means simply that one becomes aware of something in the world, which the first two steps capture: becoming aware of something in the world, in the form of a noticed-thing.

However, in the literature, *noticing* has not been restricted to these first two steps of the intuitive model. For example, van Es and Sherin proposed that noticing has three *aspects*:

> (a) identifying what is important or noteworthy about a classroom situation;
> (b) making connections between the specifics of classroom interactions and the broader principles of teaching and learning they represent; and (c) using what one knows about the context to reason about classroom events.
>
> van Es and Sherin (2002, p. 573)

Clearly, van Es and Sherin intended to include more in noticing than the simple selection of an NT. However, other researchers have explicitly chosen to associate noticing only with the earlier steps in the intuitive model. For example, Star and Strickland (2008) stated that they were restricting their notion of noticing to aspect (a) from van Es and Sherin (2002), saying, "We are interested in what preservice teachers attend to—what catches their attention, and what they miss—when they view a classroom lesson" (Star & Strickland, 2008, p. 111).

In our view, each of these two approaches has both merits and difficulties. Given the larger framing of this chapter, we think that the problem with the van Es and Sherin stance should be obvious. We have asserted that part of the reason for announcing a shared focus on teacher noticing is to somewhat narrow the task we face in understanding teaching. But, in expanding their notion of noticing to include multiple components of the intuitive model, van Es and Sherin are in danger of understanding noticing so broadly that their work does not substantially narrow researchers' task.

The problem with the stance adopted by Star and Strickland (2008) is, perhaps, more subtle than that of van Es and Sherin (2002): Researchers may be unable—both in practice and in theory—to separate the earlier steps of the intuitive model from the later ones, that is, to separate noticing from interpreting. This challenge points to a problem with not only Star and Strickland's decision but also the entire intuitive model.

We illustrate this point with a hypothetical scenario. Imagine that a teacher, Ms. Davis, is standing before a class of young students and has asked the class to find the sum of 5 and 3. A student, Julian, raises his hand. Ms. Davis calls on him and he then answers, holding up his right hand in the manner shown in Figure 5.1.

While we visualize this scenario, let us also imagine that, when Julian spoke, he did so quickly and a bit quietly, and that, when he put up his fingers, he did so in a fleeting manner. We can imagine that, for example, whether Julian meant to be holding up the thumb on his right hand was unclear.

Still, even with this ambiguity, one can imagine that Ms. Davis is relatively certain that she understands what Julian is doing; namely, he is employing a version of the *count-on* strategy to solve the problem (e.g., Fuson, 1982). In this strategy, a student begins counting from the first addend and counts on a number equal to the second addend. Finally, on the basis of this conclusion, we can imagine that Ms. Davis decides to test how widely Julian employs the count-on strategy. In particular, she gives him another problem, 2 + 6, in which the smaller addend is given first.

Let us consider this example in terms of noticing. As listed in Figure 5.2, potentially many NTs can be found here. We might say, for example, that the teacher notices Julian, one of Julian's hands, one of his thumbs, the group of three fingers on his right hand, or some words that he says. We might even want to say that the teacher notices the count-on strategy.

Clearly some puzzles exist in this scenario. For example, potentially many layers of NTs are nested one inside the other: fingers, groups of fingers, and even the count-on strategy. The puzzle, of course, is to decide which layer or layers correspond to NTs. Is it only lower level entities such as fingers? Or can something as complex as the count-on strategy count as an NT?

| You have five and then six, seven, eight (holding up one figure at a time on his right hand). Eight. | |

FIGURE 5.1   Julian's response

• Julian	• 3 fingers on his right hand
• Julian's fingers	• Some words Julian says
• Julian's thumb	• The count-on strategy

FIGURE 5.2   Candidates for noticed things

This picture is further complicated by the recognition that the flow is not all in one direction; it is not only bottom-up. The teacher would not necessarily first register fingers, then groups of fingers, and then the count-on strategy. Instead, there must be a kind of percolation up and down in layers. To see this percolation, consider why Ms. Davis can be relatively sure that Julian is holding up three fingers on his right hand: in part because this view fits with her conclusion that Julian is making use of the count-on strategy, which itself fits with her knowledge that this is a standard strategy for children of Julian's age and sophistication.

Our point here is far from novel. Decades of cognitive research have shown clearly that the recognition of pattern and structure in the world is driven, in a complex manner, by both bottom-up and top-down processes. For illustration, in Figure 5.3, we have reproduced a well-known example. (The images used are reproduced from Rumelhart, 1980.) The image on the left shows curvy lines, without context. Recognizing what these lines in isolation represent is difficult. Perhaps you can tell that the second image from the left is intended to represent an eye, but the image on the far right does not seem to be more than a short arc. However, when these curvy lines are placed in the context of the image shown on the right, what they represent becomes obvious. The short arc is now, for example, clearly a mouth.

Thus our recognition of the structure in the face diagram is driven by both bottom-up and top-down processes. We first recognize the curvy line as a mouth, and this helps us decide that the larger diagram is a face. Conversely, seeing the diagram as a face helps us to see the short arc as a mouth.

Furthermore, just as with the Julian example, what to call the NTs in the face diagram is unclear. Do we see a curvy line? A mouth? A face? Because our recognition of the face diagram involves bottom-up and top-down processes, no level of structure is clearly the primary level that we can call the NTs. This ambiguity is clearly a problem with the intuitive model of teacher reasoning in the presence of classroom phenomena presented above and with approaches to teacher noticing that rely on this model.

FIGURE 5.3 (a) Parts of a face (b) A face

Source: From "Schemata: The Building Blocks of Cognition," by D. E. Rumelhart, 1980, in R. J. Spiro, B. C. Bruce, & W. F. Brewer (Eds.), *Theoretical issues in reading comprehension.* Reprinted with permission from Taylor & Francis Group.

Note one additional problem with the intuitive model: One may interpret it as passive. In the intuitive model, teachers are simply presented with a blooming, buzzing confusion of classroom events—events that exist outside and independent of them—and then they make sense of those events. Our observation that noticing entails top-down as well as bottom-up processes points to one respect in which noticing must be active, because what the teacher sees in the world is strongly driven by knowledge and expectations.

But there are more profound respects in which the intuitive model might be overly passive. As Gibson (1958) said, "Perception is active, not passive. It is exploratory, not merely receptive" (p. 43). The teacher does not just see; she actively looks. Furthermore, and still more profoundly, the teacher is not separate from and outside of the blooming, buzzing confusion. She is a part of these events and can take an active role in shaping what occurs; she can shape the world of classroom events so that it provides her with certain kinds of observations. To take a simple example, in the hypothetical scenario described above, Julian raised his hand to signal to Ms. Davis that he wanted to answer her question. This event—Julian's raising his hand—is not just a spontaneous event that was unanticipated by Ms. Davis. Ms. Davis had just asked a question, setting the stage for Julian to raise his hand. Furthermore, she has likely made known, at least tacitly, that this is how students in her class are expected to behave. If they want to speak they are supposed to raise their hands. Thus Ms. Davis has arranged her classroom so that it produces a certain kind of event (raised hands), which she can notice and for which she has an interpretation (raised hand shows that Julian wants to speak).

This observation thus relates to another kind of problem with the intuitive model and notions of noticing that are based on this model. Noticing should probably not be treated as a passive event in which the teacher makes sense of something that happens externally to her after it occurs. Instead, the teacher constantly arranges the world so that it produces certain kinds of events, and for some of these events she establishes interpretations in advance.

Noticing as the Interface Between Automated and Controlled Processes

In the preceding section, we discussed one notion of noticing that flows from Approach 2, in which we focus on a subcomponent of the larger cognitive system. We now discuss another notion of noticing that is based on Approach 2, one that is less explicit in the literature on teacher noticing but is worth discussing, in part because it has the potential to solve some of the problems mentioned previously.

One problem we noted with the intuitive model was the difficulty in deciding what should count as an NT—a finger, a group of fingers, and so on. We introduce a possible solution to this problem by appealing to what is consciously available to the teacher. Although the teacher's cognitive systems might tacitly recognize all sorts of structure in the world (e.g., individual fingers), only some of this structure would rise to the conscious level and, hence, count as being noticed.

The idea of consciousness has something of a checkered history in cognitive science, and, indeed, much of cognitive research seems to be carried out with the hope that the issue of consciousness will somehow go away. But one well-established body of theory we can reference to make these ideas more precise is the dual-process model of cognition. Interestingly, David Feldon has used the dual-process model as a lens through which to view much of the literature on teacher thinking, with a focus on the cognitive load that teachers face while in the act of teaching (Feldon, 2007). His discussion is relevant, and in our discussion here we are inspired by his work.

According to the dual-process model, two types of cognitive processes are, at all times, going on simultaneously. The first of these, controlled processes, are slow, conscious, and effortful. In contrast, the second, automatic processes, are rapid and unconscious. These types of processes operate independently but, at some points, they intersect.

Using this model, we can, as suggested previously, use the line between automatic and controlled (conscious) processes to narrow what should count as noticing. Namely, we can choose to treat as NTs only information that is passed from automatic to controlled processes and that is, thus, available to the more slow and effortful reasoning that occurs within controlled processes.

The assumption that NTs are available to controlled conscious processing is at least implicit in much of the work on teacher noticing. For example, researchers in many studies of teacher noticing show teachers videos of classroom sessions and ask them to talk about what they notice (e.g., Borko, Jacobs, Eiteljorg, & Pittman, 2008; Sabers, Cushing, & Berliner, 1991). Thus these researchers assume, at least implicitly, that what teachers notice is available for verbalization. Similarly, other researchers show teachers videos and then ask them specific questions, such as "How many students were in the classroom?" (e.g., Star & Strickland, 2008), again, assuming that this information can be verbalized by teachers, indicating that it is available to controlled processes.

Intuitively, treating something as an NT only if it is somehow available to controlled processes—that is, if one *consciously* notices it—makes sense. For example, in our hypothetical scenario involving the count-on strategy, treating some of the structures that the teacher tacitly recognizes as appearing only inside automated processes—such as individual fingers and groups of fingers—is appealing. These structures would therefore be outside our focus. Ms. Davis, for example, might be aware only that she has seen a group of three fingers and not of the detailed way that these fingers looked on Julian's hand. If Ms. Davis is highly experienced, she might be consciously aware only of Julian's having displayed the count-on strategy.

Again, this way of restricting our notion of noticing has intuitive appeal, and it does seem, in principle, to solve some of the problems discussed in the preceding subsection. But what adopting this notion of noticing would mean, as a practical matter, for research on noticing is not entirely clear. We have perhaps traded one problem (what should count as a noticed thing) for another problem (what is conscious).

One larger problem with this notion of noticing is that we are explicitly excluding what goes on within automated processes from our treatment of noticing, which might be undesirable. In fact, as we argued earlier, much of what distinguishes expert teachers (and expert teacher noticers) from more novice teachers might be their abilities to recognize and react to complex stimuli automatically. Expert teachers might recognize and react to some aspects of classroom events with little conscious and effortful processing. A notion of noticing that excludes this type of processing might, thus, be narrower than we desire.

Approach 3: Focus on an Emergent Attribute of a Teacher's Thought and Action

Our third and final approach focused on examining emergent attributes of the larger system. For the case of an automobile engine, this approach involved focusing on such characteristics of the engine as fuel economy or temperature. Understanding how this approach would lead to a productive way of understanding teacher noticing might seem difficult. Indeed, it is a stance that, as far as we have seen, is not explicitly adopted in the literature. Nonetheless, we believe that, in some cases, this stance captures what researchers really mean to be saying.

To give a sense for how this approach might work when applied to teaching, we begin with simpler examples than those associated with teacher noticing. We might, for example, characterize a teacher's thinking as coherent or incoherent. In doing so, we are not necessarily saying anything about specific cognitive processes or subsystems; rather, we are characterizing an emergent property of the larger system, something like fuel economy. As a slightly subtler example, teachers might act as if they possess certain beliefs. For example, a teacher might act as if he believes that direct instruction is the most effective form of instruction. But, even if the teacher acts in this way, he might not have a mental representation that directly corresponds to this belief. Instead, his knowledge might take the form of specific instructional routines, and these routines would produce, in an emergent manner, behavior that is consistent with the belief that direct instruction is the most desirable.

Let us consider this approach for teacher noticing. In much research on teacher noticing, the data take the form of teachers' comments on classroom events. In some cases, for example, teachers view videos of classrooms; in other cases, the teachers draw on their own memories of classroom events. To analyze these data, researchers code these comments, placing them into categories. In many cases, we contend, these coding categories capture emergent features of teachers' reasoning about the classroom events.

We illustrate this approach with representative examples from the literature. First, to take a comparatively simple example, a number of researchers code teachers' comments about classroom events according to their level of specificity (Rosaen, Lundeberg, Cooper, Fritzen, & Terpstra, 2008; van Es & Sherin, 2008). In coding teacher comments in this way, the researchers characterize a general emergent feature of teacher reasoning processes—an outcome, like fuel economy. In more interesting—and more subtle—examples, in addition to coding for specificity, both Rosaen and colleagues (2008) and Stockero (2008) coded for the topic addressed in teachers' comments about events. For Stockero, these topics included mathematical thinking, pedagogy, climate, and management.

When used in this way, even a characteristic such as topic should, we suggest, be understood to be an emergent attribute of teacher reasoning. A teacher's reasoning process can have the characteristic that it is *about* something; it might be about, for example, pedagogy, student thinking, or classroom management. We might, alternatively, say that the teacher is "attending to" pedagogy or student thinking. But we should not be misled by the fact that the phrase *attending to* can be used here. When we say that teachers are "attending to pedagogy" in their comments, we are saying only what their comments are *about*, from a researcher's point of view, not what they were perceiving. More generally, the point is that, when researchers adopt this perspective, they are applying one type of meter to teacher comments—not a thermometer or a fuel economy meter, but a coherence meter or a topic meter. These meters tell us something about emergent features of teacher reasoning. But they do not, in any direct way, tell us anything about the underlying noticing machinery that produced those emergent features.

The Path Forward

To conclude this chapter, we note how we intend our arguments to be taken and what paths they indicate for the future. First, we hope that our comments will not be read as constituting a strong critique of the larger field of mathematics teacher noticing. We believe that no endeavor in social science would be proof against the type of analysis in which we have indulged. One can always find examples in which core theoretical constructs are fuzzy and constructs break down. These are, in our view, symptoms of social science that never go away.

And one can readily find clear evidence that the focus on teacher noticing has proved to be productive. For example, using this focus, researchers have called attention to important differences between expert and novice teachers, differences that might not otherwise have been evident (Sabers et al., 1991; Star & Strickland, 2008).

Nonetheless, we hope that the analyses we presented can help push the field forward. If the notion of *teacher noticing* is to be a stable feature of the research landscape, we believe that settling the questions we have posed will be worthwhile. As researchers, we can at least try to get beyond intuitive models of noticing and the problems they produce. In attempting to do so, we should be aware that the larger field of psychology has encountered—and, in some cases, addressed—similar problems, particularly in discussions of the psychology of perception. Looking to this existing research for answers and insights applicable to our own context would be advantageous.

Furthermore, regarding questions we have raised, we do not seek merely to reach consensus. For example, we do not think that we need to discuss only whether our notion of noticing should include interpretation, in addition to recognition of noteworthy events, and make a decision. We cannot just hold a meeting and take a vote. As we have tried to show, the problems run a bit deeper than that. Ultimately, we believe that the way to solve these questions about teacher noticing will be to address them not in isolation. Instead, we believe that, as a field, we should work toward the development of a more complete model of how teachers make sense, in the moment, of complex classroom events. Questions about noticing can then be given more precise meaning within this more complete model.

Note

1   Note, however, that Frederiksen did not explicitly address issues having to do with the timescale of callouts. Thus callouts might refer to brief events (that are either frequent or infrequent) or to longer timescale events.

References

Borko, H., Jacobs, J., Eiteljorg, E., & Pittman, M. E. (2008). Video as a tool for fostering productive discussions in mathematics professional development. *Teaching and Teacher Education: An International Journal of Research and Studies, 24*, 417–436.

Feldon, D. (2007). Cognitive load and classroom teaching: The double-edged sword of automaticity. *Educational Psychologist, 42*(3), 123–137.

Frederiksen, J. R. (1992, April). *Learning to "see": Scoring video portfolios or "beyond the hunter-gatherer in performance assessment."* Paper presented at the Annual Meeting of the American Educational Research Association, San Francisco.

Fuson, K. C. (1982). An analysis of the counting-on solution procedure in addition. In T. P. Carpenter, J. M. Moser, & T. A. Romberg (Eds.), *Addition and subtraction: A cognitive perspective* (pp. 67–81). Hillsdale, NJ: Erlbaum.

Gibson, J. J. (1958). The registering of objective facts: An interpretation of Woodworth's theory of perceiving. In G. Seward & J. Seward (Eds.), *Current psychological issues: Essays in honor of Robert S. Woodworth* (pp. 39–52). New York: Holt.

James, W. (1890). *The principles of psychology*. New York: H. Holt.

Rosaen, C., Lundeberg, M., Cooper, M., Fritzen, A., & Terpstra, M. (2008). Noticing noticing: How does investigation of video records change how teachers reflect on their experiences? *Journal of Teacher Education, 59*, 347.

Rumelhart, D. E. (1980). Schemata: The building blocks of cognition. In R. J. Spiro, B. C. Bruce, & W. F. Brewer (Eds.), *Theoretical issues in reading comprehension* (pp. 33–58). Hillsdale, NJ: Erlbaum.

Sabers, D. S., Cushing, K. S., & Berliner, D. C. (1991). Differences among teachers in a task characterized by simultaneity, multidimensionality, and immediacy. *American Educational Research Journal*, 28, 63–88.

Star, J., & Strickland, S. (2008). Learning to observe: Using video to improve preservice mathematics teachers' ability to notice. *Journal of Mathematics Teacher Education, 11*, 107–125.

Stockero, S. (2008). Using a video-based curriculum to develop a reflective stance in prospective mathematics teachers. *Journal of Mathematics Teacher Education, 11*, 373–394.

van Es, E. A., & Sherin, M. G. (2002). Learning to notice: Scaffolding new teachers' interpretations of classroom interactions. *Journal of Technology and Teacher Education, 10*, 571–597.

van Es, E. A., & Sherin, M. G. (2008). Mathematics teachers' "learning to notice" in the context of a video club. *Teaching and Teacher Education, 24*, 244–276.

6

ACCESSING MATHEMATICS TEACHERS' IN-THE-MOMENT NOTICING[1]

Miriam Gamoran Sherin, Rosemary S. Russ, and Adam A. Colestock

The mathematics classroom is a complex environment in which multiple things happen simultaneously. Teachers cannot possibly attend to all this richness equally; they must learn to filter through that complexity and decide where to place their instructional attention and efforts. A crucial part of teaching, then, involves observing the classroom and choosing and making sense of those aspects of the class that are pedagogically relevant. This book as a whole and the individual chapters within it are all predicated on the belief that this process—what has been called *noticing*—is a key component of teaching expertise and of mathematics teaching expertise in particular.

In our own work studying teacher noticing, we have had countless conversations with teachers about the kinds of things they pay attention to in class. Consider, for example, the following description that one high school teacher, Mark, gave us for how he decides what to notice and focus on during instruction:

Mark: I think it's almost a physical reaction. Where it's like . . . as a teacher I'm listening; I'm listening, and I'm sort of . . . just tracking the conversation. And then, like literally, physically, like, sort of, "wow," like something like pricks my senses.

Mark's noticing seems to rely largely on some tacit intuitions; if asked why certain things "pricked his senses" and others did not, he might be unable to articulate the reason. Instead, it is just a feeling he gets when he knows that something important is taking place.

Contrast Mark's description of his noticing with that of another teacher, Sean:

Sean: So I guess I wanted to find moments where students were figuring something out . . . and I was looking for those moments where they were . . .

they were kind of confused, going from being confused to, to understanding, either with my help or the help of . . . a classmate.

Sean said that, on this day in class, he had found himself on the lookout for a particular kind of moment. Unlike Mark, who did not describe being tuned a priori to any specific aspect of class, Sean articulated that he was specifically interested in those times when students were moving from confusion to understanding.

Although we find Mark's and Sean's comments quite interesting, we wonder how accurate their descriptions are. Mark and Sean tell us how they *think* they notice, but is that really how it happens? What we as researchers interested in understanding teacher noticing would ideally like is a way to get more directly at teachers' noticing in the moment—a way to access the process of noticing while it is occurring.

In what follows, we first draw on recent conceptualizations of mathematics teacher noticing to articulate the approach we take in this chapter. Next we describe three types of research methodologies that have been used to investigate teacher noticing and the strengths and limitations of each approach for accessing that noticing. We then explain our use of a new video technology that we believe provides greater access to teachers' in-the-moment noticing than has been available before. Finally, we discuss what we have learned about accessing teacher noticing through our ongoing work with this new technology.

Current Conceptualizations of Teacher Noticing

Researchers interested in understanding mathematics teacher noticing conceptualize the phenomenon they are studying—the *noticing*—in a variety of ways. That is, different researchers include different aspects of a teacher's thinking and practice in their definitions of *noticing*.

Some researchers understand noticing as involving only the process in which teachers initially see, or perceive, different aspects of classroom activity. For example, Star and Strickland (2008) and Star, Lynch, and Perova (this volume, chapter 8) examined "what catches their [the teachers'] attention, and what they miss . . . when they view a classroom lesson" (Star & Strickland, 2008, p. 111). This approach to teacher noticing, then, involves exploring what a teacher attends to as well as what a teacher decides not to attend to. (See Miller, this volume, chapter 4, for additional discussion of how and why teachers focus on some events and filter out others.)

Other researchers are interested not only in this initial filtering of classroom activity but also in teachers' interpretations of that activity. This is the stance that we have generally taken in prior research (e.g., Colestock & Sherin, 2009; M. G. Sherin, 2007; M. G. Sherin & van Es, 2009). Specifically, we have focused on noticing as *professional vision* in which teachers selectively attend to events that take place and then draw on their existing knowledge to interpret these noticed events. For example, teacher noticing would include not only a teacher's paying attention to a particular student idea but also the teacher's making sense of that idea on the basis of his or her knowledge of that student and the mathematics content. Our assumption is that a teacher's expectations and knowledge influence how the teacher perceives events that take place in the classroom. Thus understanding a teacher's noticing must also involve understanding how a teacher interprets what he or she perceives.

Finally, Jacobs and her colleagues (Jacobs, Lamb, & Philipp, 2010; Jacobs, Lamb, Philipp, & Schappelle, this volume, chapter 7) take an even more inclusive view of teacher noticing. They defined *professional noticing* as involving not only teachers' attention to and interpretation of classroom activity but also teachers' plans to respond to that activity. They explained that including *intended responding* in their characterization of noticing reflects the idea that all three processes are tied together conceptually and temporally.

Each of these definitions of *noticing* localizes the phenomenon to be studied in different ways, and each has contributed to our overall understanding of teacher noticing (see B. Sherin & Star, this volume, chapter 5, for further discussion of these differences). In this chapter, our approach differs from what we have done previously; we focus exclusively on a single component of noticing—that of attending to events. Our focus here on attending derives not from a theoretical shift in our understanding of noticing—we continue to view attending and interpreting as closely related processes. Instead, our reason for this focus is opportunistic. We aim to capitalize on a technology that provides a new window into teacher noticing, and teacher attention in particular.

Current Methodologies for Studying Teacher Noticing

Although researchers have made progress in studying and characterizing mathematics teacher noticing, investigating that noticing has posed formidable methodological challenges. In other domains, a common approach for studying what people notice while performing an activity is to ask them to think aloud and verbalize what they are seeing and thinking while it occurs (Ericsson & Simon, 1993). Asking teachers to verbalize their thinking in the midst of a realistic teaching situation, however, proves unfeasible because of the ongoing nature of teaching. Instead, researchers rely on three main alternatives for accessing teacher noticing.

One approach involves providing teachers with samples of others' teaching and asking them to describe what they notice. In some cases, the episodes of teaching take the form of still images of classroom instruction (Carter, Cushing, Sabers, Stein & Berliner, 1988). More commonly, they consist of video clips of lessons (Colestock & Sherin, 2009; Copeland, 1994; Kersting, 2008). The main purpose of using this approach is to investigate the kinds of interactions and events to which teachers generally attend when viewing instructional situations. One benefit of such studies is that they provide information on how a range of teachers respond to a common excerpt of instruction. One concern, however, is that a teacher's noticing in these situations may differ significantly from the teacher's noticing in the classroom. In particular, teachers consider the images without having the same level of information they have about their own instruction, such as familiarity with students and with the specific lesson.

In a second, related approach, researchers ask teachers to retrospectively recall what they were seeing and thinking during their own instruction. The retrospective recall may take place immediately following instruction without any visual reminders of what happened (Borko & Livingston, 1989); alternatively the teacher may view a video from his or her own classroom (Ainley & Luntley, 2007; Rosaen, Lundeberg, Cooper, Fritzen & Terpstra, 2008). Furthermore, in some cases, teachers are asked to discuss their instruction in individual interviews, whereas in other cases teachers are organized in groups to watch and discuss excerpts of their teaching with peers (M. G. Sherin & van Es, 2009). Teachers may find reflecting on classroom activity and articulating what they notice easier in this retrospective–recall situation because they do not have to respond immediately to what they notice. Still, a concern with using this approach is that, because the teachers have been removed from the demands of the classroom, their recollections may not accurately reflect their in-the-moment experiences.

Third, instead of relying on self-reports, some researchers explore teacher noticing by making inferences from videotapes of instruction, claiming that visible actions on the part of a teacher can provide evidence concerning what the teacher notices. For example, a teacher acting in response to a specific event constitutes evidence that the teacher attended to the event. Recently, researchers have used this methodology to investigate the extent to which teachers pay attention to students' thinking and to issues of classroom assessment (Levin, Hammer & Coffey, 2009; Pierson, 2008). Although this approach has received somewhat limited attention in the study of teacher noticing, it has been used extensively to investigate other aspects of teachers' expertise, including subject matter and pedagogical content knowledge (e.g., Putnam, 1992; Rowland, Huckstep, & Thwaites, 2005) or beliefs about teaching and learning (Cooney, 1985; Schoenfeld, 1998). Nevertheless, this approach also has limitations. Precisely characterizing what aspects of the classroom teachers are noticing on the basis of their observable responses and behaviors is difficult. Furthermore, teachers may attend to events and interactions that are not directly linked to an instructional move and, therefore, would not be identified in this type of analysis.

Applying New Technology to Study In-the-Moment Noticing

As described above, one reason these three methodologies are commonly used to study noticing is the difficulty, if not impossibility, of accessing teacher noticing while it happens naturally in the midst of instruction. Stopping a lesson midstream and asking a teacher on what his or her attention is focused is impractical, given the ongoing nature of teaching. Recent advances in technology, however, have provided a new avenue for exploring in-the-moment noticing. Specifically, some portable video cameras are now equipped with selective-archiving capability, which enables the user to select moments of video to capture immediately after they occur. Because the cameras are intended to address increasing interest in recording moments of informal interaction,[2] the burden of recording is typically fairly low so as not to interfere with the ongoing nature of activity in natural settings (Hayes, 2006).

For this chapter, we draw on data in which high school teachers used a video camera equipped with selective-archiving capability. The Deja View Camwear 100 includes two components (Reich, Goldberg, & Hudek, 2004):[3] The first is a wearable camera approximately 1-inch long that can be affixed to one's glasses or to the bill of a hat; the second is a small recording module that can be attached to a belt. The camera records continuously in a loop mode, recording over previously recorded material after a short time. Pressing the save button on the recording module interrupts this process and saves the previous 30 seconds of video in a digital-media file. The media file is stored on a video card that is housed in the recording module. Another interesting feature of the Camwear 100 is that it records instruction from the teacher's point of view in contrast to the more common back-of-the-room perspective (see Miller, this volume, chapter 4, for a discussion of teacher-perspective video). In this chapter, however, we focus only on the affordances of the camera that arise from its selective-archiving capability.

The data for this chapter were drawn from a study of 13 high school mathematics and science teachers who volunteered to use the Camwear 100. We focused on eight mathematics teachers, each of whom used the camera for one class period on up to four days. The teachers taught in two diversely populated school districts in the Midwestern United States. Their teaching experience ranged from 3 to 13 years in the classroom. In addition, three of the teachers had previous experience using video in their teacher education programs, and two had recently developed video portfolios of their teaching as part of an application for National Board certification.

Prior to each teacher's initial use of the camera, a researcher met with the teacher to introduce the camera and to find out about the class that the teacher had selected to videotape. On the day of the taping, the teacher was outfitted with the camera and was asked to "press the record button on the camera when something interesting happens in class, when something seems interesting to you."[4] The prompt was intentionally open-ended to allow the teachers to define *interesting* in their own ways while teaching. No limit was given on the number of moments the teacher could capture. Also, the researcher videotaped the entire lesson using a standard video camera stationed in the back of the room.

Later on the same day, the researcher interviewed the teacher for approximately 45 minutes. Although we had developed a standard protocol, the interviews were relatively unstructured and conversational in style. Each interview was videotaped, summarized, and partially transcribed. In total we conducted 24 interviews with mathematics teachers over the course of two school years.

The interview protocol we used with teachers consisted of three parts. First, the teacher was asked to describe the experience of using the camera that day and to say whether it had seemed to interfere with classroom instruction. Second, the researcher and teacher watched each of the captured moments, but only until the teacher remembered why that moment had been captured. Specifically, a still image of the start of the captured clip was initially displayed for the teacher. If the teacher could recall why he or she had captured the clip from the image, the video clip itself was not reviewed. Otherwise the clip was played only until the teacher recalled why it had been captured. This process was developed to avoid, as much as possible, having the teacher retrospectively develop an account of why he or she had opted to save that particular moment. The teacher was asked to describe the reasons the moment had been captured. Third, after viewing and discussing all the clips from that day, the researcher asked whether the captured clips represented what the teacher had intended and whether the teacher was aware of using any specific criteria to select interesting moments.

Capitalizing on This New Technology to Study Noticing

This new methodology provided us with a wealth of data about teacher noticing. Both teachers' captured clips and their discussion of those clips in the interviews gave us windows into their noticing. In other work, we conducted systematic analyses of the noticing of a particular teacher in our sample (Colestock, 2009; Luna, Russ, & Colestock, 2009; M. G. Sherin, Russ, Sherin, & Colestock, 2008). In this chapter, instead of attempting to characterize the noticing of a single teacher, we look across our data to consider the effectiveness of this methodology for assessing teacher noticing. In doing so, we explore what we are learning about accessing teacher noticing when we use the new camera.

Methodological Successes in Accessing Noticing

First, capturing moments with the camera was both a sensible and a feasible task to the teachers; they understood what they were supposed to do and were able to do it. On average, teachers captured 18 clips per hour of instruction. Furthermore, teachers typically captured moments throughout the lesson—at the beginning, middle, and end of class. Even though teachers' in-the-moment noticing may be so tacit that it at times is "almost a physical reaction," teachers were able to identify individual moments as worthy of capture. Thus our teachers seemed to possess what Mason has called an *awareness of awareness*; they were both noticing and conscious of the fact that they were noticing (Mason, 1998). Because of this consciousness, we were able to use our methodology successfully in capturing some component of teacher noticing. In particular, we imagine that in the midst of instruction pressing the capture button on the camera enabled the teachers to call out particular moments that stood out to them (Frederiksen, 1992).

Not only were our teachers sufficiently conscious of their noticing to be able to capture it, but they were also aware enough of those events to be able to differentiate various kinds. For example, in some cases, we asked teachers not to select everything that stood out to them as interesting but instead to focus only on those moments that were *especially* important or interesting. Although we might have imagined that noticing would be so automatic that this task would be impossible—that teachers would lack sufficient access to their thinking about their noticing to distinguish between such moments—teachers found this to be a feasible task. For instance, when talking with a researcher, Maria compared the quality of the thinking she noticed in different clips; she noted, "That [student idea] ranks up there pretty high for me" when compared with other moments. Similarly, Maria distinguished between moments by ranking them on a scale of 1 to 10; she said, "On a conceptual scale, I think [this clip] might be like a 4 whereas [this other clip] might have been around a 6 or 7." Again, our central claim is that teachers are aware both of having noticed events in class and of their thinking about those events—and using our methodology we are able to document these awarenesses.

Our data from the interviews with teachers also seem to provide a window into teachers' in-the-moment noticing. In particular, our initial concern that the interview might prompt teachers to create an ad hoc, retrospective account of their noticing that was not equivalent to their in-the-moment noticing seems not to have materialized. During the interview, many of our teachers were able to quickly recall what they had noticed and captured in the midst of instruction simply from being shown the still image or only a few seconds of video, often showing recognition of the moment by visibly reacting or saying, "Oh, yeah," before going on to describe their noticing.

In addition, some teachers correctly predicted what moment was captured in a subsequent clip without viewing it. For example, in reflecting on a clip in which students were matching slope fields to differential equations, Todd said, "So [the student] matched 7 [the slope field] and A [the differential equation], but the next clip is her saying, 'Oh, wait a second; I think I made a mistake.'" Notice that, even without viewing "the next clip," Todd was able to recall what class activity he had noticed and captured during class. The speed and ease with which teachers recognized moments from class with little (or no) aid from the video indicates that the teachers were not relying on the videos to help them recreate an account of their thinking but were instead using the video as a cue to help them recall their thinking from earlier in the day.

Finally, when teachers did not remember the moment they had captured or their reason for capturing it, they seemed to feel comfortable telling us so in the interview rather than constructing some explanation on the basis of the classroom activity they viewed in the video. Again, we believe that teachers were not using the video as a record of activity they could notice but instead were using it to cue prior noticing. Thus we assert that the interviews in fact tapped teachers' in-the-moment noticing even though they took place after instruction.

Methodological Challenges in Accessing Noticing

Despite these successes, using this methodology has not been entirely straight-forward. Specifically, we may not be accessing the full range of teachers' notic-ing—because we were unable either to capture the noticing itself or to access teachers' thinking about their noticing.

When we began using the camera with teachers, an initial concern centered on the fact that each clip a teacher captured with the camera was, by default, 30 sec-onds in duration. We imagined a number of potential problems this time restric-tion might impose. First, teachers might find it logistically difficult to know when to press the record button to capture in that 30-second window the aspect of class that interested them. In addition, we thought that 30 seconds might be either too short or too long to capture what teachers noticed—and that having too much or too little information in the video clip would obscure the very access to teachers' noticing that we were trying to achieve.

Although some teachers did initially have difficulty timing their capture to record what interested them, with practice the teachers were able to record at least a portion of the moment they intended to capture. When asked whether individual clips represented what they had intended, most teachers responded "Yes," or identified only one or two clips from each day that failed to do so. Also, when teachers had captured only a portion of the intended episode, viewing just that portion in the interview was usually sufficient to cue the entire moment. For example, when reviewing one clip, Ray said, "Oh, so I missed a lot of it. . . . I didn't get that [student talking]." Despite having missed most of the moment he had intended to capture, he was still able to talk about his noticing: "I know exactly why I [captured] that." Thus, the logistical difficulties of capturing noticed moments with the camera were at least partially overcome by talking about those moments in the interview.

Similarly, when a noticed moment was either shorter or longer than the 30-sec-ond time window, the interviews played an important role in providing access to the teachers' noticing. Specifically, at times, teachers commented that what stood out to them was, in fact, much less than 30 seconds and more like "just the last 3 to 4 seconds." In such cases, however, the teachers had no difficulty identifying that smaller moment from the 30-second clip. In other cases, although the clip was limited to 30 seconds, teachers talked about what they had noticed as extend-ing beyond that time. For instance, Ray explained, "What was happening [was that] I was going around checking homework . . . and I got to that group . . . and that was probably the fourth group in a row [that] had done the graph wrong."

Although Ray captured a moment from his conversation with the fourth group of students, he characterized what he had noticed as including events prior to that time. Similarly, for many of our teachers, the moments they had noticed extended beyond the 30-second clip, and yet the clip was sufficient to cue, in the interview, their memories of their noticing. Note that, although the time limit for the clips did place constraints on our abilities to access the entirety of teachers' noticing, through our interviews with the teachers we overcame those challenges.

However, we have yet to address other issues of accessing teachers' in-the-moment noticing with this methodology. First, at times teachers reported simply failing to use the camera because they were so involved in their everyday practices. For example, Diane said,

> Sometimes I think I just got caught up in the actual business of going about doing class, and there might have been moments that I wouldn't have thought to press, like, that were interesting if I. . . . Like, if I watched your videotape of those moments, I might be like, "Oh, yeah, actually that was something," but I didn't think to press the button then.

Diane pointed out that sometimes the work of teaching was such that she was unable to capture moments. Perhaps it was the case that Diane simply forgot to use the camera, as other teachers reported had occurred sometimes. Cassie, for example, said, "I actually forgot I was wearing it at one point, and then I suddenly thought, 'Oh wait.' I, I should be thinking about 'Should I hit the button or not?'" Alternatively, perhaps Diane was unable to use the camera because of the cognitive intensity of teaching at that moment. That is, sometimes the demands of teaching are so extreme that it is difficult to be sufficiently conscious both of what one is noticing and of the need to capture it with the camera.

Second, even if teachers capture moments they notice, we may fail to tap their thinking about those moments. As mentioned previously, at times during the interviews, teachers reported forgetting why they had captured a moment. For example, Cassie said, "I don't know why I pushed the button there, but I know I actively did because I can see myself looking at [the button as I pressed] it." Cassie knew that she had used the camera to capture something she had noticed but could not recall what it was. Thus, although the capturing technology documented her noticing, we obtained no information about the nature of her noticing in that particular moment.

Third, we suspect that the act of wearing the camera and capturing moments might change the very noticing we hope to access. Although, overall, teachers mentioned that wearing the camera did not interfere with their instructional responsibilities, a few reported that their noticing itself was altered in some ways. Some teachers reported that the camera heightened their attention in the classroom. For example, Mark said, "I felt what [the camera] did was it, it made me more aware of what I thought was important." Teachers' use of the camera may have made explicit some portions of their noticing that are normally more tacit in the classroom. Other teachers felt that wearing the camera did not heighten their noticing but instead altered their experiences of the moment. For example, Sean compared using this camera to taking pictures:

> Well, it's sort of like what, whenever you're using a camera, at least for me, I find like, I mean it's great tak −. Taking pictures is fun except that it always at some level takes you out of that moment. So instead of just living it you're focused on capturing it.

Because wearing the camera altered Sean's experience in the moments of teaching, his noticing was also likely altered. Thus, at least in his case, we might not have accessed his natural, in-the-moment noticing. In other cases, a few teachers reported not that their noticing changed but that their teaching changed as a result of using the camera. For instance, Sean noted, "The kind of capturing you're doing of your teaching . . . starts to direct the focus of your teaching." Other teachers reported changing their teaching to create moments of classroom activity to capture. For example, Ray said,

> I think I did change things a little bit. . . . I think the discussions, particularly the large class discussions that we had, probably went on longer than I would have done normally. Because I was trying to find something [interesting to capture]. . . . Actually it was a good thing . . . because I would have ploughed through that real quick and not spent as much time discussing it. . . . So I definitely modified things a bit based on [using the camera].

Similarly, Kelly said,

> Well, maybe I tried to have a little more pause time sometimes just to see like, "Is there anything interesting going to happen?" I'm going to give [the students] a little more of a chance to come up with something.

For both Ray and Kelly, trying to capture moments altered their teaching, which in turn altered the kinds of moments they were able to capture.

Because of these challenges—the ways in which our methodology occasionally influenced and changed the very phenomenon we were attempting to access—we need to be cautious in framing our data and conclusions as speaking to the character of noticing as it takes place in everyday classroom teaching.

Discussion

Although the challenges discussed previously will require our further attention while we continue this work, overall we believe that there is reason to be

Ray thought that he would be unable to recall all those moments …ought were interesting in the moment of instruction if he were to …eo of the whole lesson after class: "I think [I'd remember] only 3 or … captured]. 'Cause a lot of them are just, well, spur-of-the-moment …rly, Maria commented,

…k the thing with pressing the button is important because there is this …e meta, meta-cognition, meta-pedagogical thing happening, because …really have to be in the moment to know that last 30 seconds was …rtant. It is a lot different than watching it two days later as a whole …k and not being able to really hone in on what those were.

…tement points to the benefits of both wearing the camera and trying …re of what is happening in the moment, as well as to revisiting those …at a later time. Although part of the power of noticing, for teachers, is …scious and automatic nature, we believe that making this process more …or teachers is potentially a worthwhile form of professional development. …lar, the process of capturing moments of instruction—of making choices …en to press the save button—as well as returning to those moments out-…ass may provide needed support for teachers to define and articulate their …in ways that might otherwise be too tacit to express. Thus we imagine …methodology is valuable not only for those interested in understanding …' noticing but also for teachers who want to better harness that noticing …their classrooms in meaningful and productive ways.

…s research is supported by the National Science Foundation under Grant No. …C-0133900 and by the Edison Venture Fund. The opinions expressed are those of …authors and do not necessarily reflect the views of the supporting agencies.
…July 2008, the *Wall Street Journal* reported that the YouTube platform hosts more …n 1 billion views per day.
…other camera featuring selective-archiving potential is the POV 1.5 (www.vio-pov. …m).
…me variations of this prompt were used as well.
…primitive Pythagorean triple consists of three positive integers, a, b, c, which are …prime and satisfy the equation $a^2 + b^2 = c^2$.

…erences

…ey, J., & Luntley, M. (2007). The role of attention in expert classroom practice. *Journal … Mathematics Teacher Education, 10*, 3–22.
…ko, H., Jacobs, J., Eiteljorg, E., & Pittman, M. E. (2008). Video as a tool for fostering …roductive discussions in mathematics professional development. *Teaching and Teacher Education: An International Journal of Research and Studies, 24*, 417–436.

optimistic about the potential to study teachers' in-the-moment noticing using the methodology we introduce here. Teachers were able to use the new camera with minimal disruption to their teaching, and in the follow-up interviews they appeared to describe their thinking during instruction without much difficulty.

We wondered, however, about the relationship between the noticing we accessed with this camera and the noticing that other researchers document with their methodologies. In particular, we wondered to what extent the phenomenon we thought we were accessing—teachers' in-the-moment noticing—resembled the noticing accessed and described by other researchers.

To address this question, we examined the data we collected and compared them to the results from other work on noticing. For example, some research-ers have attempted to categorize the subject of teachers' noticing. Star and his colleagues (Star et al., this volume, chapter 8; Star & Strickland, 2008) explored preservice teachers' noticing in the areas of classroom environment, classroom management, tasks, mathematical content, and communication. In other work, Borko, Jacobs, Eiteljorg, and Pittman (2008) categorized what teachers noticed in classroom videos pertaining to teachers' thinking, students' thinking, mathemat-ics, or pedagogy. We wondered whether we would find a similar variety among the teachers' comments about the clips they had captured—and in looking across the data we saw that we did.

In some cases, teachers explained that they had selected a particular moment because it reflected a student's comment that they found interesting mathemati-cally. For example, Carla, an Algebra I teacher, commented about a clip that "was prompted by Larry's question [about parametric equations] . . . whether or not we should include t when we say the horizontal change is 4, or if it's $4t$." In other cases, teachers indicated that a moment had been noteworthy because of student participation at the time. For instance, Amy mentioned capturing a clip because "I was excited that Janelle was offering up an idea." Teachers also claimed that some moments of instruction stood out to them "more because of something I did . . . than something they did." During a geometry lesson one day, Diane chal-lenged her students to decide whether a Pythagorean triple was primitive.[5] She explained, "At the time, I was proud of myself for working that in. I was like, 'Oh yeah!'" In addition, teachers explained that some clips they had collected reflected a focus on organizational aspects of instruction such as distributing and collecting materials and monitoring the durations of particular activities.

Such comments indicate that our teachers attended to a variety of issues in the classroom. Thus at least the subjects that teachers raised as the foci of their notic-ing, using our new methodology, are similar to those that other researchers have documented. More broadly, we believe that this finding provides validation that we are working in the same territory as others who study teacher noticing.

Given this validation, we next asked whether, in this context, we have seen anything unique about teacher noticing. This issue is the focus of ongoing analy-sis, and we present just one dimension that we suspect will be important in future work. Specifically, our teachers often selected moments to capture because of how well they aligned with their expectations for their lessons. In fact, teachers commonly suggested that events captured their attention because they were surprising. The surprise might be a student's participation that was unexpected, as when Diane explained, "Sylvia's one of those students who doesn't normally raise her hand." Other times, it was a mathematical idea raised by a student that was unexpected. As Ray explained,

> I was trying to get them to discover how to solve absolute-value equations, and I didn't really expect anybody to know how to do it with a more complicated question . . . but then [Noel] explained the exact way to do it, and I was kind of like "That was an interesting thing that happened because I really didn't expect anybody to be able to do that."

Both Diane and Ray seem to have noticed the moments they did because, in those moments, the classroom activity deviated from their expectations.

In other cases, teachers captured moments because those moments reflected expected classroom activity. For example, Amy explained, "The reason I picked this is . . . Dan always asks that question. . . . And I really appreciate [when he does that]." Similarly, Ray noted a clip he had selected because it pertained to a familiar concern: "[Students] are all working on the project . . . but nobody's writing anything down. . . . I think that's a particular problem we have in this school." In these moments, Amy and Ray seemed to have been struck by how well what they perceived matched their expectations.

Thus the noticing of many of our teachers is driven by their continuous, tacit comparisons to their expectations. This finding is consistent with models of perception discussed by cognitive scientists in that one continually evaluates the goodness of fit between one's current model of the world and data perceived from the world (Rumelhart, 1980). Similar ideas have been presented in the literature on teacher cognition. Specifically, Leinhardt (1989) claimed that, for expert teachers, the process of instruction includes implicit "checkpoints" at which point teachers gather information about how a lesson is proceeding (p. 55). Our point, therefore, is not that these claims about teacher perception are new per se but rather that our methodology enabled us to uncover this process in a new way. Schoenfeld's (1998, 2010) models of teachers' in-the-moment decision making are similar to our findings, yet his inferences are based on fine-grained analyses of videos of instruction. We believe that our methodology adds a valuable layer by indicating key moments of instruction as experienced by the teacher. Furthermore, researchers studying teacher noticing have not yet explored the relationship between teachers' noticing and teachers' expectations for a lesson. We suspect that this is a productive direction for research.

The analyses that we have conducted thus far indicate that this new methodology is a worthwhile tool to add to our repertoire of strategies for investigating

---

teacher noticing. As discussed previousl
with themes reported in other research,
issues to which teachers attend while te
may be used to uncover processes, such
have been inaccessible previously. To be
these analyses, we do not expect the me
approaches. Rather, we imagine that usin
other methods will provide researchers with
sense of events that take place during instru
more work is needed to fully capitalize on th
Camwear 100. In particular, questions rem
teacher noticing as it is revealed by the camera
naturally engage during instruction.

Conclusion

At the start of this chapter, we raised questions
tions of their noticing do in fact describe their
instruction. In particular, we wondered whethe
Mark and Sean to accurately describe their in-th
were removed from that thinking and in the co
club. This question motivated us to seek a new met
to tap teachers' in-the-moment noticing without t
from examining it in a time and place removed fr
we have yet to answer our initial question about Ma
using the technology we have implemented will ulti

Specifically, we gained access to teachers' in-the-
dinating data from teachers' captured moments with
moments in the interviews. Furthermore, note that, a
gave us that in-the-moment access, the clips alone we
the teachers' in-the-moment noticing. Even though th
classroom interactions from the teacher's physical persp
teacher sees," they cannot fully account for the attention
ers engage in when they notice moments in their classro
views were essential to the methodology; it is through
during the interview that we learned what portion of the
clip had caught their attention and why those moments w

We suspect that the combination of capturing clips
reviewing those clips may be a valuable activity for teacher
previously, some teachers commented that wearing the car
awareness of when important events took place in their cla
few teachers noted the difference between commenting on
tured with the new camera and video captured with more

Borko, H., & Livingston, C. (1989). Cognition and improvisation: Differences in mathematics instruction by expert and novice teachers. *American Educational Research Journal, 26,* 473–498.

Carter, K., Cushing, K., Sabers, D., Stein, R., & Berliner, D. C. (1988). Expert–novice differences in perceiving and processing visual classroom information. *Journal of Teacher Education, 39*(3), 25–31.

Colestock, A. (2009). A case study of one secondary mathematics teacher's in-the-moment noticing of student thinking while teaching. In S. L. Swars, D. W. Stinson, & S. Lemons-Smith (Eds.), *Proceedings of the Thirty-first Annual Meeting of the North American Chapter of the International Group for the Psychology of Mathematics Education* (Vol. 5, pp. 1459–1466). Atlanta: Georgia State University.

Colestock, A., & Sherin, M. G. (2009). Teachers' sense making strategies while watching video of mathematics instruction. *Journal of Technology and Teacher Education, 17,* 7–29.

Cooney, T. J. (1985). A beginning teacher's view of problem solving. *Journal for Research in Mathematics Education, 16,* 324–336.

Copeland, W. D. (1994). Making meaning in classrooms: An investigation of cognitive processes in aspiring teachers, experienced teachers, and their peers. *American Educational Research Journal, 31,* 166–196.

Ericsson, K. A., & Simon, H. A. (1993). *Protocol analysis: Verbal reports as data* (Rev. ed.). Cambridge, MA: MIT Press.

Frederiksen, J. R. (1992, April). *Learning to "see": Scoring video portfolios or "beyond the hunter-gatherer in performance assessment."* Paper presented at the annual meeting of the American Educational Research Association, San Francisco.

Hayes, G. R. (2006, November). Documenting, understanding, and sharing everyday activities through the selective archiving of live experiences. *Proceedings of the ACM CHI 2006 Conference on Human Factors in Computing Systems (CHI),* 1759–1762.

Jacobs, V. R., Lamb, L. C., & Philipp, R. A. (2010). Professional noticing of children's mathematical thinking. *Journal for Research in Mathematics Education, 41*(2), 169–202.

Jacobs, V. R., Lamb, L. L. C., Philipp, R. A., & Schappelle, B. P. (this volume, chapter 7). *Deciding how to respond on the basis of children's understandings.*

Kersting, N. (2008). Using video clips of mathematics classroom instruction as item prompts to measure teachers' knowledge of teaching mathematics. *Educational and Psychological Measurement, 68,* 845–861.

Leinhardt, G. (1989). Math lessons: A contrast of novice and expert competence. *Journal for Research in Mathematics Education, 20,* 52–75.

Levin, D. M., Hammer, D., & Coffey, J. E. (2009). Novice teachers' attention to student thinking. *Journal of Teacher Education, 60,* 142–154.

Luna, M., Russ, R., & Colestock, A. (2009, April). *Teacher noticing in-the-moment of instruction: The case of one high-school teacher.* Paper presented at the annual meeting of the National Association for Research in Science Teaching (NARST), Garden Grove, CA.

Mason, J. (1998). Enabling teachers to be real teachers: Necessary levels of awareness and structure of attention. *Journal of Mathematics Teacher Education, 1,* 243–267.

Miller, K. F. (this volume, chapter 4). *Situation awareness in teaching: What educators can learn from video-based research in other fields.*

Pierson, J. L. (2008). *The relationship between patterns of classroom discourse and mathematics learning.* Unpublished doctoral dissertation, University of Texas at Austin.

Putnam, R. T. (1992). Teaching the "hows" of mathematics for everyday life: A case study of a fifth-grade teacher. *Elementary School Journal, 93*, 163–177.

Reich, S., Goldberg, L., & Hudek, S. (2004, October). *Deja View Camwear Model 100.* Paper presented at the First ACM Workshop on Continuous Archival and Retrieval of Personal Experiences, New York.

Rosaen, C. L., Lundeberg, M., Cooper, M., Fritzen, A., & Terpstra, M. (2008). Noticing noticing: How does investigation of video records change how teachers reflect on their experiences? *Journal of Teacher Education, 59*, 347–360.

Rowland, T., Huckstep, P., & Thwaites, A. (2005). Elementary teachers' mathematics subject knowledge: The knowledge quartet and the case of Naomi. *Journal of Mathematics Teacher Education, 8*, 255–281.

Rumelhart, D. E. (1980). Schemata: The building blocks of cognition. In R. J. Spiro, B. C. Bruce, & W. F. Brewer (Eds.), *Theoretical issues in reading comprehension* (pp. 33–58). Hillsdale, NJ: Erlbaum.

Schoenfeld, A. H. (1998). Toward a theory of teaching-in-context. *Issues in Education, 4*(1), 1–94.

Schoenfeld, A. H. (2010). *How we think: A theory of goal-oriented decision making and its educational applications.* New York: Routledge.

Sherin, B. & Star, J. R. (this volume, chapter 5). *Reflections on the study of teacher noticing.*

Sherin, M. G. (2007). The development of teachers' professional vision in video clubs. In R. Goldman, R. Pea, B. Barron, & S. Derry (Eds.), *Video research in the learning sciences* (pp. 383–395). Hillsdale, NJ: Erlbaum.

Sherin, M. G., Russ, R. S., Sherin, B. L., & Colestock, A. (2008). Professional vision in action: An exploratory study. *Issues in Teacher Education, 17*(2), 27–46.

Sherin, M. G., & van Es, E. A. (2009). Effects of video club participation on teachers' professional vision. *Journal of Teacher Education, 60*, 20–37.

Star, J. R., Lynch, K., & Perova, N. (this volume, chapter 8). *Using video to improve preservice mathematics teachers' abilities to attend to classroom features: A replication study.*

Star, J. R., & Strickland, S. K. (2008). Learning to observe: Using video to improve preservice mathematics teachers' ability to notice. *Journal of Mathematics Teacher Education, 11*, 107–125.

SECTION III

Studies of Mathematics Teacher Noticing

7

DECIDING HOW TO RESPOND ON THE BASIS OF CHILDREN'S UNDERSTANDINGS[1]

Victoria R. Jacobs, Lisa L. C. Lamb,
Randolph A. Philipp, and Bonnie P. Schappelle

> The unraveling of the math lesson is a continuously reinvented process, with dozens of decision points at which the teacher moves on to the next activity format, which has only just emerged as a likely follow-on exercise, or switches to another exercise as a result of the drift of pupils' oral response, the level of pupils' task engagement, the time remaining until recess or the end of the period, or more likely, all these factors. This continuous readjustment results from what Lévi Strauss (1962) has called, felicitously, "engaging in a dialogue with the situation" as that situation unfolds. To tinker well here seems to depend on how quickly and accurately the teacher can read the situation.
>
> Huberman (1993, pp. 15–16)

We appreciate Huberman's depiction of teaching as a fluid process requiring extensive and critical decision making on the basis of reading a situation in a specific moment (see also Franke, Kazemi, & Battey, 2007; Lampert, 2001; McDonald, 1992; Schoenfeld, 1998; Wells, 1999). Although the craft of teaching involves much more, we have chosen to focus on understanding this in-the-moment decision making both because of the centrality of this skill in effective teaching and because this expertise is so challenging to develop. In mathematics education, a particular type of in-the-moment instructional decision making has been emphasized—decision making in which children's thinking is central.

"Sizing up students' ideas and responding" has been identified as one of the core activities of teaching (Ball, Lubienski, & Mewborn, 2001, p. 453), and instruction that builds on children's mathematical thinking has been endorsed in many reform documents (National Council of Teachers of Mathematics [NCTM], 2000; National Research Council [NRC], 2001). This focus has been informed by the extensive and growing research base on children's mathematical thinking and development (Lester, 2007; NRC, 2001), and instruction that builds on children's ways of thinking has been linked to rich instructional environments and documented gains in student achievement (Bobis et al., 2005; Carpenter, Fennema, Peterson, Chiang, & Loef, 1989; Jacobs, Franke, Carpenter, Levi, & Battey, 2007; Sowder, 2007; Wilson & Berne, 1999). In addition, focusing on the thinking of children can provide a constant source of professional development for teachers throughout their careers because they can continue to learn from their students' thinking on a daily basis, even after formal professional development support ends (Franke, Carpenter, Levi, & Fennema, 2001).

Despite these documented benefits for both students and teachers, creating instruction that builds on children's thinking has proven challenging. In this chapter, we use the construct of *noticing* to begin to unpack this practice and, in particular, the in-the-moment decision making that occurs, many times a day, when a child shares a verbal or written strategy explanation and the teacher needs to respond.

Noticing

For many years, psychologists have studied how individuals notice or attend to stimuli in their environments, and, more recently, researchers have been describing the distinct patterns of noticing particular to professions (see, e.g., Goodwin, 1994; Mason, 2002; Stevens & Hall, 1998). Those studying expert/novice differences have also acknowledged these professional patterns of noticing by confirming that experts in a field are more likely than novices to focus on and remember noteworthy aspects of complex situations that are relevant to future decision making (for a summary, see NRC, 2000). Mathematics educators have shown interest in the noticing construct as a way to understand how teachers make sense of complex classrooms in which attending and responding to everything is impossible, and they have defined *noticing* in a multitude of ways (as reflected in the chapters in this volume). Some have addressed solely where prospective and practicing teachers focus their attention (Star, Lynch, & Perova, this volume, Chapter 8; Star & Strickland, 2007), whereas others have also considered how teachers reason about what they see (Sherin 2007; Sherin & Han, 2004; van Es & Sherin, 2008), including their abilities to reflect on teaching strategies and consider alternatives (Santagata, this volume, chapter 10; Santagata, Zannoni, & Stigler, 2007).

This growing body of work on mathematics teacher noticing has underscored the idea that teachers see classrooms through different lenses and that understanding these lenses can be helpful in scaffolding teachers' abilities to notice in particular ways. We applaud these researchers' attention to the important role that noticing plays in teaching, and we build on their work by selecting a particular focus for noticing—children's mathematical thinking—and a particular slice of teaching—the hidden practice of in-the-moment decision making when teachers must respond to children's verbal or written strategy explanations. This type of in-the-moment decision making is in contrast to the long-term decision making (or planning) that teachers do before or after school when children are not present. Specifically, we want to understand not only how teachers detect children's ideas that are embedded in comments, questions, notations, and actions but also how teachers make sense of what they observe in meaningful ways and use it in deciding how to respond. Thus, we are less interested in identifying the variety of what teachers notice and more interested in how and the extent to which teachers notice children's mathematical thinking. As such, we found merit in investigating a specialized type of mathematics teacher noticing that we call *professional noticing of children's mathematical thinking*. We conceptualize this expertise as a set of three interrelated skills: (a) *attending* to children's strategies, (b) *interpreting* children's understandings, and (c) *deciding how to respond* on the basis of children's understandings (Jacobs, Lamb, & Philipp, 2010).

In this chapter, we have chosen to focus on the third component skill, deciding how to respond. Note that this skill reflects intended responding, not the actual execution of the response. We recognize that intended responding is not necessarily executed as planned, but we argue that teachers are not likely to respond on the basis of children's understandings without purposeful intention to do so. We are not looking for teachers to propose any particular responses (that is, there is no checklist of desired moves) but are instead interested in whether their decision making draws on and is consistent with the specifics of children's thinking in a given situation and the research on children's mathematical development (see also Jacobs & Philipp, 2010).

Other researchers have also included issues related to responding in their conceptualizations of noticing (see, e.g., Erickson, this volume, chapter 2; Santagata, this volume, chapter 10; Santagata et al., 2007), but we recognize that many may view decision making about how to respond as something that occurs *after* noticing. Both perspectives have advantages, but we argue for its inclusion as part of noticing given that deciding how to respond is both temporally and conceptually linked to the other two component skills of professional noticing of children's mathematical thinking (attending to children's strategies and interpreting children's understandings) during teachers' in-the-moment decision making. First, when a child offers a verbal or written strategy explanation, implementation of the three component skills must occur almost simultaneously—as if constituting a single, integrated teaching move—before the teacher responds. Second, expertise in deciding how to respond is nested within expertise in attending to children's strategies and interpreting children's understandings. In other words, teachers can decide how to respond on the basis of children's understandings only if they also have attended to children's strategies and interpreted the understandings reflected in those strategies. Thus, these three component skills are inextricably intertwined. Finally, the work of teaching orients teachers to constantly consider their next moves (Schoenfeld, 1998; Sherin, 2001); thus, the skills of attending to children's strategies and interpreting children's understandings are not ends in themselves but are instead starting points for making effective instructional responses. By integrating teachers' reasoning about how to respond into the construct of professional noticing of children's mathematical thinking, we ensure that this ultimate goal of purposeful responding remains visible.

In this chapter, we characterize the component skill of deciding how to respond by investigating the expertise of four groups of participants with different amounts of experience with children's mathematical thinking. We also explore the specific connection between participants' expertise in deciding how to respond and their expertise in attending to children's strategies. Others have underscored the symbiotic relationship between the focus of attention and subsequent decision making. For example, Erickson (this volume, chapter 2) has argued that the selective attention of teachers is opportunistic in that they judiciously direct their attention to what is necessary to take action. Similarly, Sassi (2001), drawing on Aristotle's notion of *practical judgment*, argued that "learning to deliberate about the actions one should take is inseparable from cultivating perception of the salient features of one's situation" (p. 15). Thus we provide evidence for not only the developmental patterns of these two skills but also their connection.

Methods

The data were drawn from a cross-sectional study entitled "Studying Teachers' Evolving Perspectives" (STEP), in which we collected data on the professional noticing of teachers engaged in sustained professional development focused on children's mathematical thinking.

Participants

The 131 participants included three groups of practicing K–3 teachers and one group of prospective teachers who were just beginning their studies to become elementary school teachers (see Table 7.1).

Participant groups differed in their experience with children's mathematical thinking. Specifically, Prospective Teachers, by virtue of their lack of teaching experience and professional development, had the least experience with children's thinking, followed by Initial Participants, who had teaching experience but no sustained professional development, and then by Advancing Participants, who had teaching experience and 2 years of professional development. Emerging Teacher Leaders had the most experience with children's thinking because they had not only teaching experience coupled with 4 or more years of professional development but also engagement in at least a few leadership activities to support other teachers. These formal or informal activities included mentoring other teachers by visiting their classrooms, sharing mathematics problems with their grade level teams, or presenting at faculty meetings or at conferences.

Practicing teachers were drawn from three Southern California districts that

TABLE 7.1 Participant groups

Participant group	Description
Prospective Teachers ($n = 36$)	Undergraduates enrolled in a first mathematics content course for teachers
Experienced practicing teachers	
Initial Participants ($n = 31$)	Experienced K–3 teachers who were about to begin sustained professional development focused on children's mathematical thinking
Advancing Participants ($n = 31$)	Experienced K–3 teachers who had engaged with sustained professional development focused on children's mathematical thinking for 2 years
Emerging Teacher Leaders ($n = 33$)	Experienced K–3 teachers who had engaged with sustained professional development focused on children's mathematical thinking for at least 4 years and were beginning to engage in formal or informal leadership activities to support other teachers

Note: All practicing teachers had at least 4 years of teaching experience (with a range of 4–33 years), and the number of years of teaching experience in each group averaged 14–16 years.

were similar in demographics, with one-third to one-half of the students classified as Hispanic, about one-fourth classified as English language learners, and one-fourth to one-half receiving free or reduced-cost lunch. Prospective teachers were undergraduates, generally in their first 2 years of study, in a nearby comprehensive urban university, and they had just begun their first mathematics content course for teachers.

Professional Development

The professional development occurred prior to the study and was almost always facilitated by the same experienced mathematics-program specialist. It drew heavily from the research and professional development project Cognitively Guided Instruction [CGI] (Carpenter, Fennema, Franke, Levi, & Empson, 1999; Carpenter, Franke, & Levi, 2003), and the overarching goals were to help teachers learn (a) how children think about and develop understandings in particular mathematical domains and (b) how teachers can use this knowledge to inform their instruction. Participation was voluntary and consisted of about 5 full days of workshops per year (in either half- or full-day increments spread throughout the year). In workshops, teachers analyzed classroom artifacts (video and written student work), explored underlying mathematical concepts and children's understandings of those concepts, and considered how those understandings could be used to inform instruction. Between meetings, teachers were asked to pose problems to their students and bring their student work to the next meeting for discussion and reflection. (See Lamb, Philipp, Jacobs, & Schappelle, 2009, for more details about the professional development.)

Measures

We developed a written assessment to capture participants' professional-noticing expertise in terms of the component skills of deciding how to respond and attending. Specifically, participants were asked to watch a video of a one-on-one problem-solving interview between a teacher and a kindergartner (Rex), shown in two parts. After viewing each part, participants were asked to react, in writing, to a prompt. We allowed participants to view the video only once, because we wanted it to serve as a proxy for actual instructional situations in which children often share their thinking verbally and a rewind button does not exist.

Part I: Deciding How to Respond on the Basis of Children's Understandings

Participants watched Part I of the video (3 minutes), in which Rex solved two problems and was asked to solve a third problem. Unifix cubes and paper and pencil were available for Rex's use. Participants were provided background information that the video was filmed in June of Rex's kindergarten year. The three problems follow:

- Rex had 13 cookies. He ate 6 of them. How many cookies does Rex have left?
- Today is June 5 and your birthday is June 19. How many days away is your birthday?
- Rex had 15 tadpoles. He put 3 tadpoles in each jar. How many jars did Rex put tadpoles in?

On the first (cookie) problem, Rex used his fingers to count back 6 from 13 ("12, 11, 10, 9, 8, 7") to answer, "Seven." On the second (birthday) problem, Rex initially declared, "I can't figure that one out," so the teacher restated the problem and asked, "What do you think we could do to figure that out?" Rex offered, "Use our fingers or something," and then, after that minimal encouragement, was able to begin counting up from June 5th to June 19th on his fingers. When he reached June 15th and had all 10 fingers extended, he announced, "That's 10" before successfully counting up 4 more to June 19th. Next, counting on from 10, he recounted the four fingers for the dates after June 15th to answer, "Fourteen." Part I of the video concluded after the teacher had presented the third (tadpole) problem and Rex had commented, "I don't even know that one. That's hard."

To assess participants' expertise in deciding how to respond on the basis of children's understandings, we requested, "Describe some ways you might respond to Rex, and explain why you chose those responses." We coded responses on a 3-point scale that reflected the extent of the evidence we had of participants' deciding how to respond on the basis of Rex's understandings: robust evidence (2), limited evidence (1), or lack of evidence (0).

We purposefully selected Part I of the video because it included Rex's solving a series of problems so that participants could draw on Rex's previous performance when deciding how to respond to his struggles with the tadpole problem. For example, participants could not only learn that Rex successfully solved a subtraction and a missing-addend problem but also see his range of counting strategies, emerging understanding of tens, and comfort level with using fingers as a tool during problem solving. Furthermore, because of Rex's successful use of counting strategies on the first two problems, participants might reasonably assume that he should be able to solve the measurement-division (tadpole) problem. Research has shown that measurement-division problems are not substantially more difficult for young children than the other two problems when solved by direct modeling (i.e., a basic, yet powerful, strategy in which children represent all the quantities and the action or relationship described in the problem) (Carpenter, Ansell, Franke, Fennema, & Weisbeck, 1993). Thus, given that Rex solved the first two problems with counting strategies, which are more sophisticated than direct-modeling strategies,[2] one might reasonably assume that the tadpole problem was accessible because Rex could always return to a direct-modeling strategy.

Part II: Attending to Children's Strategies

After sharing how they would support Rex on the tadpole problem, participants watched Rex solve the problem in Part II of the video (1.5 minutes), which began exactly where Part I ended. Following the teacher's repetition of the problem, Rex began linking cubes into groups of 3 until he had five groups. For the first three groups, he counted by 3s ("3, 6, 9"), and then he used his fingers to count up by 1s for the last two groups ("10, 11, 12" and "13, 14, 15"). Next Rex answered "Four," but immediately self-corrected to "Five," and then recounted his 15 cubes by again counting by 3s for the first three groups and by 1s for the last two groups. When the teacher asked how many jars were needed, Rex answered "Fifteen," but again immediately indicated that he knew his answer was wrong. In response, the teacher acknowledged that there were 15 tadpoles and asked again how many jars were needed. Rex hastily answered "Four," but, when the teacher then asked how many jars he had on the table, Rex looked at his groups of cubes and confidently answered "Five."

To assess participants' expertise in attending to children's strategies, we requested "Please describe in detail what Rex said and did in response to this tadpole problem." We coded responses on a 2-point scale that reflected whether we had evidence for participants' attending to Rex's strategy: evidence (1) or lack of evidence (0).

We purposefully selected Part II of the video because it included a variety of mathematically important details that could inform a teacher's instruction. First, Rex used a direct-modeling strategy in which he represented all the tadpoles in groups of 3 cubes, with each group signifying a jar (Carpenter et al., 1999). Second, Rex's strategy included two types of counting (by 3s and by 1s), which is critical information for teachers of young children. How children count, the ability to switch between two types of counting, and the ability to recognize a group of cubes as a single entity are important indicators of emerging mathematical understandings. Finally, when asked for the number of jars, Rex showed some confusion with units when he answered 15 (the number of tadpoles) instead of 5 (the number of jars). Distinguishing these units is an important mathematical goal for children learning to make sense of this type of division problem.

Analyses

We began our analyses by coding the two professional-noticing skills of deciding how to respond and attending. We double-coded all data (in a blinded format), and interrater reliability was 80% or more. All discrepancies were resolved through discussion. We then used our cross-sectional design to capture the development of these professional-noticing skills. Means were calculated for each participant group, and group differences were tested with four planned comparisons: a monotonic trend reflecting increased experience with children's mathematical thinking and three pairwise comparisons of adjacent groups (Prospective Teachers vs. Initial Participants, Initial Participants vs. Advancing Participants, and Advancing Participants vs. Emerging Teacher Leaders). One-tailed tests were conducted, because we hypothesized that more experience with children's mathematical thinking should bring gains in professional-noticing expertise. The Type I error rate of 0.05 was split among the four comparisons using the Holm's procedure.

Findings

Using responses to the Rex video, we characterized the two skills of deciding how to respond on the basis of children's understandings and attending to children's strategies, and then, for each, we considered developmental patterns across our four participant groups.

Deciding How to Respond on the Basis of Children's Understandings

We reviewed participants' reasoning about how to respond to Rex after he had shared that the tadpole problem was hard and he did not know how to solve it. We noted (a) whether the participants' reasoning explicitly referenced Rex's thinking on the first two problems and (b) whether the proposed interaction left space for Rex's future thinking (not just the teacher's thinking). In both cases, we looked to see that the ideas were consistent with the research on children's mathematical development. Below we share sample responses for each level of the scale: robust evidence, limited evidence, and lack of evidence of deciding how to respond on the basis of Rex's understandings.

Robust Evidence of Deciding How to Respond on the Basis of Rex's Understandings

We begin by sharing an example of a response that reflected robust evidence of deciding how to respond on the basis of Rex's understandings:

> Rex really prefers to use his fingers as a tool to solve problems. In the first problem he used them to count down from 13, keeping track of when he'd counted down 6 times. In the second problem he counted on from June 5th to June 19th, but was thrown—ever so slightly—when his counting on continued beyond his 10 fingers.
>
> Considering this, I think the third problem caused some difficulty because he couldn't represent 15 tadpoles with his fingers. Also, since his other strategies involved counting on and counting back he might think he could use that here.
>
> Okay—the original question, what to do from here: I'd start by asking him why that problem was hard. Is it because of the language and context of tadpoles? Is it because he can't use a counting on or back strategy? Does he recognize that his *previous* counting strategies won't work?
>
> Where I'd go from there would really depend on his response: I'm going to assume that he understands what the problem is asking.
>
> I might adjust the numbers to (16, 2) to see if he'd skip-count by 2s up to 16 and keep track on his fingers.
>
> If Rex explained that it was hard to use his fingers for this one, I might ask if there's another tool that would help him.

In coding this response as robust evidence, we were not evaluating whether the suggested moves were the best moves (given that we do not believe that best moves even exist). Instead, we tracked this participant's extensive consideration of Rex's understandings on the previous problems and her awareness of the importance of his future thinking in solving the tadpole problem. Specifically, in the first half of the response, we learn that this participant attended carefully to how Rex solved the first two problems, including his facility and preference in using fingers to count up and down. She then used her observation that Rex was thrown "ever so slightly" when the numbers went beyond 10 in the second problem to hypothesize why Rex might be struggling with the tadpole problem ("he couldn't represent 15 tadpoles with his fingers"). Note that her reasoning is not generic reasoning about this mathematics problem but instead is particular to how she thinks Rex might engage with this problem on the basis of what she learned from his strategies on the previous two problems.

In the second half of the response, the participant returned to the original question about what she should do next and chose to explore the issue of problem difficulty with Rex ("asking him why that problem was hard"), leaving space for Rex's thinking while considering connections to his past work ("Is it because he can't use a counting on or back strategy? Does he recognize that his *previous* counting strategies won't work?"). Next, the participant explicitly stated that her responses "would really depend on [Rex's] response," indicating that Rex's thinking would play a strong role in the proposed interaction. She continued by proposing supporting moves she might consider, all of which were consistent with what the video showed about Rex's understandings and what the research shows about children's mathematical development. Specifically, she considered whether Rex understood the problem and whether she could adjust the problem so that he could use a strategy similar to one he had used earlier. When children use a counting strategy to solve measurement-division problems, they often skip-count (Carpenter et al., 1999), and this participant chose numbers (16 tadpoles with 2 in each jar) to make the skip-counting easier (2s instead of 3s) while still enabling the use of a familiar tool (i.e., Rex could use each finger to represent two tadpoles and thus count by 2s to 16 without having to count beyond his two hands). With her final suggestion, the participant acknowledged that fingers might be a challenging tool for solving the original problem and other tools might be useful.

Limited Evidence of Deciding How to Respond on the Basis of Rex's Understandings

Some responses were similar to robust-evidence responses in that they maintained a focus on drawing on Rex's understandings on the past problems and providing a space for Rex's future thinking, but they did so with less depth. Consider how the following response offers limited evidence of deciding how to respond on the basis of Rex's understandings:

> I would encourage him to try because of how successful he was with the other two questions. Then I would show him tools/manipulatives to use (connecting cubes, paper, pencil or chalkboard, yarn loops, etc.). I think he was just intimidated because it wasn't a counting question that he seems so familiar with. With tools, I believe he could at least get through the problem with or without assistance. He has a good sense of number and [is] able to count backwards from at least 13 to 6, so he seems ready for this type of problem.

This participant used Rex's understandings but in a more general way than they were used in the previous example. Specifically, she referred to Rex's success and counting strategies on the first two problems to conclude that Rex should be able to engage with the tadpole problem and that tools might be useful. However, this participant provided fewer details linking the proposed interaction to Rex's past and future thinking. Note that the length of the response was not the determining factor for robust or limited evidence; instead we focused on the depth of the use of Rex's understandings.

Lack of Evidence of Deciding How to Respond on the Basis of Rex's Understandings

Other responses provided no evidence of deciding how to respond on the basis of Rex's understandings and instead focused on either general comments or comments dominated by the teachers' (instead of Rex's) thinking.

Focus on General Comments

Some responses included few specifics in terms of the instructional next steps or the underlying reasoning. For example, they consisted of a single, general suggestion (e.g., offering tools) with little rationale, or mention of the importance of questioning without any articulation of specific questions or even types of questions to be posed (". . . I would ask questions along the way as a guide to get him started. I think questioning is a way to guide students in the process of how to start and where to go next"). Other responses focused on broad curriculum issues (". . . This question might actually be too hard for a kindergartner. I am not sure what the average kindergartner learns in a math class, but I think it's pretty basic. . .") or on nurturing Rex's affect without any reference to his past or future mathematical understandings ("'It is hard but let's try—teachers love it when you try!' I would always try to keep the child's self-esteem high. I wouldn't want him to feel like he wasn't smart"). In summary, lack of specificity with respect to Rex's mathematical understandings and the teacher's role in nurturing those understandings characterized these responses as being focused on general comments.

Focus on Teachers' Thinking

Some responses were focused on the teachers' thinking instead of Rex's past or future thinking. In these responses, reaching a correct answer was generally emphasized and details of the proposed strategies and teacher's instructional moves were provided. However, the suggested moves were typically focused on guiding Rex through the solving of the tadpole problem, with little concern for how (or even if) he was making sense of the mathematics or how these experiences would link with his work on the first two problems. In fact, it was almost as if participants could have generated these exact responses without having seen Rex's work on the first two problems. For example, one participant suggested:

I would help him draw a picture and guide him through the problem. I would ask him to draw 15 dots or lines to represent the 15 tadpoles. Then I would tell him that there will be 3 in each jar, so to represent each jar he could circle tadpoles in groups of 3. I would then ask him how many circles he has.

Another method I would guide him through would be to use the cubes that were on the table. I would ask him to count out 15 cubes, and then make them into sticks of 3 (stick them together). I would then ask him to count how many sticks he has.

Both suggestions describe specific and effective strategies for solving the tadpole problem, and these strategies are ones that children are likely to use. However, in this case, the strategies are the *teacher's* strategies, and whether any consideration has been (or would be) given to Rex's understandings of these strategies is unclear.

Attending to Children's Strategies

Because of the foundational role that attending to children's strategies plays in deciding how to respond, we also examined whether participants provided evidence of attending to Rex's strategy on the tadpole problem.

Responses that provided evidence of the participants' attending to Rex's strategy included most of the mathematically significant details of the strategy: (a) grouping of the cubes into five sets of 3, (b) counting by 3s to 9 and then by 1s to 15, and (c) demonstrating confusion about the answer (i.e., offering 4, 5, and 15 as the answer at different times). For example, a participant offered:

After the teacher reread the problem Rex started to grab unifix cubes in groups of 3. He confidently went 3, 6, 9. He then stopped to state 9 tadpoles, that's 3 (groups). He then had to use fingers to count up another group of 3—10, 11, 12. "That's 4." He did it one more time—13, 14, 15. He then stated that's 15. When the teacher prompted how many groups, he at first said 4. When she asked how many groups he had made, he recounted and then said 5.

Note that not every detail is included, but this participant showed that she attended to the mathematical essence of the strategy.

In contrast, the following response demonstrated lack of evidence of attending to Rex's tadpole strategy.

Rex said that the problem was too hard although he attempted it. He then used visual blocks to set aside 15 tadpoles. He used his counting to figure out 15 tadpoles among 5 jars. Rex then had to make sure that his process was right. He finished the problem knowing that there were 5 jars for 15 tadpoles. Rex knew how to solve the problem; he just needed the necessary help and motivation.

This participant mentioned that Rex solved the problem correctly and used blocks, but information about how Rex used the blocks, how Rex counted, and how Rex determined the answer was missing. Thus, unlike the case in the previous example, this response provided insufficient information for one to reconstruct Rex's solution. Strategy descriptions demonstrating lack of evidence of attending to Rex's strategy often included mention of the success in solving the problem but omitted details about *how* Rex solved the problem. The absence of these details is problematic, because strategy details provide a window into a child's understandings and should form the basis for teachers' decisions about how to respond.

Developmental Patterns

Using our cross-sectional design, we captured the developmental patterns of expertise in deciding how to respond and attending. Means were calculated for each participant group for the scores on each component skill, with higher numbers indicating more evidence for engagement with children's mathematical thinking (see Table 7.2). In both cases, we found a statistically significant monotonic trend, indicating that increased experience with children's thinking was related to increased engagement with children's thinking on the professional-noticing tasks.

In examining the three pairwise comparisons of adjacent groups for deciding how to respond, we found no significant differences between Prospective Teachers and Initial Participants, but we did find significant differences between Initial Participants and Advancing Participants and between Advancing Participants and Emerging Teacher Leaders, with effect sizes of 0.68 and 0.77, respectively. Thus we found no evidence that expertise in deciding how to respond on the basis of children's understandings resulted from teaching experience alone. Instead,

TABLE 7.2 Participant-group means (standard deviations) for the two component skills

Component skill	Scale	Prospective Teachers	Initial Participants	Advancing Participants	Emerging Teacher Leaders
Deciding how to respond on the basis of children's understandings	0–2	0 (0)	0.19 (0.40)	0.61 (0.80)	1.09 (0.88)
Attending to children's strategies	0–1	0.19 (0.40)	0.35 (0.49)	0.77 (0.43)	0.88 (0.33)

expertise in this skill grew with 2 years of professional development and again when teachers had engaged in 4 or more years of professional development and leadership activities.

We also examined the three pairwise comparisons of adjacent groups in attending, and we found only one significant difference—between Initial Participants and Advancing Participants, with a large effect size of 1.02. This finding is evidence that expertise in attending to children's strategies grew after 2 years of professional development. Unlike with deciding how to respond, however, there was no significant difference between the Advancing Participants and Emerging Teacher Leaders, perhaps because both were already at a high level of performance, with more than three-fourths of each group providing evidence of attending to Rex's tadpole strategy.

Discussion

Building on research that connected teachers' use of children's mathematical thinking with rich instructional environments, gains in student achievement, and teacher learning, we conceptualized the construct of professional noticing of children's mathematical thinking to begin to unpack the in-the-moment decision making that occurs when a child shares a verbal or written strategy explanation and the teacher needs to respond. This conceptualization contributes to efforts to make explicit the work of teaching, and our main focus in this chapter has been to explore one of the components skills, deciding how to respond on the basis of children's understandings.

From our cross-sectional data, we learned that developing expertise in deciding how to respond is challenging but can be achieved with engagement in professional development that is sustained over many years. We recognize that decision making in relation to Rex captures only one type of responding that teachers do, but the results shared in this chapter are consistent with patterns found with the same participants (Jacobs et al., 2010) when their deciding-how-to-respond expertise was assessed in relation to classroom video and written student work. These artifacts were different from the Rex video not only in the form of the instructional setting but also in that they depicted situations in which children generally solved problems correctly. Thus the participants' decision making was focused on extending the children's understandings rather than supporting their efforts to solve a problem correctly. Given the similarities between the developmental patterns in these supporting and extending situations, we suggest that the extent of teachers' focus on children's understandings may permeate teachers' decision making across the range of responding in which teachers engage. We reiterate that, in contrast to the typical, short-term model of professional development (Hawley & Valli, 1999; Hill, 2004), long-term support is needed for the development of this expertise in deciding how to respond on the basis of children's understandings.

Our secondary focus in this chapter was to explore the connection between participants' expertise in deciding how to respond and their expertise in attending to children's strategies. We found that 20 participants (across the 4 participant groups) provided responses demonstrating robust evidence of deciding how to respond on the basis of Rex's understandings, and 19 of those 20 also provided evidence of attending to Rex's strategy on the tadpole problem. The reverse, however, was not true. The 71 participants (across the 4 participant groups) who provided evidence of attending to Rex's tadpole strategy generated responses at all three levels of the deciding-how-to-respond scale (i.e., robust, limited, and lack of evidence of deciding how to respond on the basis of Rex's understandings). Thus, if teachers decide how to respond on the basis of children's understandings, they are likely to also attend to children's strategies. However, if teachers attend to children's strategies, they may or may not decide how to respond on the basis of the understandings reflected in those strategies. In short, expertise in attending to children's strategies is foundational to deciding how to respond on the basis of children's understandings, and our cross-sectional findings showed that neither form of expertise is something that adults routinely possess but is something they can gain with support. Participants' struggles to attend to children's strategies were particularly salient in this study, in which much of the complexity of classrooms was removed by use of a video that depicted only a single child engaged in problem solving. Therefore we argue that teachers need support in learning to attend to children's strategies, and they need additional support to learn how to use those details in deciding how to respond so that their instruction maintains children's thinking as central. We suggest that building on teachers' existing perspectives can be helpful in this endeavor.

Building Professional Development on Teachers' Existing Perspectives

Just as teachers need to first determine what children understand so that they can use that understanding as a starting point for instruction, we argue that professional developers can use an understanding of teachers' reasoning in deciding how to respond to inform their professional development. A note of caution is necessary. Although reasoning patterns existed for each participant group and can be useful as starting points, we found a range of perspectives in each group, and thus professional developers also need to look beyond group membership to consider individuals' perspectives.

When helping teachers to develop expertise in deciding how to respond on the basis of children's understandings, we encourage professional developers to recognize the positive attributes of all perspectives, including those currently demonstrating lack of evidence. In this way, responses focused on general comments and teachers' thinking can be viewed as resources rather than as ways of reasoning that need to be replaced.

Resources in Responses Focused on General Comments

Participants whose responses were focused on general comments lacked specificity about mathematics thinking and teachers' moves to support that thinking, but they also often indicated the need to promote confidence and positive feelings toward mathematics. These affective goals have been shown to be important by research connecting students' lack of confidence or dislike of mathematics with low achievement (Ma, 1999). Thus professional developers could view this concern with children's affect as a productive starting point for discussions about teaching and learning mathematics. Instead of trying to replace this concern, professional developers could work to augment it so that, in addition, children's understandings are considered when teachers decide how to respond. Our data support this additive goal in that 70% of participants who demonstrated robust evidence of deciding how to respond on the basis of Rex's understandings also made comments reflecting concern with Rex's affect.

Resources in Responses Focused on Teachers' Thinking

Participants whose responses were focused on teachers' thinking typically provided extensive details about strategies and teachers' instructional moves. Even though the specificity in these responses was related to teachers' strategies and instructional moves (rather than children's thinking), professional developers could use it as a starting point for helping teachers learn to attend to and use the specific details of children's strategies. Given that 30% of all responses (across participant groups) were focused on general comments, we know that specificity is not something that all participants demonstrated, and thus professional developers could build on this expertise.

Our cross-sectional results also revealed an interesting phenomenon related to this perspective in that almost half of the Advancing Participants—experienced practicing teachers who had completed 2 years of professional development—offered responses focused on teachers' thinking. Given that the professional development emphasized *children's* mathematical thinking, one might have expected otherwise, but we hypothesize that the Advancing Participants were in a transition period. Sustained professional development focused on children's mathematical thinking tends to fundamentally change the ways that teachers engage with children and mathematics; a shift to understanding, valuing, eliciting, and building on children's mathematical ideas is challenging and takes many years to develop (Fennema et al., 1996; Franke et al., 2001). During the first 2 years of professional development, the Advancing Participants were exposed to many new mathematical strategies, patterns of children's development in relation to these strategies, and the role of the teacher in carefully selecting tasks and posing follow-up questions to support children's construction of these strategies. We suspect that Advancing Participants may not yet have coordinated the knowledge, beliefs, and skills needed not only to believe that Rex could generate a strategy to

solve the tadpole problem on his own but also to determine their role in supporting Rex's thinking (vs. imposing their own thinking) during this problem solving. In contrast, after 4 or more years of sustained professional development and
opportunities to engage in leadership activities, the transition seems to have been
more consolidated in that fewer than one-fifth of the Emerging Teacher Leaders
generated responses focused on teachers' thinking. This shift again points to the
power of long-term professional development and the need to identify and build
on the positive attributes in teachers' existing perspectives, in part because they
may reflect skill development that is in transition.

Final Thoughts

We close by suggesting that this work on professional noticing of children's mathematical thinking may serve as a resource for professional developers beyond providing them with information about teachers' existing perspectives and expertise.
Although the construct of noticing was not explicitly discussed in the professional development in this study, we wonder about the possible benefits of talking directly with teachers about professional noticing of children's mathematical
thinking. Teachers who have engaged with our work have found our conceptualization of professional noticing of children's mathematical thinking, and in
particular our characterization of teachers' reasoning in deciding how to respond,
to be a useful self-reflection tool. By seeing themselves in each level of the scale,
perhaps in different situations or at different times in their own development,
they were able not only to see their own growth but also to consider paths for
future growth. Thus an open question remains about the multitude of ways that
the construct of professional noticing of children's mathematical thinking can be
useful in supporting teachers' development.

Notes

1   An earlier version of this chapter was presented at the 2009 annual conference of the
    American Educational Research Association. This research was supported in part by
    a grant from the National Science Foundation (ESI0455785). The opinions expressed
    in this chapter do not necessarily reflect the position, policy, or endorsement of the
    supporting agency.
2   When using counting strategies, children do not need to represent all quantities (e.g.,
    Rex did not need to represent all 13 cookies and instead started counting backward at
    12, using his fingers to represent counts rather than cookies).

References

Ball, D. L., Lubienski, S. T., & Mewborn, D. S. (2001). Research on teaching mathemat-
    ics: The unsolved problem of teachers' mathematical knowledge. In V. Richardson
    (Ed.), *Handbook of research on teaching* (4th ed., pp. 433–456). Washington, DC: American
    Educational Research Association.

Bobis, J., Clarke, B., Clarke, D., Thomas, G., Wright, R., Young-Loveridge, J., et al. (2005). Supporting teachers in the development of young children's mathematical thinking: Three large-scale cases. *Mathematics Education Research Journal, 16*(3), 27–57.

Carpenter, T. P., Ansell, E., Franke, M. L., Fennema, E., & Weisbeck, L. (1993). Models of problem solving: A study of kindergarten children's problem-solving processes. *Journal for Research in Mathematics Education, 24*, 428–441.

Carpenter, T. P., Fennema, E., Franke, M. L., Levi, L., &Empson, S. B. (1999). *Children's mathematics: Cognitively Guided Instruction.* Portsmouth, NH: Heinemann.

Carpenter, T. P., Fennema, E., Peterson, P. L., Chiang, C. P., & Loef, M. (1989). Using knowledge of children's mathematics thinking in classroom teaching: An experimental study. *American Educational Research Journal, 26*, 499–531.

Carpenter, T. P., Franke, M. L., & Levi, L. (2003). *Thinking mathematically: Integrating arithmetic and algebra in elementary school.* Portsmouth, NH: Heinemann.

Erickson, F. (this volume, chapter 2). *On noticing teacher noticing.*

Fennema, E., Carpenter, T., Franke, M. L., Levi, L., Jacobs, V. R., & Empson, S. B. (1996). Mathematics instruction and teachers' beliefs: A longitudinal study of using children's thinking. *Journal for Research in Mathematics Education, 27*, 403–434.

Franke, M. L., Carpenter, T. P., Levi, L., & Fennema, E. (2001). Capturing teachers' generative change: A follow-up study of professional development in mathematics. *American Educational Research Journal, 38*, 653–689.

Franke, M. L., Kazemi, E., & Battey, D. (2007). Mathematics teaching and classroom practice. In F. K. Lester (Ed.), *Second handbook of research on mathematics teaching and learning* (pp. 225–256). Charlotte, NC: Information Age.

Goodwin, C. (1994). Professional vision. *American Anthropologist, 96*, 606–633.

Hawley, W. D., & Valli, L. (1999). The essentials of effective professional development: A new consensus. In L. Darling-Hammond & G. Sykes (Eds.), *Teaching as the learning profession.* San Francisco: Jossey-Bass.

Hill, H. C. (2004). Professional development standards and practices in elementary school mathematics. *The Elementary School Journal, 104*, 215–231.

Huberman, M. (1993). The model of the independent artisan in teachers' professional relations. In J. W. Little & M. W. McLaughlin (Eds.), *Teachers' work: Individuals, colleagues, and contexts* (pp. 11–50). New York: Teachers College Press.

Jacobs, V. R., Franke, M. L., Carpenter, T. P., Levi, L., & Battey, D. (2007). Professional development focused on children's algebraic reasoning in elementary school. *Journal for Research in Mathematics Education, 38*, 258–288.

Jacobs, V. R., Lamb, L. C., & Philipp, R. A. (2010). Professional noticing of children's mathematical thinking. *Journal for Research in Mathematics Education, 41*, 169–202.

Jacobs, V. R., & Philipp, R. A. (2010). Supporting children's problem solving. *Teaching Children Mathematics, 17*(2), 98–105.

Lamb, L. C., Philipp, R. A., Jacobs, V. R., & Schappelle, B. P. (2009). Developing teachers' stances of inquiry: Studying teachers' evolving perspectives. In D. Slavit, T. Holmlund Nelson, & A. Kennedy (Eds.), *Perspectives on supported collaborative teacher inquiry* (pp. 16–45). New York: Taylor & Francis.

Lampert, M. (2001). *Teaching problems and the problems of teaching.* New Haven, CT: Yale University Press.

Lester, F. K. (2007). *Second handbook of research on mathematics teaching and learning.* Charlotte, NC: Information Age.

Lévi-Strauss, C. (1962). *La pensée sauvage.* Paris: Plon.

Ma, X. (1999). A meta-analysis of the relationship between anxiety toward mathematics and achievement in mathematics. *Journal for Research in Mathematics Education, 20,* 520–540.

Mason, J. (2002). *Researching your own practice: The discipline of noticing.* London: RoutledgeFalmer.

McDonald, J. P. (1992). *Teaching: Making sense of an uncertain craft.* New York: Teachers College Press.

National Council of Teachers of Mathematics. (2000). *Principles and standards for school mathematics.* Reston, VA: Author.

National Research Council (Eds.). (2000). *How people learn: Brain, mind, experience, and school.* Washington, DC: National Academy Press.

National Research Council (Eds.). (2001). *Adding it up: Helping children learn mathematics.* Washington, DC: National Academy Press.

Santagata, R. (this volume, chapter 10). *From teacher noticing to a framework for analyzing and improving classroom lessons.*

Santagata, R., Zannoni, C., & Stigler, J. W. (2007). The role of lesson analysis in preservice teacher education: An empirical investigation of teacher learning from a virtual video-based field experience. *Journal of Mathematics Teacher Education, 10,* 123–140.

Sassi, A. (2001). Cultivating perception: Helping teachers attend to the salient features of their mathematics classrooms. Newton, MA: Center for the Development of Teaching, Education Development Center. Retrieved October 29, 2005, from http://www2.edc.org/cdt/cdt/cdt_researchpapers.html#paper15

Schoenfeld, A. H. (1998). Toward a theory of teaching-in-context. *Issues in Education, 4*(1), 1–94.

Sherin, M. G. (2001). Developing a professional vision of classroom events. In T. Wood, B. S. Nelson, & J. Warfield (Eds.), *Beyond classical pedagogy: Teaching elementary school mathematics* (pp. 75–93). Hillsdale, NJ: Erlbaum.

Sherin, M. G. (2007). The development of teachers' professional vision in video clubs. In R. Goldman, R. Pea, B. Barron, & S. J. Derry (Eds.), *Video research in the learning sciences* (pp. 383–395). Mahwah, NJ: Erlbaum.

Sherin, M. G., & Han, S. Y. (2004). Teacher learning in the context of a video club. *Teaching and Teacher Education, 20,* 163–183.

Sowder, J. (2007). The mathematics education and development of teachers. In F. K. Lester (Ed.), *Second handbook of research on mathematics teaching and learning* (pp. 157–223). Charlotte, NC: Information Age.

Star, J. R., Lynch, K., & Perova, N. (this volume, chapter 8). *Using video to improve preservice mathematics teachers' abilities to attend to classroom features: A replication study.*

Star, J. R., & Strickland, S. K. (2007). Learning to observe: Using video to improve preservice teachers' ability to notice. *Journal of Mathematics Teacher Education, 11,* 107–125.

Stevens, R., & Hall, R. (1998). Disciplined perception: Learning to see in technoscience. In M. Lampert & M. L. Blunk (Eds.), *Talking mathematics in school: Studies of teaching and learning* (pp. 107–150). New York: Cambridge University Press.

van Es, E. A., & Sherin, M. G. (2008). Mathematics teachers' "learning to notice" in the context of a video club. *Teaching and Teacher Education, 24,* 244–276.

Wells, G. (1999). *Dialogic inquiry: Toward a sociocultural practice and theory of education*. New York: Cambridge University Press.

Wilson, S. M., & Berne, J. (1999). Teacher learning and the acquisition of professional knowledge: An examination of research on contemporary professional development. In A. Iran-Nejad & P. D. Pearson (Eds.), *Review of research in education* (Vol. 24, pp. 173–209). Washington, DC: American Educational Research Association.

8

USING VIDEO TO IMPROVE PRESERVICE MATHEMATICS TEACHERS' ABILITIES TO ATTEND TO CLASSROOM FEATURES

A Replication Study[1]

Jon R. Star, Kathleen Lynch, and Natasha Perova

The rapid proliferation of inexpensive and fast video technologies, as well as the widening availability of video-based case studies, has made possible a variety of new and different activities in preservice teacher education. The incorporation of video technology in preservice teacher education affords a number of pedagogical advantages. For example, although teachers completing field-observation experiences typically do so alone or with one or two other classmates, limiting the opportunity for whole class discussions of these experiences, the use of video may enable an entire class to witness the same full-length lesson and engage in a full discussion. Videos provide the additional benefit of enabling preservice teachers to witness a wider range of teachers, students, settings, pedagogies, and content than a typical field experience might. Preservice teachers may also benefit from videotaping their own field-placement classrooms and lessons, enabling them to notice things they may have missed when their attention was focused elsewhere. In recent years, teacher educators have been quick to incorporate video into their program curricula, taking advantage of its many possible uses.

In this chapter, we report on a replication study related to one particular and potentially promising use of video technology in preservice teacher education—the effect of viewing classroom videos on teachers' abilities to notice salient features of classroom instruction. We begin with the premise that, although preservice teachers spend a substantial amount of time observing other teachers' practices, what they learn as a result of these observations is unclear (Brophy, 2004). Being a good observer of another's practice is a learned skill (e.g., Berliner et al., 1988), and one reason preservice teachers' observations of practice may not be fruitful is that these teachers may not have developed the ability to understand the complexity of the classroom and the full range of events that can be observed. Only *after* developing such an appreciation of the complexity of the classroom can preservice teachers develop the subsequent and critically important skill of noticing important features of classroom instruction. In this study, we focus on ways that the medium of video can be helpful in improving preservice teachers' abilities to attend to the full range of events in classrooms, which we view as a precursor skill to noticing important features of classrooms.

We begin with an overview of the use of video in preservice teacher education in general and then discuss existing research on preservice teachers' abilities to notice salient features of classroom instruction.

Use of Video in Preservice Teacher Education

By many accounts, a useful approach for preservice teachers is to make, use, and discuss video of teaching episodes, students working, or both. A growing body of research shows the positive effect of using video to help students in introductory education courses to connect learning theory with classroom practice (Bliss & Reynolds, 2004). Viewing and discussing short, edited segments of videos has proved to stimulate conversation around the issues of teaching and learning. Viewing video was also found to have the potential to focus preservice teachers' attention on aspects of teaching and learning. Stockero (2008), for example, pointed out the benefits on teacher growth of a videocase curriculum in which preservice teachers reflected on video excerpts around a particular mathematical topic.

Preservice Teachers' Abilities to Notice

Sherin and van Es (2005) found that both in-service and preservice teachers demonstrated change in what they noticed and ways they talked about what they noticed as a result of reflecting on videos of their own teaching practices. Whereas in-service teachers' observations and conversations shifted from what the teacher in the video was doing to what the students were saying, preservice teachers had a change in focus from reporting chronological sequences in a lesson to focusing on particular moments during the lesson. Overall, the results of work by Sherin and colleagues (e.g., Sherin & Han, 2004) indicated that the video viewing of lessons has the potential to affect what preservice and in-service teachers observe in classroom practice.

Earlier work by Berliner and colleagues (Berliner et al., 1988; Carter, Cushing, Sabers, Stein, & Berliner, 1988) indicated that teachers' abilities to notice are related to teachers' classroom experiences: More experienced teachers are better observers of videos of classroom lessons than novices. Inexperienced teachers have difficulty focusing on students' (rather than teachers') actions, tend to view a lesson merely as a chronological but disconnected sequence of events, and are not particularly observant about issues of content.

These findings about preservice teachers' inattention to features of classrooms are significant when one considers the role of observation in teacher education programs. Observing other teachers' practices occupies a substantial component of preservice teachers' time in many teacher education programs, with most preservice teachers in the United States spending at least one semester observing a mentor teacher. Teacher educators expect that preservice teachers will learn from these observations, an expectation that may not be met if preservice teachers fail to notice what teacher educators hope they will notice when observing a lesson (either live or videotaped). In response to this concern, Sherin and colleagues have argued that, given preservice teachers' difficulties in noticing salient features of classroom instruction, improving the ability to notice should be an explicit focus of initial teacher preparation courses. They argued that, to this end, teacher preparation courses should provide "opportunities and structures within which teachers can develop their ability to notice" (Sherin & van Es, 2005, p. 489).

Our goal in the present study was to verify the findings of a recent study by the first author and his colleague (Star & Strickland, 2008), in which they had explored the types of classroom features and events that preservice mathematics teachers noticed before and after a semester long methods course focused on improving observation skills. The course included both specific activities designed to improve teachers' abilities to notice and the content of a typical mathematics methods course that accompanied students' initial field observations of teaching. In the present study, we sought to confirm and extend prior findings from Star and Strickland (2008), focusing on to what beginning teachers do and do not attend when viewing a classroom lesson and whether preservice teachers' abilities to notice salient features of classroom instruction improved after the completion of a methods course that included activities designed to improve observation skills.

On Noticing

In their previous work, van Es and Sherin (2002) defined *noticing* as having the following three components:

> (a) identifying what is important or noteworthy about a classroom situation; (b) making connections between the specifics of classroom interactions and the broader principles of teaching and learning they represent; and (c) using what one knows about the context to reason about classroom events.
>
> (p. 573)

Although all three of these components of noticing are important, we suggest that, particularly for preservice teachers, the first component of noticing is the most foundational. For this reason, our definition of *noticing* is limited to Part (a) of the van Es and Sherin definition. We find it intuitive that preservice teachers can make sense only of classroom features they can identify. If preservice teachers are unable even to identify that classroom events have occurred (Part [a] of the van Es and Sherin definition), it seems natural that they will be unable either to make connections between these events and broad principles of teaching and learning

(Part [b]) or to reason about these events (Part [c]). The research discussed above indicates that preservice teachers do not notice salient classroom features in a live or videotaped lesson, perhaps in part because they do not know to what to attend among the many events that occur during a classroom lesson. In the present study, we were interested in what preservice teachers did and did not attend to while viewing a classroom lesson, with the idea that their abilities to notice in the broad sense (as in van Es and Sherin's conception, *to connect and interpret events*) depend critically on what they notice in the narrow sense (*to attend to*).

Furthermore, we think that it is critical for preservice teachers to activate a focus on noticing—to begin to attend to the complexity of the classroom and the full range of events that may require a teacher's attention. To be clear, some classroom events are certainly more important than others, and it is critical that preservice teachers be able to attend to and interpret these important events. However, we believe that teachers do not have the ability to notice important events (or even to distinguish important from trivial lesson features) until *after* they have developed the ability to notice (even trivial) classroom features. We view noticing therefore as a skill that preservice teachers must learn to activate very early in their training, and only after this skill is active can teachers attempt the more sophisticated and nuanced task of determining which events are most worthy of being noticed. In line with this belief, a primary aim of the methods course described here and in our prior work was to activate or *turn on* teachers' noticing skills; determining which events were more or less important was only a secondary and peripheral goal of the course.

Star and Strickland Study

The Star and Strickland (2008) study involved two phases of data collection: (a) a preassessment in which preservice teachers viewed a video of a class session and were assessed on their abilities to notice features of the instruction they had seen in the video and (b) a postassessment of preservice teachers' abilities to notice instructional features in a (different) classroom video. The preservice teachers who served as participants were enrolled in a semester long secondary mathematics methods course (taught by Star) at a large, public Midwestern university in the United States. The course under investigation was the first methods course for preservice secondary mathematics teachers, a 15-week, one-semester course consisting of seminars, field observation, and work in a peer teaching laboratory. Participants were either mathematics majors ($n = 26$, 11 male, 15 female) or were working toward a postbaccalaureate certification in secondary mathematics ($n = 2$, both male). Participants viewed two videos from the U.S. Public Release TIMSS video series: A 50-minute eighth grade lesson on exponents was the target of the preassessment, and a 45-minute eighth grade lesson on angles, arc lengths, secants, and tangents was the target of the postassessment. The research team generated a list of assessment questions for each video; participants were asked to recall classroom features and events in five observation categories: classroom environment, classroom management, tasks, mathematical content, and communication (see Table 8.1). The preassessment was administered to preservice teachers in

TABLE 8.1   Five observation categories for preassessments and postassessments

Category	Description	Sample assessment questions
Classroom environment	The physical setting of the classroom, including desk arrangements, materials, and equipment available and utilized; demographics of students and teacher, including class size and grade level	How many students were in the room? (Fewer than 15; between 15 and 25; between 26 and 35; more than 35) On what kind of equipment did the teacher draw the graph of 2^x?
Classroom management	The ways the teacher manages classroom events, including disruptive events, pace changes, and procedures for calling on students or handling homework	Is the way the desks were arranged the common, daily arrangement? Did the teacher make it to every table group during the class?
Tasks	The activities students do in the class period (e.g., warm-ups, worksheets, taking notes, presentations, passing out papers, upcoming quizzes, and homework)	Which best describes the structure of the activities? (Students observe book's examples, then determine operation to get that result, and then develop theorem; class proves/discusses a theorem and then applies theorems to get an answer to a problem; not sure) True or false: None of the groups on camera get to the second proof.
Mathematical content	The mathematics of the lesson, including its representation of the mathematics (graphs, equations, tables, models), the examples used, and the problems posed	In one scene, a student asks if ab^3 is the same as a^3b^3. How did the teacher handle this misconception? True or false: The teacher forgot to mention that the bases must be the same to multiply two exponents together.
Communication	Communication between students or between teacher and students, including questions posed and answers or suggestions offered	True or false: When the teacher puts a problem on the screen, she gives students time to solve it before discussing the answer/solution. Record at least three questions you remember the teacher asking.

September, in one of the first classes of their methods course; the postassessment was administered in December, in one of the last classes of the semester.

The results of the preassessment showed that preservice teachers generally do not enter teaching-methods courses with well-developed observation skills. The postassessment indicated that the course led to significant increases in preservice teachers' observation skills. The largest improvements were seen in teachers' abilities to notice features of the classroom environment and tasks. More modest gains were seen in teachers' abilities to notice the mathematical content of a lesson, classroom management, and teacher and student communication during a lesson.

In their study, Star and Strickland (2008) utilized a preassessment/postassessment design, asked participants to watch full-length videos of a class period, and focused on an *attending* definition of noticing, as opposed to the more typical conception of Sherin et al., in which attending is only a subcomponent of noticing (van Es & Sherin, 2002). With the goal of confirming and extending the results from the Star and Strickland study, we replicated it, duplicating the method used by Star and Strickland in nearly every way, with only minor adjustment to the assessments for clarification, as described below.

Method

The present study, with its preassessment/postassessment design, included two phases of data collection: (a) a preassessment measuring preservice teachers' abilities to notice instructional features in a full-length video of a class period and (b) a postassessment of preservice teachers' abilities to notice instructional features in a (different) classroom video.

Participants

The participants in this study, mathematics majors in college ($N = 30$), were preservice teachers enrolled in a semester long secondary mathematics methods course (taught by Star) at a large, public Midwestern university in the United States. Although many of the participants had prior formal and informal teaching experience, none had previously participated in a formal student teaching experience. Prior to enrolling in the course, all participants had completed introductory education courses focused on learning theories, diversity in education, and literacy across subjects in the curriculum.

Measures

The assessments were written instruments designed to explore what teachers noticed (attended to) after watching full-length videos of a class period in an eighth grade mathematics classroom. Participants viewed the two TIMSS videos used by Star and Strickland (2008).

The measures used by Star and Strickland (2008) were modified for this study in the following two ways (see Star & Strickland, 2008, for details on design of the original assessment): First, in the present study 9 questions were included in each assessment for each observation category, whereas in Star and Strickland the number of questions for each observation category ranged from 6 to 15. Second, although many questions were the same in the two studies, some were refined and clarified in the present study.

Procedure

The preassessment was administered to preservice teachers in September, during the third class period of the methods course. Prior to watching the video, participants were instructed that they would watch a video of one entire class period of an eighth grade mathematics class and that after the video they would be asked questions about what they had noticed about the class. At the conclusion of the video, the preassessment was handed out. Participants were given 60 minutes to complete the assessment; everyone finished in the allotted time. The postassessment was administered in December, on one of the last classes of the semester, using the same procedure.

Members of the research team who had participated in the construction of the assessment and the scoring rubric graded all assessments.

Description of Course

The course under investigation was the first methods course for preservice secondary mathematics teachers. During each week in a 15-week semester, preservice teachers had 4 hours of seminar, 4 hours of field observation, and 2 hours in a peer teaching laboratory. The two primary aims for the course, as in the course studied by Star and Strickland (2008), were to improve preservice teachers' abilities to notice and interpret salient events in classroom lessons and to begin to develop preservice teachers' abilities to plan and implement lessons. In the first weeks of the course (after administration of the preassessment), after watching and discussing several classroom videos, the observation framework described in Table 8.1 was introduced to the preservice teachers. This framework served to organize the remainder of the course, in that subsequent class activities involved in-depth readings, small and large group discussions, role playing, and lesson-video viewing around each observation category.

Our focus in the present study was on to what teachers attended prior to the course and as a result of the course. We collected no qualitative or process data that would have enabled us to describe how the course changed preservice teachers' abilities to notice, such as which course features were most effective, how these course features were implemented, or the nature of preservice teachers' discussions that may have been instrumental in prompting preservice teachers to become more attentive to lesson features. In future studies, we plan to address the question of how course activities can affect preservice teachers' abilities to notice. The data sources for the present study are limited to the preassessments and postassessments.

Results

We first discuss results from the present study similar to those found by Star and Strickland (2008), followed by results that diverge from that prior work.

Convergent Findings

In many areas, the results from the present study converge with the findings of Star and Strickland (2008). We elaborate below on similar findings in the classroom environment and communication observation categories.

Classroom Environment

As found by Star and Strickland (2008), preservice teachers in the present study showed particularly large gains in their abilities to notice features of the classroom environment as a result of the course. On the preassessment, preservice teachers possessed relatively weak skills in observing the classroom environment, correctly answering only 46% of questions in this category (see Table 8.2). Low-scoring questions (answered correctly by fewer than 15% of the students) asked students to identify items they had noticed in the classroom, such as a chalkboard and an overhead projector; estimate how many students were in the classroom; and recall whether the teacher was left-handed. For example, on one question, although all participants correctly recalled that the classroom in the video contained a whiteboard, few noticed a computer and an overhead projector, and none noticed all three. On another low-scoring question, which asked how many students were in the room, most participants incorrectly responded that there were 26–35 students

TABLE 8.2 Results for preassessments and postassessments (percentages correct)

Category	Present study		Star and Strickland (2008)	
	Pre	Post	Pre	Post
Classroom environment	46	78	44	86
Classroom management	68	74	80	80
Tasks	57	55	65	80
Mathematical content	50	49	54	70
Communication	41	49	60	70

(19 responses) or 15–25 students (6 responses) in the room, when, in fact, there were more than 35 students in the room.

On the postassessment, by contrast, preservice teachers displayed remarkable attentiveness to features of the classroom environment. Students scored 78% correct on the classroom environment questions at postassessment, with six high-performing questions (more than 70%) and more than 50% correct on all questions. When asked to notice items on the walls in the classroom, 100% of the participants responded correctly. A second high-performing question, asking the number of students in the classroom (similar to the low-scoring question about class size on the preassessment), was answered correctly by all but 1 participant at postassessment.

Indeed, students showed substantial improvement at postassessment on questions corresponding to each of their low-performing areas at preassessment. For example, whereas on the preassessment none of the participants noticed both a computer and a projector in the classroom, on the postassessment 73% noticed both items. Students also became more observant of characteristics of the teacher; on the preassessment only 7% of participants correctly noticed that the teacher was left-handed, but on the postassessment 63% noticed that the teacher was right-handed, with many commenting additionally that her right-handedness contributed to students' difficulty in seeing what she was writing.

Communication

In addition to convergent results in the classroom environment category, we found similar results in communication. As found by Star and Strickland (2008), on questions about classroom communication, preservice teachers experienced improvements. Preservice teachers began the study with relatively weak observation skills in the area of classroom communication. Communication was the category with the lowest scores on the preassessment, with participants answering only 41% of communication questions correctly.

At the preassessment, participants scored particularly low on questions relating to how the teacher gave directions, how the teacher asked students questions and responded to their comments, and what questions the students asked the teacher. For example, when asked the first thing the teacher talked about after the bell rang to begin the class, only 27% of participants correctly noted that she told the students where to sit. When asked about the teacher's style of posing questions to her class, only 27% correctly noted that she opened her questions to everyone in the class instead of calling on specific students. Scores were particularly low on a question about how the teacher responded to a specific comment from a student; only 30% remembered that she had told the student that he was correct. The preassessment question with the lowest score asked participants to recall a question that a student had asked the teacher during a whole class discussion; none of the participants remembered that the student had asked, "Do we have to write it in words?"

At postassessment, participants' scores in observing classroom communication improved somewhat, to an average of 49%. Participants performed well on a question asking them to record at least three questions they remembered the teacher's asking; 70% of respondents were able to do this on the postassessment. In addition, on a second high-scoring question, 77% of respondents correctly noted that the teacher reminded the students at the end of class to study for an upcoming quiz.

However, participants' performance on the postassessment in the communication category continued to be somewhat mediocre, with three questions on which only 37% of participants responded correctly. For example, only 37% of participants correctly remembered the first thing the teacher talked about after the bell rang. A second low-scoring question asked participants to recall the teacher's frustration at her students' inability to find a "pattern" in the problems from the lesson. Only 37% of participants remembered that the teacher had commented, "You guys are scaring me." The third relatively low-scoring question asked how the teacher usually referred to the class as a whole; only 37% noted that she usually referred to the class as "you guys."

Thus, whereas overall teachers in both studies improved their observation skills in the area of classroom communication, the performance of teachers in the current study in this category is mixed. Participants had some increased success in noticing what kinds of questions the teacher asked and what types of reminders she gave students, but they still missed many nuances in communication, such as the teacher's word choice, how she addressed students, and how she responded to students' answers.

Divergent Findings

In several areas our present results diverged from findings of Star and Strickland (2008). In particular, we discuss below our findings that preservice teachers in the present study did *not* show improvement in the observation categories of tasks and mathematical content and *did* show improvement in classroom management.

Tasks

The tasks category refers to the instructional and assessment activities of the teacher and the students in class. Our preassessment focused on the teacher's actions that served the lesson objectives, such as the structure of the group work, presentation of the material, and assignment of homework.

In the current study, preservice teachers scored an average of 57% on the preassessment in this category. Specifically, the higher-performing questions dealt mostly with the sequence of the activities that occurred during the lesson as well as the structure of the presented material. For example, one high-performing question asked participants to arrange a series of classroom activities in the order in which they had occurred in the video; 70% of participants were able to recall the correct sequence. Another moderately high-performing question in this category asked participants to recall how many different rules for multiplying exponents the lesson covered; 63% noticed that the lesson focused on three such rules.

In contrast, the preassessment included several questions that indicated participants' difficulties in attending to features of the lesson tasks. For example, one question asked how the teacher started the lecture/discussion; only 37% of students were able to correctly recall that the teacher did a quick review of base and exponent topics from the previous grade. As another example, only 33% of students noticed that the teacher used stacks of unifix cubes and a graph as visual aids to highlight exponential growth.

Students' scores in the tasks category at postassessment ($M = 55\%$) showed no improvement from the preassessment ($M = 57\%$). (These results differed from the original study, in which participants' scores increased from a mean of 65% at the preassessment to 80% at the postassessment.) One high-performing question on the postassessment related to the type of visual aid the teacher used during the lesson; 93% of participants recalled the teacher's use of an overhead projector. However, participants continued to have difficulty noticing details about lesson tasks; for example, only 17% of students answered on the postassessment that students' homework from the previous class consisted of problems from the textbook. As another example, only 43% of students noticed that the teacher started the lesson with the problem of the day on an overhead projector.

Mathematical Content

Mathematical content included questions about the representation of the mathematics, the examples used, and the problems posed. As was the case in Star and Strickland (2008), in the present study preservice mathematics teachers began the study with relatively weak skills in observing the mathematical content of a lesson. For example, when asked, on the preassessment, whether a student had asked the teacher if $aaa/bbb = 1$ because the as cancel and the bs cancel, *all* participants in the current study said that this event had indeed happened, but no such event occurred in the classroom video. A similar pattern was seen in the results of the Star and Strickland (2008) study, in which at preassessment the preservice teachers had difficulties noticing subtleties in the ways that the teacher helped students think about mathematical content. In sum, results from both studies showed that at preassessment preservice teachers' abilities to notice features of the mathematical content of a lesson were somewhat weak.

Although Star and Strickland (2008) found that preservice teachers did show improvement in their abilities to notice issues of mathematical content, similar gains were *not* found in the present study. Perhaps the explanation for these divergent findings with respect to mathematical content is that revisions to the assessment used in the present study increased the difficulty level of questions in this observation category. Several questions in Star and Strickland (2008) that were considered part of the mathematical content observation category were closer to tasks, communication, or both, and these are the questions on which students in the original study did well at postassessment. For example, 82% of participants in the original study correctly identified as false a statement related to whether the teacher asked "why" after students offered suggestions or solutions—a question related to content but more properly classified in the communication category. Similarly, a question about how the teacher referred to the lesson content of the day (using the textbook chapter and section *number* or using the chapter and section *name*) does relate to content but is more properly categorized in the tasks category; 82% of participants in the original study answered this question correctly on the postassessment. When the prior assessment was modified, these questions were removed or modified, resulting in a more pure and difficult assessment of students' noticing of mathematical content.

Classroom Management

The preservice teachers in the current study differed from their counterparts in the original study in their level of attentiveness to classroom management events. The mean score for the preassessment in the current study was only 68%, compared to 80% in the Star and Strickland (2008) study. Note, however, that this 68% performance was the highest among all observation categories in the current study and thus is consistent with prior research findings indicating that preservice teachers are quite concerned about classroom management (Sabers, Cushing, & Berliner, 1991). Higher-performing questions about classroom management included observations of teacher actions in maintaining control of the classroom environment. For example, 93% of students noticed that the teacher went from table to table observing and answering student questions. Similarly, 77% of students noticed that the teacher took attendance in the beginning of class and visited every table group during the class. In addition, preservice teachers in the current study were also attentive to classroom procedures, such as the arrangement of desks, the distribution of lesson materials, and the taking of attendance.

At the postassessment, participants showed modest improvement in their observations of classroom procedures as well as teachers' interactions with students; mean scores in this category increased from 68% to 74%. (These results diverge from those obtained by Star and Strickland, 2008, who found no improvement from pre- to postassessment in the category of classroom management.) For example, when preservice teachers were asked about the teacher's calling on students, 93% of participants correctly noted in the postassessment that the teacher mostly called on students when their hands were raised, compared to only 57% correct on a similar question at preassessment. More generally, preservice teachers were highly observant of procedures the teacher followed, including that she prepared overheads, that she did not distribute papers during the class, and that she did not take the attendance. The divergent results from Star and Strickland (2008) may be attributed to a ceiling effect in the original study, in which the preservice teachers started with high awareness of classroom management events, with little room to improve.

Noticing of Important Classroom Features

Recall that in our assessment we intentionally included both mundane and important features of classroom lessons to enable us to explore the full range of what preservice teachers did and did not notice. To what extent did preservice teachers' abilities to notice *important* classroom events improve as a result of the methods course?

Before reporting the results of this analysis, we remind the reader that our assessment, this study, and the methods course more generally were not designed to explore this question. In particular, individual assessment items were not created and labeled a priori as assessing important or less important classroom features. Furthermore, the methods course itself was centrally concerned with improving teachers' abilities to notice all kinds of events in the classroom rather than helping preservice teachers identify a subset of noticed events that were more or less important. However, we attempted to determine post hoc which questions appeared to target important aspects of the pre- and postassessment lessons, to enable us to determine whether teachers improved in their ability to notice important events.

Two graduate students, both of whom had prior experience as middle or secondary mathematics teachers, viewed the pre- and postassessment videos, studied the pre- and postassessments, and then independently rated whether each question assessed an important facet of the lesson. No prior discussion was held to discuss the construct of *important*; rather, each rater was left to make this determination on her own. The two raters then met to compare their importance ratings. Questions that both raters independently scored as assessing important features of each lesson were classified as *important questions*. All other questions were classified as *other*.

The rating exercise yielded the following results. On the preassessment, 26 questions were deemed important by both raters. Important questions were identified in all observation categories; however, the fewest important questions came from the classroom environment category. Important questions concerned pedagogical choices made by the teacher, mathematical content addressed in the lesson, and teacher–student communication. On the postassessment, 26 questions were deemed important by both raters. Similarly to those on the preassessment, important questions were selected from all observation categories, but with the fewest from classroom environment, and important questions concerned pedagogical choices made by the teacher, mathematical content addressed in the lesson, and teacher-initiated communication, both during the lesson and while addressing individual students.

Using these importance ratings, we computed preservice teachers' mean scores for important and other questions, for both the pre- and postassessment; t-tests were used to explore whether differences in teachers' mean scores were statistically significant. On the preassessment, teachers' mean score on important questions was 53% correct, whereas the mean score on other questions was 50% correct. This difference was not significant, $p = 0.33$, indicating that preservice teachers began the study being no less (or more) observant of important lesson features than of other features.

On the postassessment, preservice teachers showed improvement on both important and other questions, with the mean score on important questions increasing to 59% correct and the mean score on other questions increasing to 65% correct. Regarding teachers' gains from pre- to postassessment (and consistent with the overall results described above), preservice teachers showed significant improvement in their performance on both important ($p < 0.05$) and other ($p < 0.001$) questions. However, at postassessment, participants' performance was significantly lower on important questions as compared to other questions, $p < 0.05$. Thus, although teachers became better observers of classroom features generally, by the end of the course preservice teachers' observation skills continued to be stronger on classroom features that were less important.

Discussion

A key premise underlying both our current and previous studies is that teachers may need explicit training in how to observe mathematics lessons. In a typical teacher preparation program, preservice teachers spend a significant amount of time observing the teaching of others, with the expectation that preservice teachers will learn by watching other teachers' lessons. Such learning is predicated, however, on the assumption that novice teachers are capable of attending to (and subsequently interpreting) salient features of mathematics lessons. Prior research indicates that novice teachers are not particularly astute observers of mathematics lessons, nor are preservice teachers capable of sorting the important from the less important aspects of classroom practice. Both the present study and our earlier work confirm that preservice secondary mathematics teachers at the beginning of a teacher preparation program are not particularly keen observers of classroom practice but that observation skills can be improved in a one-semester methods course.

Our primary goal for the present study was to replicate the results of Star and Strickland (2008). Our results indicate that this goal was met in that teachers in both courses did show overall improvements in their abilities to observe classroom interactions. Looking more closely, we found that, as shown by Star and Strickland, preservice teachers were not particularly good observers of classroom features at the beginning of the methods course, with weak performances in all observation categories. At the conclusion of the course, teachers showed substantial improvement in some areas. As was the case in our prior study, noticing of features of the classroom environment showed the most dramatic improvement. Similarly, postassessment performance on questions relating to classroom management was quite high. In the category of communication, teachers also experienced improvement, though at the end of the course their mean score was only 49%.

Some results of the present study differed from our expectations based on past work. Preservice teachers failed to show improvement in their abilities to notice features of tasks (on which they did improve in the Star and Strickland, 2008, study); similarly, performance in the mathematical content observation category was stagnant. Although some of these differences may result from modifications of the assessments for the present study, we wondered whether lower average preassessment scores played a role. Compared with teachers in the Star and Strickland (2008) study, preservice teachers in the present study began with a lower level of attentiveness to the category of tasks at preassessment. In the current study, preservice teachers scored an average of 57% on the preassessment in this category compared to the mean of 65% at preassessment in the original study. Similarly, teachers in the current study scored an average of 41% on preassessments in the communication category, as opposed to 60% in the original study. Perhaps improvements in mathematical content require a stronger grounding in tasks and communication. Or perhaps the ability to closely observe tasks, mathematical content, and communication are related. Thus, what we have observed here is initial growth in communication so that, as in Star and Strickland (2008), average scores in the categories of mathematical content and communication are about the same and the average score on tasks is slightly higher.

Note that improving preservice teachers' abilities to attend to classroom features does not eliminate the subsequent need to help teachers develop abilities to notice and interpret *important* classroom features. The assessments used here were designed to assess teachers' noticing of a wide range of lesson characteristics—including both important and relatively trivial features. Although our methods course was instrumental in helping teachers attend to a greater variety of events in a lesson, we had more limited success at improving teachers' noticing of important events. (Given that the goal of the course was to improve noticing generally and not noticing of important events, this finding is perhaps not surprising.) As found by Star and Strickland (2008), teachers made great strides in their abilities to attend to features of the classroom environment, but they continued to have difficulties noticing aspects of the mathematics content of the lesson, a lesson dimension that is arguably more critical than whether the classroom contained a chalkboard or an overhead projector.

Why might teachers show improvement in their abilities to notice classroom features but still struggle to notice *important* classroom events? Two answers are indicated by the present results. First, important events may be inherently harder to notice. The most attention-grabbing features of a lesson (to a novice) may not be those that (in the eyes of an experienced teacher) are most important. Although noticing the color the walls are painted or whether the teacher was male or female may be relatively easy, attending to the exact words, facial expression, and body language used by a student who asks a question or the specific example that a teacher uses to clarify a student misconception may be more challenging. Important classroom events may be inherently subtle, nuanced, and difficult to notice—more so than less important lesson features. Second, preservice teachers may not have developed the ability to distinguish between important and unimportant lesson features. In the absence of an observational compass that points toward important events, teachers' attention will be attracted by whatever is most visually salient, obvious, or personally compelling—independent of its importance in the lesson. Both explanations are plausible.

In either case, teacher educators need to think carefully about what it is entailed in an event's being important in a lesson. Determining what is and is not important in a lesson is a nontrivial task (even for experts). In particular, although in the present analysis important events were identified from all observation categories, recall that the fewest important events (as scored by two experienced mathematics teachers) related to classroom environment. One might reasonably conclude that certain observation categories are more densely populated with important events than are other categories; for example, one could propose that it is *always* more important to observe mathematical content carefully than to observe classroom environment carefully. However, determining what is and is not important is likely to be complex, nuanced, and fundamentally influenced by the perspective of the observer. One could imagine a scenario in which features of the classroom environment were critically important in a lesson, yet in other instances such details might be trivial. Regardless, a significant result from both the present and earlier studies is the importance of methods courses designed to explicitly focus on improving observation skills and helping teachers to be more aware of important events.

Finally, note that this study did not provide evidence in support of (or against) a central premise of our work—that teachers do not have the ability to notice important events (or even to distinguish important from trivial lesson features) until *after* they have developed the ability to notice (even trivial) classroom features. We found that preservice teachers began the methods course with relatively poor observational skills and, after a course focused on improving their abilities to notice a full range of classroom events, preservice teachers were better observers of both mundane and important events. If the ultimate goal is for teachers to be able to notice important classroom events, neither this study nor Star and Strickland (2008) tested whether it is better to focus first on improving teachers' awareness of the full range of (trivial and important) events (as was done here) or to focus explicitly on only important events from the outset. Researchers may, in the future, consider exploring this interesting issue.

Note

1   Thanks to Amanda Hawkins, Theodora Chang, Courtney Pollack, and Katy Green for their help in collecting, coding, and analyzing the data reported here.

References

Berliner, D. C., Stein, P., Sabers, D. S., Clarridge, P. B., Cushing, K. S., & Pinnegar, S. (1988). Implications of research on pedagogical expertise and experience in mathematics teaching. In D. A. Grouws & T. J. Cooney (Eds.), *Perspectives on research on effective mathematics teaching* (pp. 67–95). Reston, VA: National Council of Teachers of Mathematics.

Bliss, T., & Reynolds, A. (2004). Quality visions and focused imagination. In J. Brophy (Ed.), *Using video in teacher education* (pp. 29–52). Amsterdam: Elsevier.

Brophy, J. (Ed.). (2004). *Using video in teacher education.* Amsterdam: Elsevier.

Carter, K., Cushing, K. S., Sabers, D. S., Stein, P., & Berliner, D. C. (1988). Expert–novice differences in perceiving and processing visual classroom information. *Journal of Teacher Education, 39*, 25–31.

Sabers, D. S., Cushing, K. S., & Berliner, D. C. (1991). Differences among teachers in a task characterized by simultaneity, multidimensionality, and immediacy. *American Educational Research Journal, 28*, 63–88.

Sherin, M. G., & Han, S. Y. (2004). Teacher learning in the context of a video club. *Teaching and Teacher Education, 20*, 163–183.

Sherin, M. G., & van Es, E. A. (2005). Using video to support teachers' ability to interpret classroom interactions. *Journal of Technology and Teacher Education, 13*, 475–491.

Star, J. R., & Strickland, S. K. (2008). Learning to observe: Using video to improve preservice mathematics teachers' ability to notice. *Journal of Mathematics Teacher Education, 11*, 107–125.

Stockero, S. (2008). Using a video-based curriculum to develop a reflective stance in prospective mathematics teachers. *Journal of Mathematics Teacher Education, 11*, 373–394.

van Es, E. A., & Sherin, M. G. (2002). Learning to notice: Scaffolding new teachers' interpretations of classroom interactions. *Journal of Technology and Teacher Education, 10*, 571–596.

9

A FRAMEWORK FOR LEARNING TO NOTICE STUDENT THINKING[1]

Elizabeth A. van Es

Classrooms are complex settings, with a variety of interactions taking place at one time. Teachers need to decide to what to pay attention, and they need to reason about what they see to make decisions about how to proceed with the lesson. But learning to what events and interactions to pay attention is a complicated skill. First, teachers' knowledge and beliefs about teaching and learning, students, content, and curriculum all influence to what they attend while they teach. Second, to draw conclusions that particular teaching strategies are effective, one needs to know what counts as evidence for effective practice. Teachers often use student behavioral cues as evidence that their teaching methods were effective, but adopting cognitive perspectives to make claims about effective teaching is equally important. However, conducting such analysis proves to be a challenge because American teachers do not typically design or enact lessons in ways that provide them with windows into the development of student thinking and understanding (Stigler & Hiebert, 1999).

Given the emphasis in current mathematics education reform recommendations that teachers adopt a flexible approach to instruction that is responsive to student ideas (Ball & Cohen, 1999; National Council of Teachers of Mathematics [NCTM], 2000), I propose that teachers need to learn to *notice*; that is, they need to attend to aspects of classroom interactions that influence student learning and reason about them in the midst of instruction. My goal in this chapter is to examine the development of teachers' abilities to notice student thinking while the teachers participated in a video club. A video club consists of a group of teachers who meet regularly to view and discuss video segments from one another's teaching (Sherin, 2000). In this study, I draw on transcript data from video-club meetings and propose a framework to describe the development of one video-club group's noticing over time. I then use examples from the video-club sessions to illustrate the levels of the framework.

Noticing in the Context of Mathematics Education Reform

Noticing has been described as a component of expert practice. Just as experts have the capacity to quickly examine features that are relevant to their practices (Stevens & Hall, 1998), expert teachers have heightened sensitivities to particular aspects of their work, as well as techniques for analyzing, using, and inquiring into these features of their practices (Berliner, 1994; Mason, 2002). Ainley and Luntley (2007) described this expertise as *attention-dependent knowledge*, which includes skills that expert teachers use to attend to the cognitive and affective aspects of classrooms and that become available in the midst of instruction in response to a classroom interaction.

The construct of *noticing* has recently been characterized as consisting of three parts: attending to noteworthy events, reasoning about such events, and making informed teaching decisions on the basis of the analysis of these observations (Hiebert, Morris, Berk, & Jansen, 2007; Jacobs, Lamb, & Philipp, 2010; Jacobs, Lamb, Philipp, & Schappelle, this volume, chapter 7; Richert, 2005; Santagata, Zannoni, & Stigler, 2007; Sherin, 2007; van Es & Sherin, 2002). An important component of this research is the focus of teachers' analyses on student learning and the relationship between teaching moves and the learning that results. These studies all point to a model of *seeing* one's practice—a model that is situated in one's work and that involves attending to and making sense of important events and interactions to inform teaching decisions.

In the context of mathematics education reform, learning to notice student thinking is particularly relevant (Ball & Cohen, 1999; NCTM, 2000; Rodgers, 2002). Mathematics teachers are encouraged to adopt a student-centered, responsive approach to teaching, in which they slow the pace of their instruction and attend closely to what students say and do (Ball, Lubienski, & Mewborn, 2001; Rodgers, 2002). A variety of studies have shown that focusing on student thinking and children's learning promotes teaching and learning mathematics for understanding and leads to improved student achievement (Carpenter, Fennema, Franke, Levi, & Empson, 2000; Franke, Carpenter, Levi, & Fennema, 2001; Wilson & Berne, 1999).

Learning a new discourse for talking about teaching is also central to noticing. Nemirovsky, DiMattia, Ribeiro, and Lara-Meloy (2005) identified two types of discourse teachers use to discuss case studies of classroom episodes, *grounded narrative* and *evaluative discourse*. The former highlights the sequential nature of teachers' commentaries, similar to following the plot of a story, whereas the latter invokes comments laden with values and judgments, such as what a teacher could or should have done better. Noticing entails a third discourse structure, one that is more interpretive in nature, in which the teachers' goal is to make sense of student thinking and use evidence from practice to reason through important teaching and learning issues. This discourse is similar to that promoted by Borko, Jacobs, Eiteljorg, and Pittman (2008) and Davis (2006), in which teachers seek

to answer provocative questions, press on one another's thinking, critically analyze events they observe, and use evidence of student learning to guide teaching
decisions.

Video and Teacher Learning

In the last decade, the use of video for teacher learning has received increased attention. With recent advances in video technology, little specialized skill is required
to capture and prepare video segments for analysis. Others have examined the uses
of video in teacher education (Brophy, 2004; Miller & Zhou, 2007). In this chapter, I draw on this research to highlight particular aspects of video that make it useful for helping teachers learn to notice. First, video can be used to capture much
of the complexity of classroom interactions and to zoom in on particular aspects of
teaching to which teachers may not otherwise have access, such as discussions that
groups of students have while they collaborate to solve a problem. Second, video
segments can be reviewed several times, with teachers adopting different perspectives each time. Third, the availability for review also allows teachers time to pause
and consider events that occurred without the need to take immediate action and
may enable them to see things they did not observe when the event took place or
when they viewed the segment for the first time (Borko et al., 2008).

Video has been used to help teachers develop professional judgment and to
reason about the complex practice of teaching (Oonk, Goffree, & Verloop,
2004; Seago, 2004; Wang & Hartley, 2003) as well as to develop important skills
through observing and analyzing teaching. Research on preservice teachers' and
in-service teachers' analyses of video showed that they became more attuned to
particular dimensions of the classroom environment that influence student learning, they learned to observe the effects of teachers' actions on student learning,
they learned to ground their analyses of teaching in evidence from practice, and
their conversations became more productive over time when they adopted a
more focused, in-depth, and analytic approach to examine specific issues related
to teaching and learning mathematics (Borko et al., 2008; Santagata et al., 2007;
Star & Strickland, 2008; van Es & Sherin, 2002).

Drawing on this research base, I articulate a framework for learning to notice
student thinking. I then use data from a video-club study to illustrate how a group
of teachers developed in their abilities to notice student thinking in this context.

Research Design

Video-Club Design

The video-club design and data collection for the project have been described
elsewhere (van Es, 2009; van Es & Sherin, 2008). In this section, I briefly review
the data sources and describe the analysis procedures relevant to this study.

Participants and Setting

Seven fourth and fifth grade elementary school teachers from an urban school participated in this study. They had 1 to more than 20 years of teaching experience. The video club met for 60–75 minutes after school 10 times throughout the 2001–2002 school year, one or two times each month from October to May. Each teacher shared clips from his or her classroom two or three times throughout the year. Typically, two clips were viewed and discussed at each meeting.

The research team[2] was responsible for videotaping and selecting clips for the group to view at each meeting. In general, we attempted to capture the central activities of the lesson, and we also intentionally focused on aspects of the lesson in which students' thinking was made visible, such as when a student illustrated an invented method or a class discussed a student's questions. A 5- to 7-minute segment from each classroom was selected, and the researchers prepared a corresponding transcript.

We began the meetings with a brief overview of the topic and lesson for the first clip the group would view. Because our goal was to examine students' mathematical thinking in the clips, the facilitator prompted the group to discuss these issues. General prompts (e.g., "What did you notice?") induced the group to raise issues they found noteworthy, and specific prompts (e.g., "Let's take a look at how Lindsey solved that problem") directed the teachers to analyze student thinking. The facilitator encouraged teachers to interpret what they noticed by asking questions like "Why do you think she chose that method?" and prompted them to use evidence to support their analyses with questions like "Where do you see that in the transcript?" The facilitators had no preconceived ideas about what were correct interpretations. Rather, the goal was to help teachers learn to see interesting students ideas, to appreciate that these ideas and confusions are often expressed in subtle ways, to analyze these ideas by inquiring into the details of their thinking, and to propose, discuss, and debate a variety of interpretations of their thinking.

Data and Analysis

Data for this study include videotapes and transcripts of the 10 video-club meetings. Qualitative methods were used to conduct an analysis of the nature and development of the video-club group's noticing over the course of the 10 meetings (Erickson, 2006). Elsewhere Sherin and I have examined the shifts in individual teachers' noticing in this context (van Es & Sherin, 2008); in this chapter, I focus on the development of the group's noticing.

To begin, I examined the literature to identify areas that are central to teachers' noticing (Jacobs, Lamb, & Philipp, 2010; Rosaen, Lundeberg, Cooper, Fritzen, & Terpstra, 2008; Santagata et al., 2007; van Es & Sherin, 2008). I identified three main areas along which noticing develops: what stands out to teachers when they observe teaching, the strategies they use to analyze what they observe, and the level of detail at which teachers discuss their observations. I then turned to the video-club data and examined the group's noticing within each of these three categories. Specifically, I segmented the video-club meeting transcripts into idea units (Grant & Kline, 2004), with the segments of conversation distinguished by a shift in topic. I found 10 idea units, on average, for each clip the group discussed. In my analysis, I first characterized the group's comments in each idea unit in terms of each of the three categories. I next looked across the idea units for each clip and characterized the group's noticing at this broader level in each of the three selected categories. Finally, I looked across the characterizations per clip for all 10 meetings to identify patterns and variations in the group's noticing. To be clear, although the three categories were initially identified in the literature, the meaning and scope of each category in the context of the video club evolved during the process of analysis.

From this analysis, I then generated two central categories—What Teachers Notice and How Teachers Notice—to capture the nature of the group's noticing. The first dimension of the framework, What Teachers Notice, captured both *whom* the teachers notice in the video clip and the *topic* of their analysis. *Whom* they notice concerns whether the group focuses on the class as whole, students as a group, particular students, the teacher in the clip, or themselves. *Topic* refers to issues they identify, such as remarks focused on the pedagogical strategies, behavior or mathematical thinking, or the classroom climate. The second dimension of the framework concerns how teachers analyze what they notice, including both their analytic stances and levels of depth. *Analytic stance* refers to the approach teachers take to analyzing classroom episodes and captures whether teachers engage in a productive inquiry (Borko et al., 2008) of teaching and learning. It also captures whether the group evaluates or interprets what they observe. In *evaluating*, the group makes uninformed judgments about what was good or bad or should have been done differently. *Interpreting* refers to the group's efforts to reason about what they observe, to understand the roots of an idea, and to explain what was meant by a particular statement, drawing, gesture, or expression. Finally, the *depth of analysis* refers to whether the teachers provide few details to explain their thinking or ground their comments in evidence and elaborate on their analyses.

Additionally, for each category, I created a developmental trajectory to illustrate growth in learning to notice over time. I did so to capture teachers' development in learning to attend to the particulars of student mathematical thinking and to reason about their observations, drawing on evidence from the clips they viewed to support their analyses.

Results

The central result from this research is the framework for learning to notice student thinking. This framework is useful in that through it I articulate two central features of noticing. First, I identify the particular dimensions related to what is noticed and how teachers reason about what they observe. Second, I show a trajectory of development in these two dimensions from Baseline to Extended Noticing (see Table 9.1).

TABLE 9.1 Framework for learning to notice student mathematical thinking

	Level 1 *Baseline*	Level 2 *Mixed*	Level 3 *Focused*	Level 4 *Extended*
What Teachers Notice	Attend to whole class environment, behavior, and learning and to teacher pedagogy	Primarily attend to teacher pedagogy Begin to attend to particular students' mathematical thinking and behaviors	Attend to particular students' mathematical thinking	Attend to the relationship between particular students' mathematical thinking and between teaching strategies and student mathematical thinking
How Teachers Notice	Form general impressions of what occurred	Form general impressions and highlight noteworthy events	Highlight noteworthy events	Highlight noteworthy events
	Provide descriptive and evaluative comments	Provide primarily evaluative with some interpretive comments	Provide interpretive comments	Provide interpretive comments
	Provide little or no evidence to support analysis	Begin to refer to specific events and interactions as evidence	Refer to specific events and interactions as evidence	Refer to specific events and interactions as evidence
			Elaborate on events and interactions	Elaborate on events and interactions
				Make connections between events and principles of teaching and learning
				On the basis of interpretations, propose alternative pedagogical solutions

I begin by describing the developmental shifts from Level 1 to Level 4 for each of the two dimensions of noticing and then provide examples from the video-club data to illustrate the group's discussions at each level.

To What Teachers Attend

At Level 1, participants focused on a range of issues, including whole class behavior, participation, student learning, the overall classroom climate, and teachers' pedagogies. At this stage, video-club participants made comments like "The class is engaged. They're all following along" or "I like how you set up the problem. When I've tried that, it hasn't really worked." Similarly to the teachers studied by Kagan and Tippins (1991), the teachers appeared concerned primarily with themselves and their own practices, adopting a self-centered perspective and connecting what they observed to their own practices. At Level 2, the participants became more focused in their analyses, attending primarily to the teacher's pedagogy, student behaviors, and students' mathematical thinking. Furthermore, they began to shift from a whole class perspective to attend also to particular students in the clip. Level 3 revealed a noticeable shift in focus to examining primarily particular students' mathematical thinking as represented in the clip. This is distinct from Levels 1 and 2 inasmuch as the teacher is no longer concerned with the self and looks beyond the whole class. Finally, at Level 4, teachers noticed both particular students' mathematical thinking and the teacher's pedagogy as it was revealed in the clip, and the events they noticed directly connect teachers' pedagogies and students' mathematical thinking. At this level, for example, a teacher may notice that particular students are constructing different solutions for solving a particular problem and then examine what the teacher did in the segment to create an environment to promote students' sharing multiple solutions.

How Teachers Notice

For this dimension, at Level 1, the participants offered general impressions (e.g., "That was a nice lesson" or "That lesson did not go well at all"), often oversimplifying the complexity of the classroom episode they observed. Furthermore, the commentary was highly judgmental and evaluative in nature, with little evidence from the clip to support their critiques. At Level 2, the teachers continued to offer general impressions, but they also began to highlight noteworthy events. Furthermore, they continued to evaluate what they observed, but they also began to try to make sense of their observations. Finally, at this level, the teachers began to refer to particular events and interactions as evidence to advance an interpretation. At Level 3, the teachers' comments were highly discriminate and identified particular noteworthy events in the segment. Additionally, the discussions were grounded in the particulars of the segments they had viewed, and these particulars were used as evidence to advance an interpretation. Finally, at this level, the teachers sought to elaborate and develop the discussion with multiple interpretations and explanations. At Level 4, the conversations built on those that are characteristic of Level 3, but two additional defining features of noticing emerged at this level. First, the teachers considered and proposed alternative pedagogical solutions. This evaluation of what could be done differently is distinct from the judgmental comments teachers made in Levels 1 and 2 because it was now informed by analysis and substantive interpretation. Second, the teachers sought to make connections (a) between ideas they discussed and (b) between particular events they noticed and broader principles of teaching and learning. In other words, their discussions were based in what they had observed and different ways to interpret these interactions, but they also attempted to connect their observations to central features of teaching, such as assessment, academic language, or classroom discourse.

With these dimensions in mind, I illustrate how they coordinate and characterize noticing at each level with examples from the video–club data.

Baseline Noticing

At the first level, Baseline Noticing, the teachers' focus was primarily on the overall classroom environment, the class's behavior and learning, and the teacher's pedagogy. The teachers offered general impressions, described and evaluated what they had observed, and provided little or no evidence to support their analyses. Consider the following illustration of this focus, excerpted from the first meeting. The group viewed a clip of a whole class discussion about sets of polygons. In the segment, students raised questions concerning the use of triangles as a way to determine the angles of polygons. When the following discussion took place, the clip had just ended and the facilitator had turned to the group and asked, "What did you notice?"

Drew: I noticed they were making faces.

Daniel: I noticed the enthusiasm of the group. You know, all of the volunteering . . . a bunch of them talking at the same time. And they all wanted to volunteer.

Yvette: A good base was laid here, because they were with you or what you were talking about. . . . I look at the math group and wonder how many are in there from my group last year. . . . I was amazed with the vocabulary you were using.

Daniel: Did they all have [protractors] at their desks? I'm having the problem sometimes when they have base-10 blocks and . . . certain children are back there building teepees with the blocks while I'm talking. [In the video, students] are so focused and not playing with the [protractors].

Yvette: They were on task. I didn't see any kids fade away and poke with pencils and off-task behavior, which I see in my room all of the time. They were not making a disruption.

The teachers' initial noticing was focused on the class as a whole, referring to *they*, *the group*, or *children*, attending to issues of the enthusiasm of the class, classroom management, and on-task behavior. Two teachers also raised issues related to their own teaching. Yvette wondered how many of the students in the segment were in her class the previous year, and Daniel commented on the challenges he encountered with students when he used base-10 blocks with his class. In terms of *how* they noticed, the comments were quite general: "A good base was laid." "They all wanted to volunteer." "They were on task." Additionally, their comments were both descriptive (e.g., "They were making faces" or "They were not making a disruption") and evaluative (e.g., "I was amazed with the vocabulary " or "The students are so focused") in nature. Finally, they offered few details, and the observations were vague. For instance, Yvette stated, "A good base was laid here, because they were with you or what you were talking about." However, both what base was established and what she meant by "they were with you" were unclear. Later, she commented on the vocabulary but did not articulate to which vocabulary words she was referring. In addition, she stated that "they had an idea," but what idea they had and how it related to the overall mathematical goals of the lesson were also unclear.

Further in the discussion, in an effort to focus the group's analysis, the facilitator asked the group to consider how one student, Khianna, understood the relationship of the triangles to the angles of the polygon.

Facilitator:	What about at the end, is it Khianna? When she drew, she said, "I have triangles; I got triangles." Do they want to have those separate triangles?
Wanda:	No.
Facilitator:	Because that adds more angles, right?
Wanda:	To me, she's building on what we've been talking about with the triangles, but, yeah, the way she's drawn it is incorrect, and that's not what I was talking about. I was talking about, at that point, a quadrangle. And so she wasn't listening, and the person who had given that [answer] was actually sitting right beside her.
Frances:	She didn't make the connection.
Yvette:	But I look at it differently. She at least had geometry on her page, and she made a connection that may have been a week or a lesson ago. And to me, it's like, "Okay, she's in the right ballpark."

Although the facilitator had focused the group on Khianna's statement, they discussed a behavioral issue: that she was not listening. Frances offered a general assessment when she remarked, "She didn't make the connection," but Frances did not elaborate on this assessment or offer evidence to support her claim. Finally, although Yvette offered an alternative perspective, she did so in a way that maintained the overly general impressionistic stance toward the analysis.

Mixed Noticing

In the next phase of the video club, which correlates with the next stage of the framework, Mixed Noticing, the participants focused primarily on the teachers' pedagogies, but they also began to attend to students' mathematical thinking. They continued to offer general impressions, but they also identified noteworthy events. Furthermore, although they continued to evaluate what they had observed, they adopted an interpretive stance as well. Additionally, they began to refer to specific moments or children in the segments they viewed, but they were inconsistent in elaborating and providing details to develop their analyses. The following example illustrates this level of analysis.

During Meeting 3, the group viewed two clips in which the class worked on addition and subtraction of decimals and writing values in decimal form. In the first clip, two students showed the class their solutions for an addition and a subtraction problem. For each, the student explained the solution and the teacher led a brief whole class discussion. One student, Derrell, solved the problem 9.4 − 9.25 using tally marks to represent the numbers he subtracted. For example, he drew nine tally marks to represent 9 ones and then crossed out all nine marks when he subtracted the numbers in the one's place. After the viewing of the clip, when asked what they noticed, the teachers responded with issues about what the class as a whole appeared to understand, commenting that they seemed to know to line up the decimal point when adding and subtracting and that they appeared to have trouble understanding the difference between whole numbers and decimals. The facilitator then asked the group, "What about Derrell?" in an effort to focus them on a particular student's thinking. The following discussion ensued:

Yvette: He's phenomenal, because he started in my math group, and I thought there were a lot of small tasks there you had to [do] to get to that [answer].

Facilitator: What are some of those small tasks?

Yvette: Um, lining up the decimal when you have different number of digits, so he may not understand tenths and hundredths, but at least you have a base to work from. You're lined up. The idea that he stayed up there and borrowed correctly was very good.

Wanda: And I liked how he borrowed. I liked that he didn't put the zero [in the hundredth's place], which we tend to tell them to do. He borrowed a 10 from the 4, and wrote down 10, because there was nothing there and he said, "I need something there," and he borrowed the 10.

Facilitator: I thought it was interesting how he drew the sticks and was crossing them out. What role did that play for him?

Drew: He's a visual learner, so he probably wanted to see 9 and 4, and it probably helped him out just seeing the tally marks.

Elena: I agree with that. And for fourth grade, we allow them to work with those strategies they feel real comfortable with. For him though, I think he could have done it, but it was the whole teacher piece, presenting a visual there.

In this excerpt, the respondents first referred to the whole class's mathematical understanding: "They understand you have to line up the decimals" and "They don't understand the difference between whole numbers and decimals." Furthermore, instead of providing detail to support their interpretations, the teachers commented about the whole class, giving general impressions. When asked to focus on Derrell, they examined his mathematical thinking, but their approaches were mixed. They continued to evaluate what they had observed (e.g., "He's phenomenal" and "I like how he borrowed"). Although Wanda's statement "He may not understand tenths and hundredths" was a preliminary interpretation about Derrell's thinking, she provided no evidence to support her claim. Additionally, Drew's statement that Derrell is a visual learner and the tally marks probably helped him was unsubstantiated, and Drew did not inquire into the specifics of Derrell's solution strategy or how it assisted him in solving the problem. Similarly, toward the end of the conversation, Elena talked about her pedagogical approach, which is to let students choose their own strategies, but she did not provide insight into Derrell's mathematical thinking or his use of tally marks. Moreover, when the group later discussed another student's strategy for solving a subtraction problem, Linda remarked, "I still think they don't get it. I work in Yvette's room, and I still don't think the kids understand that 1.3 is one and three-tenths. They don't visualize tenths, hundredths, and thousandths." Linda's comment that "they don't get it" indicates that she is viewing the class as an undifferentiated group instead of as a set of individual students. Thus the teachers began to attend to student thinking, and, although they had focused minimally on individual students, they continued to refer to the whole class. Furthermore, although they began to offer preliminary interpretations of their thinking, they did so in general ways, and they continued to evaluate student thinking.

The teachers also continued to raise pedagogical issues for discussion at this level. For instance, after discussing Derrell's strategy, Frances commented, "I noticed they all went right to left. Do you teach them to go from right to left?" And after a brief response she asked the group, "How do you feel about teaching the traditional algorithm and partial products?" Wanda also raised a teaching issue when she stated, "We do say line up the decimals, but what we need to reiterate to the students is we need to line the like things up: the tenths, the hundredths, the ones." These comments raised legitimate concerns; however, they were not grounded in or informed by interpretations of student thinking.

This mixed approach to the analysis was characteristic of Level 2, with the teachers focused on both teaching and student learning issues, but maintaining a broad, evaluative approach to the analysis that was not supported or developed with evidence.

Focused Noticing

Level 3 discussions indicated a substantive shift across the two main categories. In particular, in terms of what was noticed, the discussions became centrally focused on specific students and their mathematical thinking. Regarding how they noticed, the teachers reasoned primarily through what they had observed, and the participants examined specific events from the clips and used these details to draw inferences about student understanding. Consider this example from Meeting 6. The teachers viewed a clip in which the teacher, Elena, posed the following problem to the students:

> Jake wants to make at least 160 brownies for the bake sale. Each batch makes about 12 brownies. He plans to charge 35 cents per brownie. How many batches does he make?

The teacher invited Kamilah to the board to share her method. Kamilah prepared to divide 160 by 12. First, she tried to estimate and multiplied 12×1 to see if that is close to 160. She changed to use a traditional algorithm. She divided 16 by 12 and then said that she had to "divide 12 into 40." A student suggested that she use a strategy they had learned in class, create a hint list, with different values to estimate—multiplying the given value, in this case 12, by 1, then 5, and then 10. Kamilah intended to follow this suggestion but instead multiplied 10×5 and then 10×10. When reminded that she was supposed to be working with 12, Kamilah responded, "No, they told me to try 5s." Kamilah then returned to the traditional algorithm, dividing 40 by 12. After viewing this clip, the group had the following discussion:

Frances:	She lost me. Is she going for 160?
Wanda:	I thought she was trying to estimate the answer, [asking] 12 times what equals 160?
Daniel:	Why is she multiplying by 5? Where did that come from?
Drew:	She's trying to do this method that we just learned, if 12 times something will give you 160, try 1: 12 times 1 is 12; that's too small. . . . But it looks like she's mixing it up with [another method].
Daniel:	Right, because she did the old school method.
Frances:	She's got two different algorithms it looks like here. She started with the conventional method of division, and then got stuck, and so she's going to this other method, partial products.
Elena:	She started out saying um, "Twelve into 1." And then she said . . .
Drew:	Then she moved over to 16.

Elena: "Twelve into 16." So, she didn't really do the 12 times 10. She started
              with "Okay, there are no 12s in 1; let's see how many 12s there are in
              16." Then she put 1. And then she had 40, and then she went to . . .
Daniel: Partial quotients. Then she wanted to do partial quotients.

In this discussion, the teachers reasoned through the strategies Kamilah had used
to solve the problem. Frances initiated the discussion by announcing that she was
confused about Kamilah's thinking, and the teachers used the details from the
clip to explain that she was using two different approaches, estimation and the
traditional algorithm, to solve the problem. This focused analysis on a particular
student's approach is an important shift from Level 2 to Level 3. The teachers
referred to specific events in the clip to explain student thinking, trying to com-
prehend, on the basis of the evidence from the transcript and the video clip, what
the student appeared to understand.

This discussion was particularly noteworthy because it raised an important tension the group members experienced related to using a new curriculum that
introduced teachers and students to a variety of approaches to solving problems.
Thus viewing this clip enabled the teachers to observe how a student might confuse these approaches and where the specific confusions arose in that process.

Extended Noticing

In the final stage of their experiences, the teachers reached the final level in the
noticing trajectory: The participants continued to examine the details of students'
mathematical thinking, considering a variety of explanations or interpretations,
using the details from the clip to reason through what they had observed and to
support their ideas. However, in their Level 4 discussions, teachers extended their
analyses to consider the relationship between student thinking and the teachers'
pedagogy. The important distinction between this stage and Mixed Noticing (in
which teachers focused primarily on pedagogy and began to consider student
thinking) is that the teachers connected their analyses of particular student thinking to specific approaches observed in the clip and proposed alternative teaching
approaches on the bases of their analyses. For example, if teachers noticed that a
student offered an extended explanation about a solution strategy, they examined
how the teacher's moves helped provide opportunities for thinking to emerge
(e.g., "When you asked her to share her solution again, it seemed like she could
better explain it"). Additionally, upon analysis of student thinking, they revisited
the tasks in the curriculum and examined how they helped or hindered students
in making progress toward the learning goal. Finally, at this level, the teachers
connected what they had observed and broader principles of teaching and learning. In particular, they couched their discussions in terms of broader issues they
discussed, such as assessment or equity in learning (e.g., "So maybe we need
to really rethink our assessment of students"). These discussions extended their

analyses from a focus on student thinking to consider how the particulars in teaching influenced student learning.

In looking at how the teachers moved through these levels over the course of the video club, one sees that their development was not linear (see Table 9.2). It is not the case that the group noticed at Level 1 for the first two meetings, then moved to Level 2 and remained at this level for a few meetings, and then proceeded to Level 3 and engaged in focused analysis before shifting to Extended Noticing at Level 4. Instead, the group's discussions had the characteristics of Baseline Noticing for the first two meetings. Then, between Meetings 3 and 8, the discussions cycled back and forth between Mixed Noticing and Focused Noticing before shifting to Extended Noticing in the final two meetings. This movement between levels indicates that the shift from Mixed Noticing to Focused Noticing is a major one and that it takes time. Consistent with the literature on professional development (Garet, Porter, Desimone, Birman, & Yoon, 2001), the video-club group's developmental trajectory shows that teachers need extended opportunities to learn to notice the particulars of student thinking and the relationship between one's teaching and student learning.

Additionally, this research raises questions about how the design of the video club may have influenced the development of the group's discussions and their noticing of student thinking over time. If we consider the two dimensions of noticing defined here, what is noticed and how it is noticed, it appears that two elements of the video club helped the group learn to attend to and interpret the specifics of student thinking and to consider the relationship between particular teaching moves and student thinking. One aspect of the video club that appears to influence the group's noticing over time is the video clips they viewed (Sherin, Linsenmeier, & van Es, 2009). What was captured and selected for the group to view informed the extent to which they (a) had windows into student thinking that would enable them to engage in in-depth analysis of student thinking and

TABLE 9.2 Analysis of video-club group's learning to notice student thinking

Level 1 Baseline	Level 2 Mixed	Level 3 Focused	Level 4 Extended
Meeting 1			
Meeting 2			
	Meeting 3		
		Meeting 4	
	Meeting 5		
		Meeting 6	
		Meeting 7	
	Meeting 8		
			Meeting 9
			Meeting 10

(b) had access to images of teacher practice that promoted student thinking to emerge in the classroom discourse.

Moreover, the facilitators appear to have played a central role in helping the group home in on the particulars of student thinking represented in the video clip (van Es, 2010). They accomplished this both through highlighting specific student moves, ideas, and strategies that are worthy of attention (e.g., "Let's take a look at Joaquin's drawing. What do you think the four squares mean?") and through modeling and requesting the group to refer to evidence in the transcripts and clips to develop their analyses (e.g., "When did that happen? Can we find that in the transcript?"). The facilitators also made specific moves to establish a norm that the goal was not to evaluate or critique the students or teacher in the clip, but rather to try to understand what happened and why ("We didn't select this clip to show what Michael did wrong. Instead, we thought it was interesting that he used all these different strategies"). Thus the group's discussions became more interpretive, with the goal of making sense of what was observed. Finally, the facilitators acted as participants in the meeting, offering ideas and interpretations and taking positions about the issues the group discussed (e.g., "Ah, that's interesting. I was thinking she meant something else"). Typically, facilitators of professional development try to remain neutral, but in this video club the facilitators offered opinions, and in some cases alternative perspectives, in order to stimulate discussion. In this way, the facilitators modeled how to engage in the practice of reasoning about student ideas. Additionally, their offering alternatives helped the group recognize multiple valid interpretations of a student idea and the value of further inquiry as ways to clarify the issue under discussion. Finally, proposing alternatives showed the group that disagreement is not only accepted but also expected of the group. Through exploring different explanations, the group engaged in more substantive analyses of student thinking, turning to the video to provide evidence to support interpretations.

Discussion and Conclusion

My goal in this chapter is to offer a framework for learning to notice student thinking. In this framework, I highlight two central dimensions of noticing: what teachers observe in classroom episodes and how they reason about these features of instruction. Furthermore, I propose a trajectory of development and use the video-club data to illustrate the nature of the teachers' discussions at each level and their development over the course of the 10 meetings.

As a result of this analysis, I raise several issues. First, what is noticed is related to how teachers reason about what they observe. Generally, the levels of *what* teachers noticed were the same as the levels of *how* they noticed. For example, I found no evidence that the teachers noticed a range of issues and topics (Level 1 of What Teachers Notice) while also primarily interpreting what they observed and elaborating on their analyses with specific details (Level 3 of How Teachers

Notice). Learning to attend to the particulars of student mathematical thinking may help teachers reason about what they observe, whereas noticing a range of issues involves adopting a broader, more general stance. Second, the video club supported the group's shifting to advanced levels of noticing. In examining the development of teachers' analyses over the course of the club, I identified particular meetings at which change occurred. Understanding what occurred in these meetings and how particular features, such as the clips the group viewed, the nature of facilitation, and the discourse for analyzing video, worked together to mediate these shifts is an important subject of future research. Third, this framework does not specify the kinds of student thinking that groups of teachers may analyze, such as student errors or solution strategies, nor does it identify particular teaching moves that may be worth attending to as they relate to promoting visible student thinking. Particular representations of student thinking in video or specific teaching moves may yield more specialized noticing than others, an object of future investigation. Fourth, this framework evolved from my analysis of one video-club group. In analysis of another video-club group, one might identify other relevant dimensions for capturing the development of learning to notice student thinking and gain insight into the extent to which teachers progress through other levels in their development or follow alternative paths while they learn to notice student thinking.

Through this framework, I begin to articulate how groups of teachers who analyze video in focused ways over time can develop in noticing student thinking. The framework can also serve as a useful tool for scaffolding teacher learning. In spite of the widespread use of video for reflection, few frameworks exist that can structure teachers' analyses. This framework shows important features for noticing that, when coordinated, can support teachers in engaging in productive reflection of teaching and student learning.

Notes

1 This research is supported by the National Science Foundation under Grant No. REC-0133900. The opinions expressed are those of the authors and do not necessarily reflect the views of the supporting agency.
2 The research team consisted of the principal investigator, two graduate students, one of whom is the author of this chapter, and one undergraduate student who assisted with videotaping in the teachers' classrooms.

References

Ainley, J., & Luntley, M. (2007). The role of attention in expert classroom practice. *Journal of Mathematics Teacher Education, 10,* 3–22.
Ball, D. L., & Cohen, D. K. (1999). Developing practice, developing practitioners: Toward a practice-based theory of professional education. In G. Sykes & L. Darling-Hammond (Eds.), *Teaching as the learning profession: Handbook of policy and practice* (pp. 3–32). San Francisco: Jossey-Bass.

Ball, D. L., Lubienski, S., & Mewborn, D. (2001). Research on teaching mathematics: The unsolved problem of teachers' mathematical knowledge. In V. Richardson (Ed.), *Handbook of research on teaching* (4th ed., pp. 433–456). New York: Macmillan.

Berliner, D. C. (1994). Expertise: The wonder of exemplary performances. In J. M. Mangier & C. C. Block (Eds.), *Creating powerful thinking in teachers and students: Diverse perspectives* (pp. 161–186). Fort Worth, TX: Holt, Rinehart, and Winston.

Borko, H., Jacobs, J., Eiteljorg, E., & Pittman, M. E. (2008). Video as a tool for fostering productive discussions in mathematics professional development. *Teaching and Teacher Education, 24*, 417–436.

Brophy, J. (2004). *Using video in teacher education.* San Diego, CA: Elsevier.

Carpenter, T. P., Fennema, E., Franke, M. L., Levi, L., & Empson, S. B. (2000). *Cognitively Guided Instruction: A research-based teacher professional development program for elementary school mathematics. Research report.* Madison: NCISLA, Wisconsin Center for Education Research, University of Wisconsin.

Davis, E. A. (2006). Characterizing productive reflection among preservice elementary teachers: Seeing what matters. *Teaching and Teacher Education, 22*, 281–301.

Erickson, F. (2006). Definitions and analysis of data from videotape: Some research procedures and their rationale. In J. L. Green, G. Camilli, & P. B. Elmore (Eds.), *Handbook of complementary methods in education research* (pp. 177–192). Washington, DC: American Educational Research Association.

Franke, M. L., Carpenter, T. P., Levi, L., & Fennema, E. (2001). Capturing teachers' generative change: A follow-up study of professional development in mathematics. *American Educational Research Journal, 38*, 653–689.

Garet, M. S., Porter, A. C., Desimone, L., Birman, B. F., & Yoon, K. S. (2001). What makes professional development effective? Results from a national sample of teachers. *American Educational Research Journal, 38*, 915–945.

Grant, T., & Kline, K. (2004, April). *The impact of long-term professional development on teachers' beliefs and practice.* Paper presented at the annual meeting of the American Educational Research Association, San Diego.

Hiebert, J., Morris, A. K., Berk, D., & Jansen, A. (2007). Preparing teachers to learn from teaching. *Journal of Teacher Education, 58*, 47–61.

Jacobs, V. R., Lamb, L. C., & Philipp, R. A. (2010). Professional noticing of children's mathematical thinking. *Journal for Research in Mathematics Education, 41*, 169–202.

Jacobs, V. R., Lamb, L. L. C., Philipp, R. A., & Schappelle, B. P. (this volume, chapter 7). *Deciding how to respond on the basis of children's understandings.*

Kagan, D. M., & Tippins, D. J. (1991). Helping student teachers attend to student cues. *The Elementary School Journal, 91*, 343–356.

Mason, J. (2002). *Researching your own practice: The discipline of noticing.* London: RoutledgeFalmer.

Miller, K. F., & Zhou, X. (2007). Learning from classroom video: What makes it compelling and what makes it hard. In R. Goldman, R. Pea, B. Barron, & S. Derry (Eds.), *Video research in the learning sciences* (pp. 321–334). Mahwah, NJ: Erlbaum.

National Council of Teachers of Mathematics. (2000). *Principles and standards for school mathematics.* Reston, VA: Author.

Nemirovsky, R., DiMattia, C., Ribeiro, B., & Lara-Meloy, T. (2005). Talking about teaching episodes. *Journal of Mathematics Teacher Education, 8*, 363–392.

Oonk, W., Goffree, F., & Verloop, N. (2004). For the enrichment of practical knowledge: Good practice and useful theory for future primary teachers. In J. Brophy (Ed.), *Using video in teacher education* (pp. 131–167). San Diego, CA: Elsevier.

Richert, A. (2005). Inquiring about practice: Using web-based materials to develop teacher inquiry. *Teaching Education, 16*, 297–310.

Rodgers, C. R. (2002). Seeing student learning: Teacher change and the role of reflection. *Harvard Educational Review, 72*, 230–253.

Rosaen, C., Lundeberg, M., Cooper, M., Fritzen, A., & Terpstra, M. (2008). Noticing noticing: How does investigation of video cases change how teachers reflect on their experiences? *Journal of Teacher Education, 59*, 347–360.

Santagata, R., Zannoni, C., & Stigler, J. (2007). The role of lesson analysis in pre-service teacher education: An empirical investigation of teacher learning from a virtual video-based field experience. *Journal of Mathematics Teacher Education, 10*, 123–140.

Seago, N. (2004). Using video as an object of inquiry for mathematics teaching and learning. In J. Brophy (Ed.), *Using video in teacher education* (pp. 259–286). San Diego, CA: Elsevier.

Sherin, M. G. (2000). Facilitating meaningful discussions about mathematics. *Mathematics Teaching in the Middle School, 6*, 186–190.

Sherin, M. G. (2007). The development of teachers' professional vision in video clubs. In R. Goldman, R. Pea, B. Barron, & S. J. Derry (Eds.), *Video research in the learning sciences* (pp. 383–396). Mahwah, NJ: Erlbaum.

Sherin, M. G., Linsenmeier, K. A., & van Es, E. A. (2009). Issues in the design of video clubs: Selecting video clips for teacher learning. *Journal of Teacher Education, 60*, 213–230.

Star, J. R., & Strickland, S. K. (2008). Learning to observe: Using video to improve pre-service mathematics teachers' ability to notice. *Journal of Mathematics Teacher Education, 11*, 107–125.

Stevens, R., & Hall, R. (1998). Disciplined perception: Learning to see in technoscience. In M. Lampert & M. L. Blunk (Eds.), *Talking mathematics in school: Studies of teaching and learning* (pp. 107–149). Cambridge, England: Cambridge University Press.

Stigler, J., & Hiebert, J. (1999). *The teaching gap.* New York: Free Press.

van Es, E. A. (2009). Participants' roles in the context of a video club. *Journal of the Learning Sciences, 18*, 100–137.

van Es, E. A. (2010). A framework for facilitating productive discussions in video clubs. *Educational Technology Magazine, 50*(1), 8–12.

van Es, E. A., & Sherin, M. G. (2002). Learning to notice: Scaffolding new teachers' interpretations of classroom interactions. *Journal of Technology and Teacher Education, 10*, 571–596.

van Es, E. A., & Sherin, M. G. (2008). Mathematics teachers' "learning to notice" in the context of a video club. *Teaching and Teacher Education, 24*, 244–276.

Wang, J., & Hartley, K. (2003). Video technology as a support for teacher education reform. *Journal of Technology and Teacher Education, 11*, 105–138.

Wilson, S. M., & Berne, J. (1999). Teacher learning and the acquisition of professional knowledge: An examination of research on contemporary professional development. *Review of Research in Education, 24*, 173–209.

10

FROM TEACHER NOTICING TO A FRAMEWORK FOR ANALYZING AND IMPROVING CLASSROOM LESSONS

Rossella Santagata

To a certain extent, every teacher engages in acts of noticing. However, there is evidence that expert teachers' noticing skills are more refined than those of novices (Berliner, 2001). For example, when asked to view a series of slides taken in mathematics and science classrooms, expert teachers were able to apply richer schemata than were novices to make sense of the visual information provided. They used their knowledge of classrooms and instructional strategies to focus their attention on important elements of the images and to make multiple hypotheses and interpretations of what they saw. Novice teachers were more hesitant in their descriptions of what was depicted in the images, and their interpretations were not always as accurate and rich as those provided by experts (Carter, Cushing, Sabers, Stein, & Berliner, 1988). Similarly, when viewing videotapes of classroom instruction, expert teachers could monitor, understand, and interpret multiple events occurring in the classroom in more detail and with more insight than novices (Sabers, Cushing, & Berliner, 1991).

Because of these differences in expert and novice teachers' abilities to notice, researchers have been interested in investigating ways to improve teachers' noticing skills. I first describe a framework my colleagues and I have used to guide teachers' analysis of teaching and to improve their noticing skills. I then situate this work in the broader field of noticing by highlighting similarities to and differences from others' approaches to teacher noticing. I conclude by summarizing findings about improving teacher-noticing skills from the implementation of our framework in a professional development project with in-service teachers from an urban district.

Improving Teacher Noticing: A Lesson Analysis Framework

My colleagues and I (Santagata, Zannoni, & Stigler, 2007) have conducted research on what we call *teachers' abilities to analyze classroom lessons*. These lesson analysis abilities are in many respects similar to *teachers' noticing skills* as defined by Sherin and van Es (Sherin, 2007; van Es & Sherin, 2002). Typically, we present teachers with videotapes of actual lessons and ask them to analyze what is happening; that is, we focus primarily on teachers' abilities to reason about classroom events. Like the teachers in other work on teacher noticing (Jacobs, Lamb, Philipp, & Schappelle, 2009; van Es & Sherin, 2002), teachers participating in our professional development experiences used their knowledge and understanding to interpret particular moments of the teaching and learning process, with a particular focus on student thinking and learning.

Teaching as a Cultural Activity and Implications for Lesson Analysis

In our approach to lesson analysis as a form of noticing and reflection on classroom instruction, we draw from international research on mathematics teaching. In particular, we build on findings from the Third International Mathematics and Science Video studies (Hiebert et al., 2003; Stigler & Hiebert, 1999) that underline the cultural nature of teaching. Teaching practices are more similar within countries than between countries. Because daily classroom routines have deep roots in beliefs and practices specific to each culture, teachers often do not perceive them as pedagogical choices but adopt them because as students they have experienced these routines themselves, making instructional practices hard to see.

This view of teaching highlights difficulties teachers encounter in efforts to implement new, research-based practices into their daily routines (Gallimore & Santagata, 2006), leading to the unchanging persistence of U.S. teaching across centuries (Cuban, 1984, 1990; Feiman-Nemser, 1983; Tyack & Tobin, 1994) and minimal effect of professional development on teachers' practices and on student learning (Cohen & Hill, 2000; Porter, Garet, Desimone, Yoon, & Birman, 2000; Wilson, 2003). One obstacle is that teachers tend to adapt new strategies into the familiar, often missing key elements that made those new strategies effective for student learning (Cohen, 1990). Another is that teachers seldom have opportunities to observe alternative strategies being implemented in real classrooms and with students similar to their own.

New strategies can be portrayed in video of classroom lessons, and professional development experiences can assist teachers in isolating interesting moments and revealing practices that would otherwise remain unnoticed. Despite the clear advantages and appeal of using video in the context of professional development, watching videos of classroom instruction can be overwhelming for teachers. Teaching is complex, and many things occur at once during a classroom lesson. We have focused on finding ways to structure teachers' analyses to maximize their learning from videotaped instruction.

The Lesson as Unit of Analysis and the Lesson Analysis Process

One way in which our approach differs from that employed by others interested in the improvement of teacher noticing is our use of entire classroom lessons rather than short video clips. Lessons are natural units in the process of teaching. The essential elements of any instructional effort are included in the lesson: goals for students' learning, instructional activities, strategies for monitoring students' thinking and assessing their learning, and a closure (Hiebert, Morris, Berk, & Jansen, 2007; Santagata et al., 2007). Most teachers plan and teach through daily lessons and reflect on the interrelations among all these elements. If watching the entire lesson is impossible because of time constraints, we select clips in sequence to reproduce the essential parts of the lesson, so that the viewer has a picture of the lesson as a whole.

The decision to use the lesson as unit of teacher analysis is also related to the teacher reflections we request. The process of analysis is more structured than in other video-based professional development experiences (e.g., Sherin's, 2007, video clubs) and is guided by the teacher's learning goals. Teachers are asked to assess the extent to which these goals were achieved, their evidence of student learning, and how the lesson could be improved. We have summarized this approach to video-based lesson analysis into a framework that we have used to design video-based prompts for teachers. See Figure 10.1 for the framework as we originally conceived it.

Undertaking the kind of inquiry into the process of teaching promoted by the Lesson Analysis Framework—guided by the teacher's learning goal(s) and focused on the effect that teaching has on student learning—enables teachers to acquire analytic tools to independently assess the extent to which a certain act of teaching was effective in terms of student learning. Through this process of analysis,

---

LESSON LEARNING GOAL(S)

What are the main ideas students are supposed to understand through this lesson?

ANALYSIS OF STUDENT LEARNING

Did the students achieve the learning goal(s)? What evidence do we have that students achieved the learning goal(s)? What evidence do we have that students did not achieve the learning goal(s)? What evidence is missing?

ALTERNATIVE STRATEGIES

What alternative strategies could the teacher use? How do you expect these strategies to impact students' achievement of the lesson learning goal(s)? If any evidence of student learning is missing, how could the teacher collect that evidence?

FIGURE 10.1 Lesson Analysis Framework

teachers may develop the professional judgment necessary to make their own decisions about changes that can positively affect their instructional strategies. In other words, they may learn to learn from their practices. After reflecting on the effect of specific instructional decisions on student learning, teachers propose alternative strategies and generate hypotheses on the effects of these alternatives on student learning. This last phase of the lesson analysis process constitutes both the direct link to future action and the beginning of a new cycle of analysis. Hiebert and colleagues described a similar process of analysis and argued that preservice teachers would be better positioned when they enter the teaching profession if they had learned to learn from their practices (Hiebert et al., 2007). Although initial research on the Lesson Analysis Framework was conducted in the preservice context as well (Santagata et al., 2007), here I focus on its use with in-service teachers.

Empirical Basis for the Lesson Analysis Framework

Research on expert/novice teachers' differences provides support for three particular features of the Lesson Analysis Framework: (a) the use of the lesson learning goals as the criteria for analyzing the effectiveness of the lesson, (b) the focus on noticing and reasoning about student learning, and (c) a flexible approach to teaching that builds on the analysis of student thinking and learning to devise new instructional moves both during instruction and in the context of reflection after instruction.

A classic study conducted by Borko and Livingston (1989) revealed that expert teachers, when reflecting on their own lessons, selected classroom events that they thought affected the achievement of the lesson learning goals. Berliner (2001), in a review of several studies, reported that, whereas novice teachers tended to adhere rigidly to lesson plans, expert teachers were more flexible; they adapted and responded to students' needs during instruction. In other words, during their teaching, expert teachers attended to student learning, reasoned about it, and immediately made decisions to respond to students' specific difficulties. Researchers who followed teachers trained in the Cognitively Guided Instruction approach to mathematics teaching have provided evidence that teachers who are highly engaged with students' mathematical thinking have an attitude of inquiry into their teaching process and see "themselves as constantly testing their knowledge, learning from their students" (Franke, Carpenter, Levi, & Fennema, 2001, p. 669), both when planning and during instruction.

Situating the Lesson Analysis Framework Within the Field of Teacher Noticing

To highlight the theoretical contribution of the Lesson Analysis Framework to the broader conceptualization of teacher noticing, I discuss how the particular notion of noticing promoted through this approach relates to two fundamental questions researchers ask: What processes are included in noticing? And why should one notice the work of teaching?

Authors differ in the processes they include in noticing. On the one hand, Sherin (2007) described teacher noticing as *professional vision*, which consists of two subprocesses: selective attention and knowledge-based reasoning. Selectively attending is isolating, focusing on, and tuning to a specific event or feature from the complex reality of teaching during live observation or through the viewing of a videotape of classroom instruction. Knowledge-based reasoning is the interpretation of what was observed through the application of one's knowledge and understanding.

On the other hand, Star and colleagues (Star, Lynch, & Perova, this volume, chapter 8; Star & Strickland, 2008), in their studies on preservice teachers' noticing skills, defined *noticing* as the process of attending to important elements of classroom teaching. These authors argued that preservice teachers need to be able to focus on certain details of a classroom lesson before they can reason about them. Their notion of noticing is, thus, limited to the first element of Sherin's notion. Although I agree with Star and colleagues that selective attention is conducive to a productive analysis of teaching, I propose that what one notices and the kind of reasoning one performs on what one notices are interrelated processes. That is, when one's purposes for noticing go beyond the intellectual exercise of studying teaching, or teachers' conceptions of teaching, and include reflection on teaching guided by the goals of learning from it, the two processes—attending and reasoning—inform each other. For example, a teacher who is interested in investigating the effectiveness of a particular teaching move on student learning might look for specific evidence of student learning (such as questions students ask) that she would have not attended to otherwise.

The notion of noticing promoted through the Lesson Analysis Framework not only includes both selective attention and knowledge-based reasoning but also extends teacher noticing to a third process: the generation of new knowledge. In the third phase of the Lesson Analysis Framework, teachers are prompted to think about strategies alternative to those used by the teacher in the lesson under study. This phase was designed to guide teachers through the generation of hypotheses about which instructional strategies might improve the effectiveness of the lesson. When this cycle is applied to the work of teaching, teachers can test these hypotheses in their classrooms, use the Lesson Analysis Framework questions to analyze their effect on student learning, and, by doing so, add to their knowledge bases. This broader notion is similar to the conception of teacher noticing embraced by Jacobs and colleagues (Jacobs, Lamb, Philipp, Schappelle, & Burke, 2007) in their work on professional noticing of children's mathematical thinking. These authors included in their definition of noticing the decision of how to respond to student thinking. Their conception of noticing and the one at the basis of the Lesson Analysis Framework differ in the grain size of the response. Jacobs and colleagues' work is focused on responses at the level of discursive interaction with students; the Lesson Analysis Framework includes prompts for teachers to generate alternatives that can range in grain size from phrasing questions to students differently to designing a new instructional activity for students.

I next describe use of the Lesson Analysis Framework to design a video-based professional development program. I then discuss how data from the implementation of that program prompted a revision of the Lesson Analysis Framework to better assist teachers in improving their noticing skills in the second year of the study.

Lesson Analysis in the Context of Teacher Professional Development

My colleagues and I implemented the Lesson Analysis Framework with in-service teachers in the context of a 2-year professional development program we developed and studied.[1] The program objectives were drawn from results of the Third International Mathematics and Science Video study, which showed that U.S. teachers, in contrast to teachers from countries with higher-achieving students, rarely maintained the cognitive demand of the problems they presented to their students (Hiebert et al., 2003).

One goal for the professional development program was, therefore, to provide participating teachers with opportunities to study videotaped lessons that portrayed strategies for maintaining the complexity of the mathematics when asking students to solve problems. Merely exposing teachers to models of effective instruction through video does not guarantee that teachers will attend to features of that instruction that are essential for effective implementation or that they will reason about various elements of that instruction in an interrelated manner. The professional development program, therefore, included explicit guidance, supported by the Lesson Analysis Framework, on the targets for the teachers' attending and reasoning in the videotaped lessons.

Teaching for understanding also requires teachers to master the mathematical concepts they teach, know how students learn those concepts, and be aware of difficulties they are likely to encounter. A second goal for the professional development program was thus to deepen teachers' content knowledge and pedagogical content knowledge.

The program was tailored to sixth grade mathematics teachers working in a high-poverty, low-performing district. Three content-specific modules (focused on fractions, ratios and proportions, and expressions and equations) were designed. For each topic, a video-based module was developed. Each module was structured into three phases: (a) Content Exploration, (b) Lesson Analysis, and (c) Link to Practice. A multimedia online platform developed by LessonLab (Visibility) was used to structure participants' viewing and analyses, guided by predefined sets of questions. Teachers typed answers to the questions in the provided text boxes. A feature of the software enabled them to click on a button that inserted in their text a time stamp corresponding to a moment of the video they had chosen to cite. Written responses were saved on a server accessible by both the facilitator during the professional development sessions and the researchers for later analysis.

Teachers met in small groups (of 8–10 people) led by a facilitator and, for each topic, spent one pull-out day (i.e., approximately 6 hours) exploring content and one pull-out day (usually 1 week after the content exploration) analyzing a videotaped lesson. They then taught the lesson they had studied during the professional development to their students and later met at their school sites to share their experiences and the work their students had completed during the lesson. Following is a brief description of the activities included in each phase of the program (for more details, see Santagata, 2009).

Content Exploration

This phase of the professional development was designed to use written documents and video to deepen teachers' understanding of core mathematics concepts and of how students learn these concepts. The video portrayed a mathematics-focused discussion, led by a mathematics educator, among other teachers, (a) to provide a dynamic setting for teachers to learn mathematics concepts that would make the task more engaging than simply reading mathematics-content documents and (b) to create an atmosphere in which teachers felt comfortable sharing their doubts about their understanding of mathematics concepts.

Teachers participating in the professional development program watched selected segments of the videotaped discussion and completed online tasks designed to deepen their conceptual understanding. Their written responses were then shared in a face-to-face group discussion led by a facilitator.

Lesson Analysis

This phase included a videotaped lesson centered on a word problem that made use of one or more of the core concepts studied during the content exploration day. Teachers were asked to solve the problem and reason about various strategies students might use to solve it. They then studied the lesson plan and watched the video. The videotaped lesson provided teachers with a model for engaging students in conceptual thinking. Lessons were designed by the research team and taught by either a collaborating teacher or one of the professional development facilitators. The videos were collected in the local district so that the student population was representative of the participating teachers' students. We used the videos unedited to provide a window into the reality of the classroom and to assure the teachers that we had not selected only moments of the lessons that served our purposes.

Teachers' analyses of the lesson were guided by the Lesson Analysis Framework and included a series of questions focused on students' learning and understanding as evidenced in the video and in samples of students' work. Teachers answered questions independently online in written form before sharing their answers with their colleagues in a face-to-face group discussion led by the facilitator. After completing this phase, teachers proposed modifications for improving the lesson before teaching it to their students. During each year of the program, teachers analyzed three videotaped lessons, one for each topic area.

Link to Practice

During this phase, teachers taught the lesson they had analyzed and participated in a facilitator-led 1-hour meeting at their school sites as a way to facilitate the application of their learning during the professional development sessions to their daily practices. At the meeting, teachers were asked to share with their colleagues samples of student work from the lesson they had taught.

Context of Implementation and Larger Study

The program was implemented for 2 consecutive years in five middle schools. Thirty-three teachers participated during the first year, and 60 teachers (including the 33 returning teachers) began the program the second year. In an experimental study of the impact of the first year of the program, my colleagues and I compared teachers who participated in the intervention to a control group and found some effects on teacher practice and students' learning (Santagata, Kersting, Givvin, & Stigler, in press). In the second year of implementation, all participating teachers received treatment. Pre-/post-test analyses, limited by issues of teacher compliance, found modest effects on teacher knowledge and student learning. Here I concentrate on the lesson analysis portion of the professional development program and on what we learned about guiding teachers' analysis of videotaped lessons.

Using the Lesson Analysis Framework to Design Video-Based Prompts for the First Year of Program Implementation

As mentioned previously, in the first year of implementation the Lesson Analysis Framework served as a guide in the design of video-based lesson analysis questions for teachers. The modules included fairly broad questions analogous to the ones listed in Figure 10.1. To assess whether the questions we designed elicited a productive analysis of teaching and learning, we followed a three-step procedure to examine teachers' responses to these questions. First, teachers' responses that were not appropriate (i.e., did not answer the question) or revealed difficulties (an example of this will be provided later) were marked. Second, when at least two-thirds of teachers had difficulties with a particular question, the question was included in a list of problematic questions. Third, the list of problematic questions was reviewed and questions were grouped into categories on the basis of the kinds of analyses teachers were required to complete and the knowledge and skills necessary to complete them in effective ways. Finally, memos and field notes from professional development sessions, classroom lessons, and meetings were reviewed in search of confirming and disconfirming evidence of teachers' difficulties that emerged from the review of teachers' responses. Field notes were structured to include comments both on aspects of the professional development that had been successfully implemented and on aspects that had not. These comments were used as disconfirming and confirming evidence.

This close analysis of teachers' responses revealed that teachers had difficulties with most lesson analysis questions, particularly those related to assessing the effectiveness of the lesson in achieving the learning goals and to proposing alternative instructional strategies to those shown in the video. Specifically, when asked to broadly assess the effectiveness of a lesson, teachers did not spontaneously focus on student learning; instead they spoke about the actions of the teacher. Any analyses of students' learning tended to be superficial and to focus on general issues of attention and motivation instead of on the learning of specific mathematics content (Givvin, Santagata, & Kersting, 2005; Santagata, 2009). I provide an example to illustrate this point.

The ratio and proportions module used in the first year of implementation included a videotaped lesson centered on the following problem:

> Your class has been asked to organize a project called "Holding Hands Across L.A." You will need to have people line up and hold their hands from Downtown to Long Beach. Your job is to determine how many people you will need in order to form the line.

The teacher begins the lesson by clarifying the problem statement and asking the students to think about the problem for a couple of minutes before the class discusses what piece of information they need to solve the problem. When the students agree that they need the distance between Downtown Los Angeles and Long Beach, the teacher provides it (i.e., 87,000 ft). The question "How can we find out how many people we need without lining up?" precedes an activity in which five students hold hands and stand on a premeasured 20-ft line in the classroom. Students are next asked to think for themselves for 2 minutes and then discuss with their neighbor this question: "If we need five people for a 20-ft line, how many people do we need for a line that goes from downtown L.A. to Long Beach (i.e., 87,000 ft)?" The students share their solution methods and the teacher builds on them to introduce the concepts of ratio and proportion. Multiple exchanges between the teacher and the students provide opportunities to assess students' understanding and difficulties. The lesson ends with students' individually solving two additional problems: (1) How many people would you need for a 5,200-ft line? (2) If we lined up every student at your school (2,700 students), how long would the line be in feet?

Teachers' analysis of student learning from this lesson was guided by questions focused on both teacher–students interactions and samples of student work. The following prompts targeted student learning as evidenced in the video:

> View the following video segments and verify whether the learning goals were achieved: Did the students understand that ratios are multiplicative comparisons? Did the students understand that proportions are equivalent ratios? Did students understand how to set up a proportion with a variable? Have students learned to use various strategies to solve problems involving proportions?
>
> Please cite evidence from the video (by marking specific moments of the video) to answer these questions.

Teachers' responses to these questions varied in quality, but overall they lacked evidence to support their claims. Most teachers thought that the lesson had achieved its goals and any evidence from the video mentioned was mainly focused on the teacher's behaviors instead of on student learning. The following teacher's comments illustrate the average type of responses teachers provided:

> When the teacher made a T chart on the board, the students saw a multiplicative pattern.
>
> Writing the chart horizontally and putting equal signs between each ratio helped students realize that the ratios are equivalent.
>
> Students used cross-multiplication to find the value of the variable.
>
> Students worked in groups to come up with solutions.

The first two comments indicate that, because the videotaped teacher did something that the participating teacher valued as effective, students learned. Students' comments provided evidence of both understanding and difficulties, but this evidence was not cited by the participant, who instead focused only on the teacher's actions. The two comments focused on students' behaviors do not directly relate to the questions asked. The respondent identified one strategy used by the students to solve the proportion, cross-multiplication, but did not discuss, as requested, strategies students used to set up the proportion. Finally, working in groups instead of a specific mathematical strategy was given as a strategy for solving the problem.

Revising the Framework for the Second Year of Implementation

These findings prompted a revision of the Lesson Analysis Framework and of the video-based prompts for the second year of implementation. Two changes were made to the framework. First, the questions in the Analysis of Student Learning section of the framework were revised to focus teachers' analyses on the process of learning rather than the outcomes. Thus, the expression "achieve the learning goals" was changed to "make progress toward the learning goals." Second, because teachers had difficulty building on the analysis of student learning to propose alternative strategies as requested (see Figure 10.1), a prompt was added to scaffold teachers' transitions from considering evidence (or lack thereof) of student learning to the generation of alternative teaching strategies: "Which instructional strategies supported students' progress toward the learning goals and which did not?" This prompt was intended (a) to facilitate teachers' integration of various elements of teaching (i.e., teacher's actions, student learning, and specific mathematics content) (Davis, 2006; Lampert, 2001) when reflecting on the effectiveness of a lesson and (b) to assist teachers in their analyses by focusing their reasoning on the effect that specific instructional strategies had on students' learning of the mathematical content targeted by the lesson. Figure 10.2 shows the revised version of the Lesson Analysis Framework.

Introducing Additional Guidance by Focusing Teachers' Attention and Scaffolding the Generation of Alternatives

In addition, in designing questions to be included in the revised modules for the second year of implementation of the program, we used the framework only as a guide to formulate more specific questions. Specifically, moments of the lesson during which student learning and thinking were made visible were isolated[2] into short clips and shown to teachers. Teachers were then asked to analyze students' contributions and to reflect on the effect of a particular teacher's choices on students' progress toward the goals of the lesson. As a result, instead of answering the

---

LESSON LEARNING GOAL(S)

What are the main ideas students are supposed to understand through this lesson?

ANALYSIS OF STUDENT LEARNING

Did the students *make progress* toward the learning goal(s)? What evidence do we have that students *made progress* toward the learning goal(s)? What evidence do we have that students *did not make progress* toward the learning goal(s)? What evidence is missing? *Which instructional strategies supported students' progress toward the learning goals and which did not?*

ALTERNATIVE STRATEGIES

What alternative strategies could the teacher use? How do you expect these strategies to impact students' achievement of the lesson learning goal(s)? If any evidence of student learning is missing, how could the teacher collect that evidence?

FIGURE 10.2 Lesson Analysis Framework revised

Note: Changes from initial framework are highlighted in italics.

few broad questions included in the first version of the modules on large portions of the lesson video, teachers answered several questions on shorter video segments that focused their attention on specific instances of the lesson. Note that teachers still watched the lesson in its entirety, but their viewing was structured into short clips interspersed with more focused questions.

Another change we introduced consisted of following the analysis of student learning during specific moments of the lesson with a question about alternative strategies the teacher could have used. In the first version of the program, this question was asked only after the teachers had completed the analysis of the entire lesson; in the second version, it was both interspersed between student learning analysis questions and repeated at the end to focus on the lesson as a whole. As a result of this change teachers could derive alternative instructional decisions directly from the analysis of student learning and as a result of reflections on the effect of specific teachers' instructional choices on student outcomes. Because approximately half of the participating teachers in the second year were returning teachers, we included a new lesson in the ratio and proportion module. Sample questions from the revised version of the ratio and proportion module follow the problem central to this new module:

> Alberto and Kisha are in charge of bringing lemonade to their class party. They each made a pitcher of lemonade. Alberto's lemonade has 3 lemons and 2 cups of water. Kisha's lemonade has 4 lemons and 3 cups of water. They only want to take the most lemony lemonade to the party. Whose lemonade is the most lemony?

At the beginning of the lesson, the teacher posed an introductory problem to the students by using cutout drawings of lemons and cups of water: Two pitchers of lemonade have an identical number of lemons. Which pitcher is more lemony? Students shared their ideas. Next, a different amount of water was added to each of the pitchers of lemonade, and students were asked again which pitcher was more lemony. Students discussed their answers and their rationales. Then the teacher presented the "lemonade for a party" problem accompanied by visual representations of lemons and cups of water. In pairs, students wrote their solutions and rationales while the teacher took note of their solutions. The teacher then led a discussion of students' solutions by noting on the board the rationales students provided. She then facilitated a discussion in which students were asked to prove or disprove their conjectures about which pitcher was more lemony. For example, a few students argued that Kisha's lemonade was more lemony because it had more lemons. The teacher presented a counter-example in which students were asked to compare Pitcher A, which included 3 lemons and 6 cups of water, and Pitcher B, which had 2 lemons and 2 cups of water. Students could easily see that, although Pitcher A included more lemons, Pitcher B was more lemony because it contained more lemons per unit of water. The teacher then formalized the discussion by explaining the idea of *fair share*. She demonstrated the distribution of lemons into the cups of water on the board by physically moving drawings of lemons into cups of water and by cutting lemon figures into equal parts. She then defined a *ratio* as the relationship between two quantities. The lesson concluded with students' revisiting the problem, using what they had learned about fair share. Students individually solved additional problems comparing the lemoniness of two pitchers of lemonade.

Following are two sample questions that guided participating teachers' analyses of student learning from this lesson:

1. As you watch the following clip where the teacher presents examples to disprove the students' conjectures, choose a comment made by a student that helps move the reasoning of the class forward. Discuss how this comment is important in developing understanding about the proportional relationships in this problem.
2. The teacher has prepared counter-examples to test conjectures she had anticipated that the students would make. How important do you think this portion of the class discussion is to student understanding? If you would have handled this differently, explain what you would have done, and why.

These more focused questions helped teachers to attend to specific students' contributions and to provide in-depth analyses of the teaching and learning process, considering specific mathematics content. Following is a representative teacher's comment:

1. I think Markisha's comment about it having to do with the water while disproving the first conjecture is important to the students' understanding. This is the first student comment that was made that hints at the relationship between the lemons and the water. The relationship is central to the idea of ratio and this is the first time the students are beginning to see that the lemons and the water are related.
2. I think this part is very important because it clarifies and gives the students the opportunity to see the relationship of how both the lemons and the water depend on each other to make the lemonade more lemony; in addition, they can start realizing that, while they are interdependent of each other to make the lemonade more lemony, they can also start paying attention to how ratios work: a certain amount of (A) can be affected by a certain amount of (B). Ex. 3:2 for Alberto's lemonade to 6:3 for Kisha's lemonade can determine how lemony the lemonade is.

To summarize, the implementation of the Lesson Analysis Framework with teachers participating in a professional development program highlighted the difficulties teachers may encounter in attending to and reasoning about student learning. These findings have led us to make more explicit the kind of reasoning we believe—and research on novice–expert differences indicates—is conducive to effective reflections on teaching. Specifically, we have redesigned questions that guided teachers' analyses to better assist them to attend to the specifics of student thinking and to focus on the effect that the videotaped teacher's instructional decisions had on students' learning of the mathematics. In addition, we have facilitated their analysis of the video by structuring their viewing through shorter clips and interspersing between clips questions about possible alternatives.

Conclusions

Research on expert- and novice-teacher differences shows the importance of teachers' noticing skills. This research has raised interest in finding ways to improve teacher noticing. In this chapter, I presented a particular approach to teacher noticing centered on the analysis of classroom lessons and described an observation framework that has been used to improve teachers' analysis skills. Findings from a study with in-service teachers were reported to outline the difficulties teachers might encounter when asked to notice and reason about teaching and learning. Steps taken to increase the effectiveness of the Lesson Analysis Framework by increasing guidance provided to teachers in two fundamental ways were also described. First, my colleagues and I focused teachers' attention on specific evidence of student thinking and learning by showing teachers the lesson through sets of short video clips. Second, we posed questions specific to the effect of teachers' actions on student learning of the mathematics (or lack thereof) as evidenced in the clips and used those reflections to prompt for possible alternative strategies at multiple points during the analysis process.

In sum, our findings support the design of video-based prompts designed to explicitly direct teachers' attention and scaffold their reasoning about teaching. Whether the nature of the scaffolding provided to teachers should vary depending on the participants' knowledge and skills and, thus, evolve while teachers gain expertise is an open question. The participants in our study were particularly disadvantaged in that respect, as teachers working in urban settings often are (Hill, 2007). Jacobs et al. (2009) found that teachers who had engaged with sustained professional development focused on students' mathematical thinking were more likely to attend to student thinking than were participants who had not had opportunities to acquire that kind of knowledge. Would the same types of prompts benefit both groups of teachers, or would customized prompts be more beneficial? Regardless of the exact prompts, we argue that U.S. teachers could benefit from guidance and explicitness. As a country, in fact, we have yet to develop a common knowledge base for the teaching profession (Hiebert, Gallimore, & Stigler, 2002) and a language to describe and reason about teaching. Our lack of a common vocabulary for describing features of common instructional practices is reflected in numerous labels researchers use in observation rubrics they develop to describe teaching (Grossman & McDonald, 2008). Thus I argue that the average teacher will benefit from noticing prompts that direct her or his attention to the specifics of student thinking and highly scaffold reasoning about the teaching and learning process.

The kinds of questions we designed for the revised version of the professional development program seem particularly promising for eliciting a productive analysis of teaching that generates knowledge for improvement. Specifically, in our study, questions that focus teachers' reflections on the specifics of student learning and impel teachers to make hypotheses on particular teaching choices that might have affected student learning facilitated teachers' proposition of alternative strategies. On the one hand, I believe this process of analysis to be essential for teachers to learn to reflect on and improve their teaching over time. On the other hand, other productive ways to guide teachers' analyses of teaching might be found. Thus, in sharing the work that my colleagues and I have conducted, I invite other researchers and practitioners engaged in this kind of work to make public their approaches to the improvement of teacher noticing skills.

Notes

1   The Algebra Learning for All study was funded by the Institute of Education Sciences through the Teacher Quality Program, under Grant R305M030154. James Stigler was the principal investigator on the project; the author served as co-principal investigator, and Ronald Gallimore, Karen Givvin, Nicole Kersting, Joi Spencer, and Belinda Thompson were key collaborators.
2   The Visibility software enabled us to mark entry and exit points of lesson segments we wanted to show teachers and to create within a module page clickable links that opened the video-segment window.

References

Berliner, D. C. (2001). Learning about and learning from expert teachers. *International Journal of Educational Research, 35*, 463–482.

Borko, H., & Livingston, C. (1989). Cognition and improvisation: Differences in mathematics instruction by experts and novice teachers. *American Educational Research Journal, 26*, 473–498.

Carter, K., Cushing, K., Sabers, D., Stein, P., & Berliner, D. C. (1988). Expert–novice differences in perceiving and processing visual classroom information. *Journal of Teacher Education, 39*(3), 25–31.

Cohen, D. K. (1990). A revolution in one classroom: The case of Mrs. Oublier. *Educational Evaluation and Policy Analysis, 12*, 327–345.

Cohen, D. K., & Hill, H. C. (2000). Instructional policy and classroom performance: The mathematics reform in California. *Teachers College Record, 102*, 294–343.

Cuban, L. (1984). *How teachers taught: Constancy and change in American classrooms, 1890–1990* (2nd ed.). New York: Teachers College Press.

Cuban, L. (1990). Reforming again, again, and again. *Educational Researcher, 19*(1), 3–13.

Davis, E. A. (2006). Characterizing productive reflection among preservice elementary teachers: Seeing what matters. *Teaching and Teacher Education, 22*, 281–301.

Feiman-Nemser, S. (1983). *Learning to teach.* East Lansing, MI: Institute for Research on Teaching.

Franke, M. L., Carpenter, T. P., Levi, L., & Fennema, E. (2001). Capturing teachers' generative change: A follow-up study of professional development in mathematics. *American Educational Research Journal, 38*, 653–689.

Gallimore, R., & Santagata, R. (2006). Researching teaching: The problem of studying a system resistant to change. In R. R. Bootzin & P. E. McKnight (Eds.), *Measurement, methodology, and evaluation: Festschrift in honor of Lee Sechrest* (pp. 11–28). Washington, DC: APA Books.

Givvin, K., Santagata, R., & Kersting, N. (2005, August). *"Do they really get it?" Using video to help teachers identify students' misunderstandings.* Presentation at the annual meeting of the European Association for Research on Learning and Instruction, Nicosia, Cyprus.

Grossman, P., & McDonald, M. (2008). Back to the future: Directions for research in teaching and teacher education. *American Educational Research Journal, 45*, 184–205.

Hiebert, J., Gallimore, R., Garnier, H., Givvin, K., Hollingsworth, H., Jacobs, J., et al. (2003). *Teaching mathematics in seven countries: Results from the TIMSS 1999 Video Study* (NCES 2003-013). Washington, DC: National Center for Education Statistics.

Hiebert, J., Gallimore, R., & Stigler, J. W. (2002). A knowledge base for the teaching profession: What would it look like and how can we get one? *Educational Researcher, 31*(5), 3–15.

Hiebert, J., Morris, A. K., Berk, D., & Jansen, A. (2007). Preparing teachers to learn from teaching. *Journal of Teacher Education, 58*, 47–61.

Hill, H. C. (2007). Mathematical knowledge of middle school teachers: Implications for the No Child Left Behind policy initiative. *Educational Evaluation and Policy Analysis, 29*, 95–114.

Jacobs, V., Lamb, L. C., Philipp, R., & Schappelle, B. (2009, April). *Professional noticing of children's mathematical thinking.* Paper presented at the annual meeting of the American Educational Research Association, San Diego, CA.

Jacobs, V., Lamb, L. C., Philipp, R., Schappelle, B., & Burke, A. (2007, April). *Professional noticing by elementary school teachers of mathematics.* Paper presented at the annual meeting of the American Educational Research Association, Chicago, IL.

Lampert, M. (2001). *Teaching problems and the problems of teaching.* New Haven, CT: Yale University Press.

Porter, A. C., Garet, M. S., Desimone, L., Yoon, K. S., & Birman, B. F. (2000, October). *Does professional development change teaching practice? Results from a three-year study.* Report to the U.S. Department of Education, Office of the Under Secretary on Contract No. EA97001001 to the American Institutes for Research. Washington, DC: Pelavin Research Center.

Sabers, D. S., Cushing, K. S., & Berliner, D. C. (1991). Differences among teachers in a task characterized by simultaneity, multidimensionality, and immediacy. *American Educational Research Journal, 28*, 63–88.

Santagata, R. (2009). Designing video-based professional development for mathematics teachers in low-performing schools. *Journal of Teacher Education, 60*(1), 38–51.

Santagata, R., Kersting, N., Givvin, K., & Stigler, J. W. (in press). Problem implementation as a lever for change: An experimental study of the effects of a professional development program on students' mathematics learning. *Journal of Research on Educational Effectiveness*.

Santagata, R., Zannoni, C., & Stigler, J. W. (2007). The role of lesson analysis in preservice teacher education: An empirical investigation of teacher learning from a virtual video-based field experience. *Journal of Mathematics Teacher Education, 10*(2), 123–140.

Sherin, M. G. (2007). The development of teachers' professional vision in video clubs. In R. Goldman, R. Pea, B. Barron, & S. J. Derry (Eds.), *Video research in the learning science* (pp. 383–396). Mahwah, NJ: Erlbaum.

Star, J. R., Lynch, K. & Perova, N. (this volume, chapter 8). *Using video to improve preservice mathematics teachers' abilities to attend to classroom features: A replication study*.

Star, J. R., & Strickland, S. K. (2008). Learning to observe: Using video to improve preservice mathematics teachers' ability to notice. *Journal of Mathematics Teacher Education, 11*, 107–125.

Stigler, J. W., & Hiebert, J. (1999). *The teaching gap: Best ideas from the world's teachers for improving education in the classroom*. New York: Free Press.

Tyack, D., & Tobin, W. (1994). The "grammar" of schooling: Why has it been so hard to change? *American Educational Research Journal, 31*, 453–479.

van Es, E. A., & Sherin, M. G. (2002). Learning to notice: Scaffolding new teachers' interpretations of classroom interactions. *Journal of Technology and Teacher Education, 10*, 571–596.

Wilson, S. M. (2003). *California dreaming: Reforming mathematics education*. New Haven, CT: Yale University Press.

11

USING CLASSROOM ARTIFACTS TO FOCUS TEACHERS' NOTICING

Affordances and Opportunities[1]

Lynn T. Goldsmith and Nanette Seago

Fifteen high school mathematics teachers sat chatting at their monthly after-school professional development seminar while Mark, the seminar leader, passed out five samples of students' work on the Crossing the River problem. Mark asked the teachers to form small groups to examine the worksheets and identify the algebraic thinking reflected in each solution. While the teachers worked, Mark reminded them to point to evidence from the student work to support their ideas. "Try to start with descriptions of what you see and then use those descriptions to reach an interpretation of the students' thinking. Then see if you can develop an alternative interpretation."

One student had recorded her strategy on the back of her worksheet using colored pencils to indicate who was in the boat for each trip across the river. Mark stopped in on the group just when Lorena, a veteran teacher, was glancing over the worksheet. "This student is a visual learner. He has difficulty with abstract concepts," she declared, releasing the paper and reaching for the next work sample. Without comment, her group mates began to follow suit. Mark, however, stepped into the conversation: "Lorena, your comment about being a visual learner sounds like you're making an interpretation of this student's work, but I don't know what your evidence is. What are you noticing about the work that led you to this conclusion, and how does it help you think about this student's algebraic thinking?"

Scenes like this one—teachers working together to examine classroom work as a part of professional development experiences—are enacted regularly in schools across the country. Teacher educators often use classroom artifacts such as student work samples or videotaped segments of lessons to help teachers learn to make sense of the complex practice of teaching (Kazemi & Franke, 2004; Little, 2002; Sherin, 2001; Smith et al., 2005). Professional development facilitators have gravitated to using classroom artifacts in part because they are ecologically valid—they capture aspects of authentic practice, yet by being removed from the immediacy of the classroom itself they can be examined and reflected upon in a more deliberate and considered manner (Ball & Cohen, 1999; Wilson & Berne, 1999).

Learning to notice classroom events and students' mathematical thinking is a key component of teaching expertise (Berliner, 1994; Mason, 2002), and classroom artifacts provide a valuable context for honing that expertise. According to van Es and Sherin (2008), an important aspect of noticing involves the ability to attend to what is significant in a complex situation. Our view of the importance of noticing is consistent with these claims, and we use the term *noticing* to capture the work that teachers do in identifying and interpreting key features of classroom interactions and student work. This work involves attending to both the mathematical content of the task and students' mathematical thinking, for example recognizing similarities and differences among mathematical representations and arguments, generating plausible interpretations of students' work, and seeing strengths as well as weaknesses in students' thinking.

We caution, however, that organizing professional development around the examination of classroom artifacts does not in itself guarantee that teachers will develop their abilities to identify and interpret student thinking. Artifacts are simply tools for teachers' professional development, just as manipulatives are tools for students' mathematical development (Ball, 1992; Ball & Cohen, 1999). Like manipulatives, classroom artifacts do not intrinsically carry information that will help teachers improve their practices; they are effective only when used skillfully (Nikula, Goldsmith, Blasi, & Seago, 2006). Many teachers approach artifacts with the mindset of judging the quality of the work they capture. A common goal of professional development facilitators is to help teachers take a more inquiry-based stance toward artifacts—to shift from evaluating student work to identifying and interpreting it for evidence of students' mathematical reasoning and teachers' decision making. The assumption underlying this goal is that teachers' careful analysis of the cognitive, mathematical, and pedagogical features of artifacts will help them develop the disposition to attend more closely to the mathematical thinking of their own students and the skills needed to make instructional decisions that will advance their students' thinking.

Teachers' interpretations of classroom artifacts are influenced by the very ways they think about mathematics and mathematics teaching and learning. Teachers view video or read a student's worksheet through the lens of their own knowledge, beliefs, and experiences; this lens shapes their very perception of the artifacts themselves (Heid, Blume, Zbiek, & Edwards, 1999). In this chapter, we present findings from our Turning to the Evidence project regarding shifts in the work teachers do in identifying and interpreting classroom artifacts. We further consider how different kinds of artifacts shape what teachers tend to notice.

Turning to the Evidence Project

In the Turning to the Evidence (TTE) project, we examined teachers' use of classroom artifacts in two professional development programs, *Fostering Algebraic Thinking Toolkit* (Driscoll et al., 2001) and *Learning to Teach Linear Functions* (Seago, Mumme, & Branca, 2004). These two programs share an underlying philosophy and a number of critical goals and design features. Common goals include a focus on extending teachers' understanding of algebraic thinking, increasing their sensitivities to students' mathematical ideas, promoting teachers' deeper understandings of the algebra they teach, and developing their abilities to use classroom records and artifacts to inquire into their practices. Despite the many similarities, the programs differ in important ways. Learning to Teach Linear Functions (LTLF) is organized primarily around work with videocases that capture classroom discussions. Each videocase highlights aspects of student thinking about linear relationships; all video clips feature classrooms that are unfamiliar to participants. The Fostering Algebraic Thinking Toolkit (ATT) uses a variety of kinds of artifacts to explore algebraic habits of mind (e.g., written student work, transcripts of students' small group problem solving, records of teachers' questions to students in the classroom). Most of the artifacts used in the ATT program come from participating teachers' own classrooms.

In the study, we followed four groups of teachers: two groups participating in LTLF seminars and two groups of teachers enrolled in ATT seminars. In all, 49 middle and high school teachers participated in the seminars. Additionally, a group of 25 teachers from the same districts served as a comparison group for pre-/post-program paper-and-pencil measures. Groups were facilitated by the lead authors of the respective programs (Driscoll for ATT and Seago for LTLF) in order to ensure fidelity of implementation.

We collected both quantitative and qualitative data for the study. Quantitative data included (a) a background questionnaire and (b) a multiple-choice/open-response mathematics survey that was based largely on items under development for the Learning Mathematics for Teaching instrument (Hill, Rowan, & Ball, 2005) and emphasized teachers' knowledge of algebra and linearity. Qualitative data sources included (a) a pre- and post-program Artifact Analysis assessment (a TTE-developed paper-and-pencil measure for which participants responded to both video and written artifacts), (b) video of all the professional development sessions, and (c) video of at least two classroom lessons, with pre- and post-lesson interviews, for each professional development participant. In this chapter, we report on data from the pre-/post-program Artifact Analysis and from analyses of four professional development sessions: two sessions from one of the LTLF groups and two sessions from one of the ATT groups.

Identifying Shifts in Teachers' Noticing: Responses to the Artifact Analysis

We administered the paper-and-pencil Artifact Analysis to all seminar participants and all comparison teachers at the beginning of the project (Fall 2003) and again in Spring 2004. Teachers viewed a 5-minute video clip of sixth grade students presenting solutions to a linear-function problem and responded in writing to a series of increasingly specific questions about the video. They also commented on three samples of written student work for the same problem.

We developed a scoring rubric that was based on five areas the LTLF and ATT developers had identified as central to productive work with artifacts:

- use of evidence to support statements;
- tone of statements (inquiring, prescriptive, descriptive);
- subject of statements (specific students, the class as a whole);
- focal aspect of student thinking (deficits, strengths/potential in understanding);
- content focus (specific mathematics, generic mathematics, or non-mathematical content).

These areas were identified largely on the basis of the craft knowledge of project members and advisors, inasmuch as we found little in the way of a research base upon which to draw when we began the project. Nonetheless, these areas coincide with those recently studied by other researchers (Borko, Jacobs, Eiteljorg, & Pittman, 2008; van Es & Sherin, 2008).

We scored teachers' responses holistically for each of the five goal areas on the basis of whether teachers' comments fell primarily into one category or another. After achieving interrater reliability of 93% on scoring for the video and 82% for the student work on a subset of the data (and discussing and resolving any disagreements), we each individually scored half of the remaining set of pre- and post-program data, blinded to treatment condition and time.

We conducted logit analysis of teachers' responses, treating them as repeated measures of teachers' response tendencies in each of the five coded areas. Although the teachers were not randomly assigned to the treatment and comparison groups, the pretreatment measures could be compared to examine initial equivalence of the groups. Responses for each of the five goal areas were analyzed separately using hierarchical generalized linear modeling (HGLM) for the categorical outcomes obtained from the coding of responses. The data were nested in that multiple measures came from each teacher and each teacher belonged to either a professional development or a comparison group. The hierarchical analysis partitioned the total variance in the data appropriately into a within-teacher and an across-teacher component and used dummy-coded time (pre-/post-program) and group (treatment/comparison) variables to predict differences in responses of teachers in the professional development and comparison groups. Tables 11.1,

11.2, and 11.3 present results for analyses of those areas which yielded significant results.

Each row indicates the estimated probabilities, given a teacher's group membership and the time of response, that a teacher's response would fall into each of the coded categories. Statistically significant posttest values indicate that the probabilities are different for treatment- versus comparison-group teachers, controlling for those teachers' pretreatment values. For example, for the category "using evidence to support claims" (see Table 11.1), the probability that a treatment teacher supported statements with evidence on the posttreatment assessment (0.42) was significantly greater than the probability of a comparison teacher's doing so (0.18), controlling for pretreatment responses. A similar pattern can be observed for focus on students' thinking (see Table 11.2): On the posttest, treatment teachers were more likely than comparison teachers to focus on the mathematical potential in students' responses. The treatment teachers were also significantly less likely on their postassessments to make comments that had no mathematical focus (e.g., to comment on students' cooperation or their willingness to speak in class; see Table 11.3). Further, this decreasing probability appears to correspond to an increase in the probability of making comments with a specific mathematical focus. In contrast, the probability of comparison teachers' making non-mathematical comments increased from pretest to posttest. Overall, these findings are consistent with van Es and Sherin's (2008) results regarding shifts in teachers' professional

TABLE 11.1 Estimated probability that a response related to evidence for claims is coded in each category by group and time of response

	Pretreatment		Posttreatment	
Group	No evidence used to back claims	Evidence used to back claims	No evidence used to back claims	Evidence used to back claims
Treatment	0.65	0.33	0.56	0.42★
Comparison	0.70	0.28	0.81	0.18★

★ $p < 0.05$

TABLE 11.2 Estimated probability that a response related to focus is coded in each category by group and time of response

	Pretreatment		Posttreatment	
Group	Focus on students' deficits	Focus on understanding/ potential	Focus on students' deficits	Focus on understanding/ potential
Treatment	0.50	0.45	0.35	0.61★
Comparison	0.49	0.47	0.61	0.37★

★ $p < 0.05$

TABLE 11.3 Estimated probability that a response related to mathematical focus is coded in each category by group and time of response

Group	Pretreatment			Posttreatment		
	Non-mathematical focus	Generic mathematical focus	Specific mathematical focus	Non-mathematical focus	Generic mathematical focus	Specific mathematical focus
Treatment	0.18	0.14	0.68	0.10★	0.15	0.75
Comparison	0.11	0.26	0.63	0.16★	0.22	0.61

★ $p < 0.05$

vision after participation in a video club and Borko et al.'s (2008) analysis of teachers' participation in problem-solving cycles.

Although the paper-and-pencil Artifact Analysis indicated that teachers participating in the professional development programs were more likely than nonparticipants to attend to those aspects of the artifacts that we conjecture help promote deeper understanding of students' mathematical thinking, it fails to provide a nuanced picture of how teachers' analyses of artifacts changed over time. To explicate these changes more fully, we contrasted discussions of artifacts in early and late professional development sessions for two of the four groups we studied: one LTLF seminar and one ATT group.[2]

A Deeper Analysis of the Shifts in Teachers' Noticing

The LTLF group was composed of teachers from the Atwood Unified School District, an urban West Coast district that serves approximately 18,000 students. Seven middle school teachers and two high school teachers participated in the seminar. The ATT seminar took place in the Bristol School District, a small urban district in the Northeast; it serves approximately 6,200 students. Seven middle school and six high school teachers attended this seminar.

We analyzed Sessions 1 and 8 (of 12) of the Atwood seminar and Sessions 3 and 13 (of 13) from the Bristol group. Within each group, teachers worked with the same artifact in the two sessions analyzed: Atwood teachers viewed and discussed a video clip of two students, Danielle and James, presenting their solutions to the Growing Dots problem; the Bristol teachers worked with three written student work samples of the Crossing the River problem (see the Appendix).

We began our coding and analysis of transcripts of seminar discussions with close reading and notation of sections that related to the goal categories explored in the written Artifact Assessment. In subsequent passes through the data, we elaborated on these initial categories, made connections among them, and looked for patterns in the data within and across sessions, as well as across the professional development groups. Despite the differing focal artifacts used in the ATT and LTLF seminars, we found a number of common shifts in teachers' noticing over time—shifts that enabled us to elaborate on the study's written assessments.

Using Evidence to Support Claims

Both the ATT and LTLF programs were designed explicitly to support development of teachers' dispositions to use information in artifacts to inquire into practice. As veteran professional development facilitators, both Driscoll and Seago expected that teachers would tend to use artifacts as bases for discussing their own experiences and opinions instead of as data sources to be analyzed and explored. For this reason, they both actively guided and supported teachers in identifying evidence from artifacts to support claims about students' mathematical thinking.

Both spent time in early seminar sessions framing group discussions to ensure they were grounded in the artifacts the groups were investigating. For example, in the Atwood group, Seago opened the first video discussion with explicit instructions to use the transcript in thinking about the video they had just watched. She then reinforced this request by asking the first person who commented on the video to tie those comments to the transcript.

Nanette: I'll let you look over the transcript and think about what were mathematically interesting and important moments . . .

Bruce: I just think that, identifying the variable again. 'Cause there were two different variables.

Nanette: Can you . . . tell us what time [code on the transcript]—what were the two variables?

Although, in early sessions, teachers in both the Atwood and the Bristol group made observations that were connected to evidence in the artifacts, they also offered comments that were not grounded in data. These comments seemed to be triggered by an association between the artifact and their own experiences or beliefs. For example, in the Atwood discussion, Bruce continued his thought by moving from the particulars of James's work to a broader, unsubstantiated claim about students:

> I just think it's one of the common mistakes that the students don't read what the question says. When they get to looking at a problem, sometimes the directions go out the window and they're just looking to see what it's doing and not answering the question.

In the Bristol group, we observed associations similar to Bruce's. For example, when Shirl opined that Student A had not answered the question posed on the worksheet because he had failed to write an algebraic expression, George replied, "This is the kind of kid you got to, like, drag [the answer] out of him." Later, Maureen commented:

> It's like he's starting to try to use variables, to get a little abstract. But . . . he's still very concrete. You know, he needs to have the chips moving back and forth. . . . So he . . . starts [to] try to use variables as part of rules but he couldn't. . . . And if you said, "[How many trips for] a million adults?," he'd be sitting there with a million adult chips moving and counting, tallying.

Unsubstantiated generalizations and comments like these were absent from group discussions in the later Atwood and Bristol sessions, in which teachers focused on interpreting the particulars of the mathematical thinking captured in the artifacts. For example, teachers in the Bristol group spent much of their second discussion of the problem trying to understand the reasoning behind Student A's solution to the third part of Problem 5.[3]

Grace: We were just trying to figure out . . . where they were getting their 7 times the *A* minus 1—the two kids across—just what exactly was the logic going on here? . . .We kind of figured out where the "7 times" comes from but I don't think we figured out where the "*A* minus 1" came from.

Miki: Wasn't their "*A* minus 1" the number of adults minus 1? Because they acted out getting the first adult over, so there's your 4 trips, and then repeat it *A* minus 1 times.

Debbie: If there is, because if there's only one adult, so 1 minus 1, you repeat it 0 times, and then 2 kids cross.

Grace: Oh! . . . Maybe they were thinking there weren't any adults. Is that what you're saying?

Over the course of the professional development, teachers in both groups needed fewer prompts from the facilitators to explore the logic of students' thinking or to ground their conversations in specific details from the artifacts. Van Es and Sherin (2008) have reported shifts in teachers' stances toward video over time, moving from comments that are largely evaluative of classroom events to comments that are more often interpretive. Our data indicate that for our teachers the shift was not in the types of their comments (from evaluation to interpretation) but in how teachers interpreted artifacts. The teachers in our groups engaged in interpretation from the very first; the change was in the degree to which these interpretations were close to, and warranted by, evidence in the artifacts themselves.

Noticing the Potential in Students' Thinking

The shift toward noticing potential in students' thinking that we observed in teachers' written responses to the Artifact Analysis was evident in richer detail in the professional development sessions and seems to have been stimulated by a broadening sense of what they considered productive mathematical thinking.

In both the Atwood and the Bristol seminars, teachers in the early session primarily took a normalizing view of students' solutions: They interpreted the work in terms of a standard correct answer, expressed in formal algebraic notation. Consider, for example, the following discussion about Student A among Bristol teachers.

George: He recognizes there's a pattern, and then he also recognizes the fact that then it's going to start repeating.

Shirl: The problem then becomes, though, on Number 2, that he doesn't recognize that what they're asking is not just "What's the pattern?" then, but "What's the answer?" He never answers the questions.

George: Well, it looks like he never came up with a rule.

Kristen: He does, here. He somewhat comes up with a rule.

Shirl: No, and he never comes up with a rule. . . .

George: Yeah, because it says right here [in the directions]: "Write a rule for any number of adults and two children." . . .

George: But he never did.

Kristen: Oh no, he just says to repeat it, "adults minus one times." . . .

George: Actually, he never answered Question 4.

Shirl: He never answered Question 2 either.

Despite Kristen's brief effort to give Student A credit for describing the algorithm for solving the problem, the group concluded that the work was inadequate because of the lack of algebraic notation, dismissing the student's articulation of the procedure as a potential answer to the questions.

Similarly, in the first Atwood seminar, teachers focused on the problems with James's recursive solution ("add 4 to the previous figure," which he expressed as $x + 4$) and overlooked ambiguities in Danielle's explanation for her solution $x \cdot 4 + 1$.

Seago: What about Danielle? Did anybody—?

Janice: I thought she did a great job with that.

Tom: She . . . has an A on it.

Annie: At first I didn't know what she was talking about, about 4, and she drew a little "4" on the end. . . . I knew what she was *trying* to do.

We suspect that, because Danielle's solution was correctly expressed in standard algebraic notation, teachers assumed that her communication, not her thinking, was unclear.

In the early sessions of both the Atwood and the Bristol group, teachers seemed to privilege standard representations of problem solutions such as tables and algebraic notation. These are the representations that are regularly presented in teachers' textbooks, that the teachers themselves produced when solving problems, and that they considered a primary goal of instruction in their own classrooms. We suggest that the tendency to compare students' work against normative representations led the Bristol teachers to focus on the shortcomings in student work samples and the Atwood teachers to both overestimate the clarity of Danielle's reasoning and underestimate James's reasoning.

As facilitators, both Seago and Driscoll had explicit goals for supporting teachers' shifts from focusing on deficits in students' thinking to noticing the mathematical potential captured in the artifacts under study. Both believed that the latter perspective is the stronger, more generative one to take for planning instruction. During the professional development, therefore, both encouraged teachers to approach students' work with genuine curiosity and a mindset to impute to students a certain intentionality and logic in their problem solving, even when students' solutions seemed incorrect or incomplete. Driscoll and Seago encouraged teachers to articulate the details of students' solutions and to consider connections between students' thinking and the mathematical goals for the activity. In this way, the facilitation helped teachers to expand their normative stances toward students' work and to look more deeply for the reasoning behind students' solutions.

For example, when the Atwood teachers revisited the Growing Dots video in Session 8, they were less puzzled by James's recursive solution and more willing to see it as an approach that captured some, but not yet all, of the critical features of solutions to linear-function problems. In the Bristol group's final session, in analyzing Student A's work, teachers focused primarily on understanding the solution as presented rather than on the student's failure to write an algebraic expression. Toward the end of the professional development, both the Atwood and the Bristol teachers were more intent than they had been at the beginning of the seminars on looking for the logic in students' solutions, even if the logic differed from their own reasoning about the problem.

More Detailed Attention to the Mathematics

The Artifact Analysis data indicated that, at posttest, the seminar participants were significantly less likely than were the comparison teachers to comment on non-mathematical aspects of the artifacts (see Table 11.3). Furthermore, the probability of commenting on specific mathematics was greater for seminar participants than for the comparison teachers. We also observed a shift in the mathematical focus in the seminars in terms of participants' greater attention to the mathematical meaning of solutions. We posit that Seago's and Driscoll's ongoing focus on analyzing artifacts in terms of student thinking encouraged teachers to probe more deeply the underlying mathematics, looking for the common mathematical threads in solutions and for connections among representations.

For example, in the later ATT session Miki credited her examination of student work with elucidating the mathematical meaning of her own answer to the Crossing the River problem. "[I] had solved the problem . . . and the numbers worked out and I accepted that as the answer, but I didn't know where the "minus 3" came from until I looked at [the student's work.]" The Atwood teachers, too, concentrated on mathematical meaning when they revisited James's explanation of his solution, discussing his decision to focus on the pattern of change and ignore the constant.

Walter: He thought that, if he counted the center [dot], you would be counting something that had not been added. And his interpretation was "How many had been added? . . .

Trevor: He was looking at the growth . . .

Walter: But to do that would kind of help him understand that the center [dot] is part of the pattern.

Nanette: Or potentially related to what Trevor was saying [earlier], "What does it start with? . . .

Walter: And, instead of extending it, you could retract it and say, "How far can you retract it? . . . And then you could kind of help him see that that 1 was indeed part of it.

Nanette: Yeah, potentially, it might be . . . a matter of order. Instead of adding the 1 at the end as Danielle did and the rest of the class appeared to be working on, it could be starting with the 1. . . . So the 1, where it's placed, . . . might matter in how kids are making sense of it.

Trevor: So b plus mx.

Summary

Teachers in both the Atwood and the Bristol group shifted the ways they attended to, and worked with, classroom artifacts over the course of the seminar. Over time, teachers increasingly grounded their discussions in evidence from the artifacts themselves, noticed more potential in students' thinking, and focused more deeply on the mathematical details in students' work.

Given the similarities between the LTLF and ATT programs in terms of overall philosophy, mathematical focus, and design features (particularly the central role that classroom artifacts play in grounding inquiry into issues of mathematics learning and teaching), the observation that teachers in the two groups developed similar stances toward artifacts may be unsurprising. In fact, their growing attention to the mathematical reasoning and representations captured by the artifacts can be ascribed to the effectiveness of the seminars themselves. Yet the kinds of artifacts that teachers encountered in the two programs differed, and these differences likely affected the aspects of students' thinking to which the teachers attended.

Characteristics of Artifacts That May Afford Differences in Noticing

The previous sections focused on common changes we found in teachers' noticing across the two programs. When we analyzed the LTLF and ATT sessions, we also found differences between the two groups in terms of teachers' focus on students' mathematical thinking—differences that we suspect relate to the kinds of artifacts they used. In this section, we briefly explore two aspects of the artifacts that seemed to affect teachers' noticing: the artifact medium and teachers' familiarity with the students who generated the artifacts.

The Artifact Medium

The teachers working with video began their analyses of artifacts differently than those working with written work: The Atwood group focused immediately on analyzing students' reasoning, whereas the Bristol teachers first focused on developing plausible accounts of the reasoning process itself. We think that this difference was due largely to the kinds of information available in the two kinds of artifacts. While the video included students' descriptions of their solution processes, the written work provided fewer clues about students' thinking.

In Session 1, the Atwood teachers began their discussion of the video on the Growing Dots problem by focusing on James's use of x, using his explanation to help them understand his thinking:

Janice: [The teacher asked James,] "At one minute, what would x be in your equation?" "To *me*?" [James] says. . . . "[It's] the number that I was adding it to. Like what was in the previous picture." So his variable is not consistent throughout. . . . The variable changes from the beginning to Minute 1 to Minute 2. . . . [His x] has to equal 1 or 5 or 9 or 13.

Session 8 also began with a discussion of the mathematical ideas underpinning James's solution, with several teachers offering interpretations of James's work:

Janice: [The teacher] posted instructions on the board to "describe the pattern." James wasn't all that wrong. He just didn't look at it more long-term. . . .

Walter: [James] saw "Oh, plus 4."

Janice: He was looking at each step as an independent . . . of the previous [step]. . . . As soon as James got from Point A to Point B . . . Point A became Point B, and he moved on.

In contrast, before the Bristol teachers could explore the mathematical ideas at play in students' written solutions, they first needed to determine how students might have arrived at their answers. In Session 3, for example, much of the group's discussion of the Crossing the River problem revolved around trying to understand how Student B had formulated answers to Question 5. Questions about the meaning of some of Student C's work arose in Session 13 as well:

Miki: In [Problem Number] 4, I thought the C was for the number of children . . . but if it's a different number of children it doesn't work.

Debbie: Right, it doesn't work. But if you go to [Problem] Number 5 and it says 6 adults plus 3 children, they get the answer 27. . . . They must have gone 4 times 6 and then just added 3, and they must have figured out that . . . when you add 1 more child you're adding 2 more trips to it. I mean, it works for 4 adults and 7 children, but . . . [for] 1 adult and 9 children that 13 doesn't work . . .

Jordan: When they did the ACC—adults times children squared plus 1—when they change the number of children it doesn't work.

Maureen: But do you think they meant "adults times children *squared*"?

Jordan: That's what they wrote.

Maureen: That's what they wrote, but, I think they were thinking children times—

Debbie: Who knows, but I'm making the jump that they noticed that it's 4 times adults, because 4 times 6 is 24. We know that. . . . And their formula pretty much works for 4 adults and 7 children; the only thing it doesn't work on is that last one, but they're not showing us what they're doing to get the answer.

Conversations in which teachers used computations to try to reconstruct students' reasoning were common among Bristol teachers but were virtually absent from the video-based work in Atwood.

We attribute these differences to the kinds of information about students' thinking that are typically available in video and written artifacts. The written work used in the Bristol seminar rarely included students' explanations of the reasoning behind their solutions. With little access to the particulars of students' thinking, the teachers had to work through how students had arrived at their answers before they could focus on why students might have thought about the problem as they did. Therefore much of the analysis undertaken by Bristol teachers involved using the written evidence to fashion a plausible story line about students' thinking. In contrast, the video artifacts in Atwood captured students' explanations of their solutions and, therefore, provided teachers with at least initial access to their thinking. The Atwood teachers did not, for example, have to determine whether James had included the center dot in the pattern because he explicitly stated that he did not: They could move directly to exploring connections between James's understanding of the pattern of growth and his representation of that pattern as $x + 4$.

We must note a caveat: We do not claim that having access to students' explanations of their solution processes obviates the need to unpack the logic of their solutions, since students' explanations may be incomplete, imprecise, or ambiguous. Furthermore, students' public, post hoc explanations may not reflect their actual solution processes. Our data do indicate, however, that working with video artifacts reduces the burden of following students' reasoning more than when working with students' written work.

Familiarity With the Classroom Producing the Artifact

The differences in Atwood and Bristol discussions that we attributed to different artifact media involved teachers working with artifacts that came from unfamiliar classrooms. Additionally, our examination of discussions *within* the early Bristol session suggests that teachers' familiarity with the classrooms producing the artifacts may affect their attention to student thinking. In particular, we found that the Bristol teachers' examination of familiar student work would often include commentary about students and classroom events that were not captured in the artifacts themselves but that teachers would use in making claims about students' work. The clearest evidence for this conjecture comes from Bristol teachers' work in Session 3: In this session, they first discussed unfamiliar student work on the Crossing the River problem (from Students A, B, and C) and then discussed artifacts from their own students' work on the problem.

When teachers examined the unfamiliar work, they often puzzled over how students had arrived at their responses and worked to follow students' reasoning by trying to re-enact their methods, performing indicated computations or using the students' approaches to work another problem. A conversation among three Bristol teachers working with Student B's answer for Question 5c illustrates this kind of work:

Kristen: But 7 and 8—where do you get 9 children? . . .

Shirl: I think he made a mistake here and then tried to adjust because he wanted them to always be 1 different . . . . Even though that wouldn't work. But this one [answer], I don't know. . . . I have no idea how he got that . . .

Grace: Well, the 8 maybe he got from 1 less of the number of children, because that's his pattern. Then 7—because I think you're right. And 6 is, and 5 is 1 less than 6; 1 is 1 less than 2. So he just said, "It's doing a pattern."

In contrast, when the teachers broke into small groups later to discuss their own students' work on the same problem, they barely focused on the work captured in the artifacts. Teachers provided narrative accounts of their students' approaches, recalling the lesson itself to describe the gist of solutions they had observed instead of focusing on the specifics of the work they had brought. When Kristen shared her students' work, she began with the following observation:

> Now this girl basically sounded just like us. And I actually think [her group] got it quicker than we did. . . . Most of the groups got similar answers . . . but a couple of groups couldn't come up with a formula.

Somewhat later, Kristen raised a question about another group's answer, but rather than try to work through the puzzling part—as she and her colleagues had done with the unfamiliar work less than an hour before—Kristen relied on her knowledge of her students to resolve her question:

Kristen: My two math whizzes ended up in the same group, and they were able to do it. And then when I gave them [the problem] . . . they did something. . . . I'm not quite sure. That's telling me that there's 6 times the adults plus 3 times the children—that would give me 27 trips. That's

> how I would determine it if it was an algebraic equation. But knowing they don't know algebraic equations I think they're just labeling 6 adults plus 3 children.

The point here is not whether Kristen's interpretation is correct but that *because* she knew the students she seemed comfortable drawing a conclusion about their thinking before she had explored other possibilities. Yet part of the power of using artifacts to investigate students' thinking lies in suspending one's biases or prior expectations (both about the students and about productive approaches to the mathematics) and exploring the ways students call upon and apply their mathematical knowledge and understanding. When working with artifacts from familiar classrooms, teachers may need to work harder to suspend these biases than when working with artifacts from students (or contexts) they do not know.

Conclusion: Using Artifacts Artfully

In this chapter, we have explored teachers' shifts in noticing over the course of artifact-rich professional development experiences and the effects of different types of artifacts in shaping teachers' attention. The findings from our study show that using classroom artifacts provides opportunities for teachers to increase their use of evidence, notice potential in student thinking, and focus on specific mathematics while they inquire into students' mathematical thinking.

In closing, we briefly highlight the role of the facilitator in promoting the shifts in noticing that we, and other researchers, have reported. We believe that these shifts occurred not only because teachers had opportunities to work with artifacts but also because facilitators actively promoted teachers' increasingly targeted and sophisticated analysis of students' thinking (Goldsmith & Seago, 2008; Nikula et al., 2006). Facilitators' artful use of artifacts in professional development requires that they have clear goals for directing teachers' attention to mathematically important elements of the artifacts and that they make considered decisions about the kind of artifacts to use.

Different kinds of artifacts seem useful for meeting different kinds of professional development goals. If one's goal is to follow or unpack students' thinking, working with written artifacts may be preferable, whereas study of video may be best for delving into the details of students' understanding. Second, knowing where teachers' attention is likely to be drawn by an artifact enables the facilitator to focus on those aspects of the artifact that are most likely to be productive. Although video offers multiple channels of information, it also has multiple channels for distraction. Skillful facilitators remain alert to the possibility that the aspects of the video they consider noteworthy may not be the ones that initially draw the teachers' attention. Similarly, skillful facilitators recognize that teachers investigating students' written work may initially focus on the correctness of answers instead of unpacking the thinking that led to the answer.

The more deeply facilitators understand how teachers take up work with different kinds of artifacts, the better prepared they can be for taking advantage of the strengths of the medium and for shaping teachers' noticing about learning and teaching mathematics. Regardless of the kind of artifact being investigated, a major reason to organize professional development around the study of artifacts is to encourage teachers to develop the dispositions to value and inquire into students' mathematical thinking as a regular part of their classroom practices.

Notes

1   In this chapter, we report on the work of the Turning to the Evidence project, which was funded by the National Science Foundation (NSF) under Grant REC-0231892. Any opinions, findings, and conclusions or recommendations expressed in this material are those of the authors and do not necessarily reflect the views of the National Science Foundation. Project members also included Mark Driscoll, Johannah Nikula, and Zuzka Blasi; Daniel Heck conducted statistical analyses. We extend special thanks to Mark Driscoll for advice about this chapter.
2   Names of teachers and districts are pseudonyms.
3   The Crossing the River problems presented in this chapter have been slightly modified from those used with the Bristol teachers. However, the student solutions included here parallel the solutions in the samples with which the teachers worked.

References

Ball, D. L. (1992, Summer). Magical hopes: Manipulatives and the reform of math education. *American Educator, 16*, 14–18, 46–47.

Ball, D. L., & Cohen, D. K. (1999). Developing practice, developing practitioners: Toward a practice-based theory of professional education. In G. Sykes & L. Darling-Hammond (Eds.), *Teaching as the learning profession: Handbook of policy and practice* (pp. 3–32). San Francisco: Jossey-Bass.

Berliner, D. C. (1994). Expertise: The wonder of exemplary performances. In J. M. Mangier & C. C. Block (Eds.), *Creating powerful thinking in teachers and students: Diverse perspectives* (pp. 161–186). Fort Worth, TX: Holt, Rinehart, and Winston.

Borko, H., Jacobs, J., Eiteljorg, E., & Pittman, M. E. (2008). Video as a tool for fostering productive discussions in mathematics professional development. *Teaching and Teacher Education, 24*, 417–436.

Driscoll, M. D., Zawojewski, J., Humez, A., Nikula, J., Goldsmith, L., & Hammerman, J. (2001). *Fostering algebraic thinking toolkit*. Portsmouth, NH: Heinemann.

Goldsmith, L. T., & Seago, N. (2008). Using video cases to unpack the mathematics in students' mathematical thinking. In M. S. Smith & S. N. Friel (Eds.), *Cases in mathematics teacher education: Tools for developing knowledge needed in teaching* (Association of Mathematics Teacher Educators Monograph No. 4) (pp. 135–145). San Diego, CA: Association of Mathematics Teacher Educators.

Heid, M. K., Blume, G. W., Zbiek, R. M., & Edwards, B. S. (1999). Factors that influence teachers learning to do interviews to understand students' mathematical understandings. *Educational Studies in Mathematics, 37*, 223–249.

Hill, H. C., Rowan, B., & Ball, D. L. (2005). Effects of teachers' mathematical knowledge for teaching on student achievement. *American Educational Research Journal, 42*, 371–406.

Kazemi, E., & Franke, M. (2004). Teacher learning in mathematics: Using student work to promote collective inquiry. *Journal of Mathematics Teacher Education, 7*, 203–235.

Little, J. W. (2002). Locating learning in teachers' professional community: Opening up problems of analysis in records of everyday work. *Teaching and Teacher Education, 18*, 917–946.

Mason, J. (2002). *Researching your own practice: The discipline of noticing.* London: RoutledgeFalmer.

Nikula, J., Goldsmith, L. T., Blasi, Z. V., & Seago, N. (2006). A framework for the strategic use of classroom artifacts in mathematics professional development. *National Council of Supervisors of Mathematics Journal of Mathematics Education Leadership, 9*(1), 57–64.

Seago, N., Mumme, J., & Branca, N. (2004). *Learning and teaching linear functions: Video cases for mathematics professional development, 6–10/facilitator's guide.* Portsmouth, NH: Heinemann.

Sherin, M. G. (2001). Developing a professional vision of classroom events. In T. Wood, B. S. Nelson, & J. Warfield (Eds.), *Beyond classical pedagogy: Teaching elementary school mathematics* (pp. 75–93). Hillsdale, NJ: Erlbaum.

Smith, M. S., Silver, E. A., Stein, M. K., Henningsen, M. A., Boston, M., & Hughes, E. K. (2005). *Improving instruction in algebra: Using cases to transform mathematics teaching and learning* (Vol. 2.). New York: Teachers College Press.

van Es, E. A., & Sherin, M. G. (2008). Mathematics teachers' "learning to notice" in the context of a video club. *Teaching and Teacher Education, 24*, 244–276.

Wilson, S. M., & Berne, J. (1999). Teacher learning and the acquisition of professional knowledge: An examination of research on contemporary professional development. In A. Iran-Nejad & P. D. Pearson (Eds.), *Review of research in education* (Vol. 24, pp. 173–209). Washington, DC: American Educational Research Association.

Appendix: Mathematical Tasks and Student Work

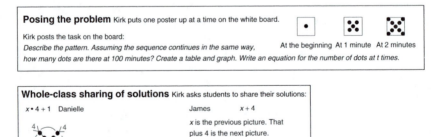

FIGURE 11.1 Growing dots

Source: Reprinted with permission from *Learning and teaching linear functions: Video cases for mathematics professional development, 6–10/Facilitator's guide,* by Nanette Seago, Judith Mumme, & Nicholas Branca. Copyright © 2004 by San Diego State University Foundation. Published by Heinemann, Portsmouth, NH. All rights reserved.

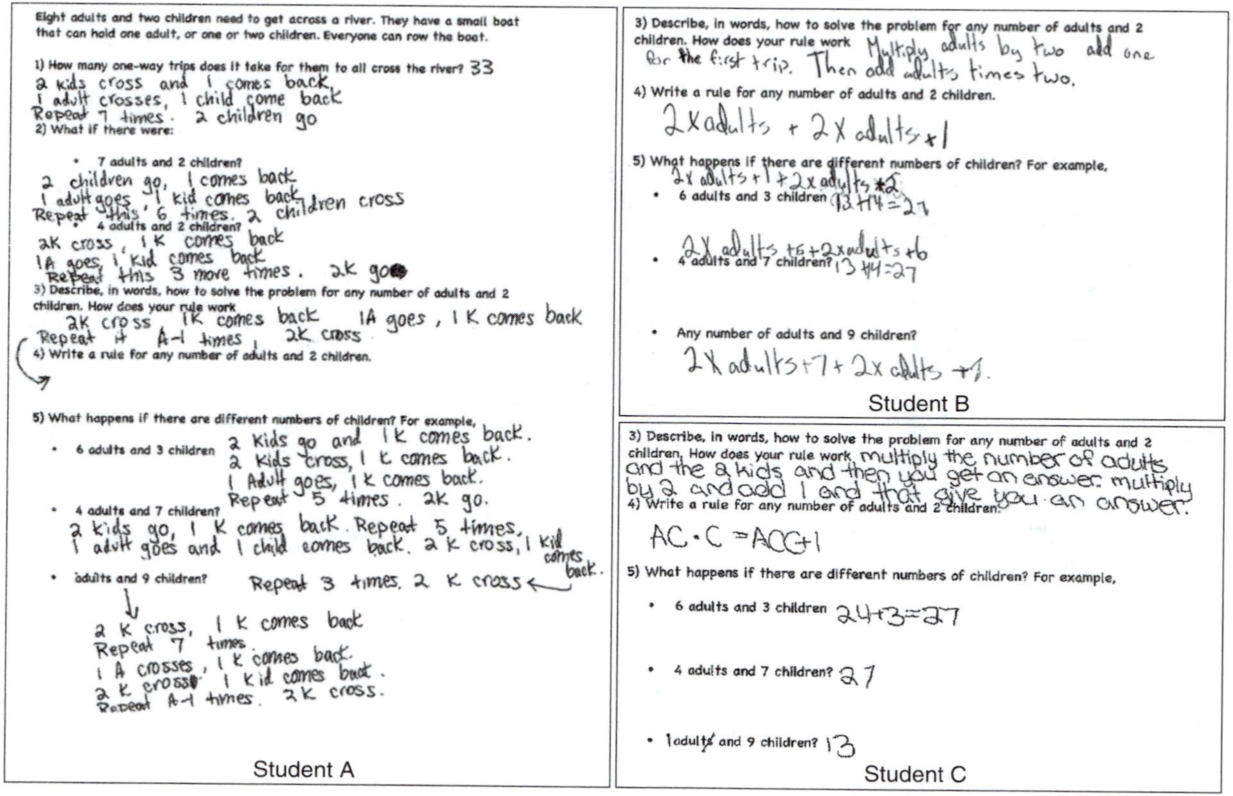

Eight adults and two children need to get across a river. They have a small boat that can hold one adult, or one or two children. Everyone can row the boat.

1) How many one-way trips does it take for them to all cross the river? 33

2 kids cross and 1 comes back.
1 adult crosses, 1 child come back
Repeat 7 times. 2 children go

2) What if there were:

• 7 adults and 2 children?

2 children go, 1 comes back
1 adult goes, 1 kid comes back 2 children cross
Repeat 4 times, 6 times, 2 children?

4 adults and 2 children?

2k cross, 1k comes back
1A goes, 1k comes back. 2k go
Repeat this 3 more times.

3) Describe, in words, how to solve the problem for any number of adults and 2 children. How does your rule work

2k cross 1k comes back 1A goes, 1 k comes back
Repeat it A-1 times 2k cross

4) Write a rule for any number of adults and 2 children.

5) What happens if there are different numbers of children? For example,

• 6 adults and 3 children
  2 kids go and 1 k comes back.
  2 kids cross, 1 k comes back.
  1 Adult goes, 1 k comes back.
  Repeat 5 times. 2k go.

• 4 adults and 7 children
  2 kids go, 1 k comes back. Repeat 5 times, 1 kid
  1 adult goes and 1 child comes back. 2k cross, 2k comes back.

• adults and 9 children?   Repeat 3 times, 2 k cross
  2k cross, 1 k comes back
  Repeat 7 times.
  1 A crosses, 1 k comes back.
  2 k cross. 2k cross.
  Repeat A-1 times. 2k cross.

Student A

3) Describe, in words, how to solve the problem for any number of adults and 2 children. How does your rule work Multiply adults by two add one for the first trip. Then add adults times two.

4) Write a rule for any number of adults and 2 children.

$2 \times adults + 2 \times adults \times 1$

5) What happens if there are different numbers of children? For example,
$2 \times adults + 1 + 2 \times adults$
• 6 adults and 3 children $13 + 14 = 27$

$2 \times adults + 6 + 2 \times adults + 6$
• 4 adults and 7 children? $15 + 14 = 27$

• Any number of adults and 9 children

$2 \times adults + 7 + 2 \times adults + 1.$

Student B

3) Describe, in words, how does your rule work. multiply the number of adults and the 2 kids and then you get an answer. multiply by 3 and add 1 and that give you an answer.

4) Write a rule for any number of adults and 2 children

$AC \cdot C = ACC + 1$

5) What happens if there are different numbers of children? For example,

• 6 adults and 3 children $24 + 3 = 27$

• 4 adults and 7 children? 27

• 1 adult and 9 children? 13

Student C

FIGURE 11.2 Crossing the river

12

NOTICING LEADERS' THINKING ABOUT VIDEOCASES OF TEACHERS ENGAGED IN MATHEMATICS TASKS IN PROFESSIONAL DEVELOPMENT

Elham Kazemi, Rebekah Elliott, Judith Mumme, Cathy Carroll, Kristin Lesseig, and Megan Kelley-Petersen

This chapter is focused on building teachers' content knowledge through professional development. Through our leadership-preparation project (Researching Mathematics Leader Learning [RMLL]), we are creating resources for leaders of professional development to engage teachers with mathematics by solving and discussing solutions to mathematical tasks. We aim to support leaders in cultivating mathematically rich learning environments for teachers by focusing leaders on the normative ways teachers engage with mathematical explanation. Our approach to making sense of leaders' thinking is based on the contention that we need to identify important features in professional development for leaders if they are to reason about, act on, and learn from these professional development experiences. Research on teacher noticing supports this goal through a focus on identifying and making sense of complex teaching situations (Jacobs, Lamb, Philipp, & Schappelle, 2009; Sherin, 2007; Star & Strickland, 2007). In particular, Jacobs and colleagues (2009) described three components of teachers' noticing that are relevant to our work with leaders: attending, interpreting, and deciding how to respond. In their work, the three components relate to teachers' noticing of children's mathematical thinking. In our work, the three components relate to our own noticing of leaders' thinking while they participated in professional development. In other words, we focus on *our* noticing as leaders of leaders (LOLs). In this chapter, we show how our noticing of leaders' thinking about videocases of teachers engaged in mathematics in professional development helped us consider novel ways to support leaders in facilitating mathematical tasks in professional development. We argue for the importance and utility of developing a framework to orient leaders to a particular and focused purpose for engaging in mathematics with teachers. How phenomena are framed is of central concern in understanding the disciplined perception that expertise builds (Erickson, 2007; Stevens & Hall, 1998).

The Problem of Engaging in Mathematics in Professional Development

We began our project with several key premises:

1. How leaders of professional development engage teachers in mathematics is important. In the professional development context, teachers have unique opportunities to learn what is entailed in developing such mathematical habits of mind as generalizing, proving, engaging in argumentation, and connecting representations to their symbolic equivalents.
2. We find a dearth of research specifically on how to structure and lead mathematical work with teachers (Even, 2008). We have much to learn about how engagement with mathematical reasoning in professional development helps teachers create learning environments for their students.
3. Wilson and Berne (1999) and Lord (1994) suggested that what is typically defined as *competent participation* in professional development is engaging colleagues in social pleasantries and avoiding dialogue that may prove uncomfortable for participants. Moreover, Remillard and Rickard (2001) suggested that teachers' inquiring into practices and engaging in depth with mathematical ideas were not typical norms in the professional development seminars they facilitated unless teachers were provided support and scaffolding. Although social norms, such as being polite and considerate of colleagues, are often the focus of teachers and professional development facilitators, they do not expressly support the deepening of mathematical knowledge. Among the activities we have seen when leaders engage in mathematics with teachers, the most relevant to our project is the tendency for leaders to give teachers a rich task, work on solving the problem, and then go around the room having groups share their solutions. We worried that important mathematical ideas might get lost in this kind of serial sharing.

Given these issues, we began our project by explicitly introducing leaders to the construct of *sociomathematical norms* for explanation (Yackel & Cobb, 1996). We framed our discussion of videocases of professional development with leaders by identifying the sociomathematical norms for what constitutes a good explanation that seemed to govern mathematical discussions among teachers. Leaders' capacities to cultivate deep understanding of mathematics depend on their abilities to know what and how to press for mathematical understanding. We wanted them to be more intentional in how their facilitation of professional development cultivated norms for mathematical explanation. When leaders work with colleagues in professional development, tension is likely to arise when they focus on teachers' mathematical understandings and uncover teachers' mathematical confusions. Leaders are likely to grapple with navigating the use of errors, negotiating teachers' social and intellectual status among colleagues, and connecting mathematical work done in the professional development context to work that teachers do with their students.

To engage leaders in considering how to foster productive sociomathematical norms and orchestrate discussions in professional development to support teachers' mathematical reasoning (Stein, Engle, Smith, & Hughes, 2008), we collaboratively designed a series of six full-day seminars across the academic year. Two members of our team took primary responsibility for facilitating the seminars while other members of the team documented them. We use the terms *LOL facilitator* to point to an action of the facilitator of the seminar and *we* to indicate our collective engagement with designing the seminars and discussing the challenges of facilitating this kind of work with leaders. Because (with few exceptions) we were all present during the enactment of the seminars, we were able to discuss and consider our in-the-moment ideas about how leaders were thinking about the cases. The issues we discuss here reveal what we attended to in the moment. This chapter is written from our perspective as facilitators who have had multiple opportunities to design and lead mathematics professional development for leaders. In this chapter, unlike the other chapters in this book, we focus on our own noticings as professional educators. Our discussion of leader preparation, then, emerges out of our practice as professional educators rather than our skills as researchers. In this chapter, our goal is not to present research findings that resulted from systematic data analysis but to convey how our noticing of leader thinking has influenced our own growing practice.

Each seminar began with solving and discussing a mathematical task of generalizing from arithmetic solutions as a way to investigate algebraic reasoning. Leaders' collective mathematical work and discussions of their methods for solving the task set the stage for the centerpiece of the seminar—a videocase of a mathematics professional development leader engaging teachers in the same task. Tasks and videocases were drawn from a larger set of materials developed for leaders of mathematics professional development (Carroll & Mumme, 2007). Leaders discussed both what mathematical explanations were shared in the videocase and how participants in the videocase engaged in sharing explanations. Between seminars, leaders carried out professional development with classroom teachers as part of their various leadership positions (see also Elliott et al., 2009). In the next section, we provide an example of these videocases and describe the types of ideas we chose to highlight in the videocase to help leaders cultivate sociomathematical norms. We then discuss to what we attended, how we interpreted leaders' thinking about the videocases, and how these interpretations have influenced our future plans for supporting leaders to effectively engage teachers in mathematics.

Videocase: Janice's Method

Consider the following summary of a videocase. It is a 9-minute excerpt from the second morning of a 5-day workshop designed to help teachers learn to use new instructional materials. Twenty-three K–5 teachers from several districts participated in this session on developing computational fluency in subtraction. Participants were asked to compute 92 − 56 mentally. A few teachers shared their thinking, and the facilitator, Casilda, recorded their approaches on the board. In the videocase clip, one of the teachers, Janice, answered 36 and shared her strategy. In explaining that she rounded 92 down to 90 and 56 up to 60, she said, "I know 90 is 2 from 92, so I put 2 plus the 4 that I needed to add to 56 to get 60, which equals 6. And add 30 and 6 together will give you that 36." The facilitator asked Janice, "Why did you add the 2 and the 4?" Janice answered by saying that she needed to "recover" the 2 and the 4.

A conversation ensued about what Janice meant by the term *recover*, prompted by the facilitator asking participants if they had questions for Janice. One teacher articulated her confusion about this method: "I see that it turns out right, but I don't understand—90 is smaller than 92, and we're adding 2. And 60 is 4 bigger than 56, but we're still adding. That's the confusing part for me." The discussion continued, and the following ideas were offered by the group as a way of making sense of Janice's method:

Mary: They're both in the hole. It's kind of like a checking account. You're minus 2 here, and you're minus 4 here, and you put them together and you get even.

Chris: (Saying that he had overheard another participant say, "It's minus minus"). You're really subtracting negative 4. . . . When she rounded 90 down and had the 2 left over and she rounded 56 up, she did not have 4 left over. She had negative 4 left over, so she's got to do something with the 2 and the negative 4, and the problem is still 2 minus 4, so it's 2 minus negative 4 or 2 plus 4.

The group appeared to understand more clearly why Janice added 2 back in from 92—"She still has the 2 to put back in"—but the group remained unsure about the 4. Laughter about Chris's comment about the "minus minus" indicated that many in the group were not convinced by his explanation. Someone asked whether the "minus minus" idea will work all the time.

Casilda, the facilitator, presented another idea to help the participants think about adding in 4:

> She took away 4 too many when she subtracted 60. The problem was only subtract 56. So she subtracted too many. This would be like, she was paying 56 but she gave the clerk 60 and so the clerk has to give her back 4. So the 2 she has in her pocket, the 4 the clerk gave her back, plus 30.

Some participants began trying this method with other numbers, and Betty asked whether the facilitator could show it on a number line. Casilda drew a number line (see Figure 12.1), indicating that Janice went from 92 down to 90 and from 56 up to 60.

FIGURE 12.1 Number line drawn to explain the method for 92−56

She asked the group, "What happened to the difference?" Beth answered, "You took less of it because you're shortening the distance." Casilda affirmed this by saying, "The difference made was much smaller because she moved both numbers in." Casilda pointed to how much the difference was lessened on the number line, 2 on one side and 4 on the other, resulting in 6 that needed to be added back to 30. The videocase ends after these comments.

Our Initial Views of the Videocase

Prior to using this videocase with leaders, our team discussed it to consider the potential benefits of its use. We had identified a range of mathematical and interactional issues that merited leaders' consideration. Specifically, we saw a group of teachers trying to make sense of a method and convince themselves that it was mathematically sound by appealing to a range of representations, situations, and mathematical ideas: paying a cashier who wants $56 with $60 instead, drawing a number line to show how the distances between the numbers were changed, and evoking previously learned rules (minus minus). Some teachers appeared to have determined whether the method was generalizable. Interactionally, teachers appeared willing to ask questions about what they were uncertain of and to engage in making sense of the method.

When we began using this videocase, we wanted leaders to attend to sociomathematical norms for explanation—what seemed to count as a sufficient explanation and how that contributed to the mathematical ideas that were articulated in whole group discussions. The LOL facilitators highlighted the way the facilitator in the videocase took the time to probe Janice's meaning of her use of the word *recovery*, probing for a conceptual explanation for what she did. In addition, the LOL facilitators marked that teachers implicitly drew on different models for subtraction and noted that the teachers were polite with one another but also responded with laughter when Chris said, "You're really subtracting a negative 4." The laughter conveyed the group's collective response, making fun of what is typically viewed among elementary school teachers as complicated mathematics.

These ways of working with this videocase reflect merely one of many readings of the case. We have highlighted mathematical entailments of the case, demonstrating our own professional vision (Goodwin, 1994) for what might be considered salient for leaders of mathematics professional development. However, when leaders at varying levels of experience talked about this same videocase, we learned what was actually salient to leaders.

Our Noticing of Leaders' Thinking About the Videocase

We worked with three groups of leaders. The first group was a highly experienced group of mostly elementary teacher leaders ($n = 11$) with whom we piloted our materials; typically they had 7 to 9 years of leadership experience. The second group ($n = 24$) had about 4 years of leadership experience and spanned the K–12 grades. The third group was our least experienced group of elementary teacher leaders ($n = 12$), who typically had 1 or 2 years of leadership experience.

We cannot claim that what these groups noticed is representative of what other groups of leaders with similar levels of experience would notice. Taken together, however, they helped us consider the frames that leaders brought to watching a group of teachers work.

In the next sections, we describe how focusing on the three components of noticing (attending, interpreting, and deciding how to respond) helped us better understand leaders' needs and how we might better address those needs. Table 12.1 summarizes what the LOL facilitators noticed about leaders' thinking about the videocase.

Attending to and Interpreting Leaders' Thinking About the Videocase

When we attended to and interpreted the leaders' thinking about the videocase, we identified three themes that merited consideration: issues related to engaging leaders in mathematics, the social climate of professional development, and the facilitator's role.

Leaders Demonstrated a Range of Ways of Engaging with the Mathematics

Prior to watching each videocase, the LOL facilitators engaged leaders in solving and discussing a mathematical problem related to the one that appeared in the videocase. The LOL facilitators attended to how the leaders' responses were similar to the ways teachers might engage with the tasks. In fact, many leaders were also classroom teachers or were out of the classroom temporarily to take on new roles as mathematics coaches or teachers on special assignment. Among our most seasoned leaders, some described themselves in small group discussions as saturated with the mathematics and not interested in comparing ways of solving the task. At the same time, other leaders took up the idea of modeling subtraction as an operation (as removal vs. difference on the number line) and began to consider whether their approaches would generalize to decimals. The familiarity of the task to leaders seemed important because we also observed leaders who, when discussing the videocase, were still trying to make sense of Janice's method, not having seen such a compensating method before.

TABLE 12.1 Summary of LOL facilitators' noticing of leaders' thinking about videocases

	Attending	Interpreting	Deciding How To Respond
	To what do LOLs attend in leaders' thinking about videocases of teachers engaged in mathematics in professional development?	How do LOLs interpret leaders' thinking about videocases of teachers engaged in mathematics in professional development?	How could LOL facilitators use what they learned from attending to and interpreting leaders' thinking about the videocases to better support leaders in facilitating mathematical tasks in professional development with teachers?
Mathematics theme	Leaders demonstrated a range of ways of engaging with the mathematics (e.g., some tried to understand it, some engaged beyond finding the answer, some quickly stopped engaging, etc.).	Leaders (and teachers) hold mathematical knowledge differently than do K–12 students.	LOL facilitators need to cultivate an appreciation that teachers' motivations to engage in mathematics in professional development is different from students' motivations in classrooms. Part of the mathematical knowledge on which teachers draw is a specialized form of knowledge that is unique to teachers' work with learners of mathematics. The purpose for engaging teachers in mathematics in professional development should be to develop this specialized form of mathematical knowledge.
Social-Climate theme	Leaders highlighted issues of safety and risk taking.	Leaders have a different relationship with teachers than teachers have with students and this relationship can open up or close down opportunities for learning.	
Facilitation theme	Leaders noted the facilitator's role in general terms.	Leaders' seemed to have an unclear understanding of why teachers should engage in mathematics in professional development.	

We interpreted these observations of leaders by recognizing that *leaders (and teachers) hold mathematical knowledge differently than K–12 students*. Leaders (and teachers) have often experienced and come to an understanding of the mathematics in the K–12 curriculum. They often have facility with the content, enabling them to solve the problems they give to their students. They have progressed at least once through the curriculum as students and potentially many more times as teachers. Because leaders (and teachers) may already know the mathematics, many can quickly find a solution or be less interested in working with explanations once they have solved the problem. To solve the problem, they may use procedures, algorithms, or symbolic manipulations without attention to the underlying ideas. As one leader explained to her small group:

> When [you] asked me how I did it, I wasn't expecting to explain how. I thought that once I explained what I did, I had already done it. I wasn't thinking like I would think [about] it when I was teaching. If I was teaching, I would have prepared for my explanation in some way.

Our leaders identified strongly with their roles as teachers even while they participated in professional development designed for learning to facilitate professional development, not just to engage in it as a learner.

We now recognize that in professional development for leaders we need to help them anticipate how teachers will engage with mathematical tasks. Leaders may need to be prompted to consider their own reactions and abilities to engage with mathematical tasks as an indicator of how teachers will respond. Not all the leaders with whom we worked were familiar with Janice's method, and some were expanding their knowledge when they tried to make sense of the method. Despite this, we see the need to be more intentional in how leaders are asked to work with mathematical tasks. They need to be able to anticipate how teachers will approach mathematics tasks and be able to pose tasks and orchestrate discussions in professional development to make evident the important ideas that teachers need to support student learning. Later in this chapter, we return to this issue of framing and working with mathematical tasks and what it means to design learning environments for teachers (National Research Council, 2000).

Leaders Focused on the Social Climate of the Professional Development Environment

After facilitating the leaders' work on the mathematics, the LOL facilitators showed the videocase and provided the prompt "How is the group engaging in mathematics?" In listening to the leaders' responses, we attended to their focus on the social climate of a session. Specifically, leaders sensed that this was a group in which teachers felt safe to take risks, and leaders made general statements, whether true or not, about adults as participants in professional development. These statements were typically stated as barriers, for example "adults shut down faster than children," "a lot of people won't put confused faces because they want to pretend they get what the person is saying," "some groups of individuals have such a block against math . . . they are going to feel threatened." Some of the leaders also evaluated how they thought Janice might have felt, whether she herself was confused or intimidated by the facilitator's questions. This concern about the social climate may show what is culturally valued in the United States. Miller and Zhou (2007), for example, compared how U.S. and Chinese teachers commented on the same classroom video. U.S. teachers were more likely to comment on teacher personalities and the social climate of the classroom, whereas Chinese teachers were more likely to comment on the mathematics of the observed lessons.

During the professional development sessions, we noted that leaders made evaluative statements about teachers judging whether they were engaged, intimidated, or confused. New leaders, especially, also cast doubt on their own abilities to push on teachers' understanding, and leaders, in general, were struck by how tenacious the facilitator in the videocase seemed to be when she asked teachers to explain why Janice's method was mathematically sound. In addition to these comments about how the facilitator in the videocase contributed to the social climate, in every group of leaders some noted who talked and how many times as evidence of whether the teachers in the group were engaged. This kind of counting was less critical to us, in part, because a videocase may not provide an accurate picture of frequency and quality of interaction across an entire professional development experience.

We have interpreted these leader reactions by reflecting on how *leaders' relationships with teachers are different from teachers' relationships with students*. Leaders' relationships with teachers in professional development have an added layer of complexity. When engaging in mathematics together in professional development, some teachers may feel as though they should, or already do, know the mathematics and may resist completing mathematical tasks or try to disguise any uncertainty or confusion. Thus, in comparison to teachers who are assumed to have more authority than students, leaders may often be cautious when working with colleagues in discussing mathematics because they do not want to appear as though, or seem to suggest that, they know more than a colleague. Leaders and teachers can negotiate themselves and each other into particular kinds of identities with respect to doing mathematics, and leaders need to be aware of and attend to the ways that teachers position themselves and use status differentials during professional development. For example, teachers may mark their contributions to discussions in one or more of the following ways: (a) I'm not a math person; (b) those teachers know math because they are the middle school teachers (and we're elementary school teachers); (c) that's Christopher talking—he's really smart (i.e., in some professional development contexts men can take and hold more status); and (d) I don't know math but I'm learning, and here's a question that occurs to me.

We became aware over the course of our professional development seminars of how status differentials may open opportunities for learning. For example, a teacher who declares, "I'm not good at math," and goes on to ask what she or he believes to be a naive question may open up a deeper mathematical conversation among her peers. At other times, status remarks may close opportunities, such as (a) when an elementary school teacher defers to a secondary school teacher simply because the latter is perceived to have more mathematical knowledge or (b) a teacher dominates a conversation and attempts to make the mathematical questions seem obvious and self-explanatory. Leaders may disrupt these displays of status by explicitly communicating to teachers that the work they are doing with mathematics is not just about finding solutions but is also about developing a kind of mathematical knowledge that they need as professionals but did not gain from being students. Teachers' motivations for engaging in mathematics during professional development may not correspond with this view of needing to develop mathematical knowledge specific to teaching, and, therefore, leaders may need to be explicit about their purposes for engaging teachers in mathematics.

Leaders Discussed the Facilitator's Role in General Terms

We attended to how some leaders tended to talk about the role of the facilitator in the videocase in general terms when, for example, they were discussing the facilitator's questions. They recognized that the videocase facilitator's purpose in expressing confusion about what Janice had said was to slow the conversation and that she feigned a lack of understanding to elicit additional explanations. For some leaders, these moves were natural links to similar moves they would make in a classroom so that students would provide more detailed reasoning. In small groups, the LOL facilitators heard leaders ask whether the videocase facilitator was attempting to model classroom teaching; they noted her persistence in paraphrasing, suggesting analogies, and questioning teachers' meanings. Only the most experienced leaders explicitly discussed the use of the removal and distance models as a way of making sense of what was shown on the number line. Even so, the conversations among leaders about how the videocase facilitator engaged the teachers in mathematics remained at a general level. We interpreted these leaders' observations by recognizing that *many leaders may hold an unclear understanding of why teachers should engage in mathematics in professional development.*

Deciding How to Respond on the Basis of Leaders' Thinking About the Videocase

When we attended to and interpreted the leaders' thinking about the videocase in the moment and in collective reflection after the seminars, we clarified our own reasons for providing opportunities for leaders and teachers to engage in mathematics in professional development. We now see the need to cultivate an appreciation that *teachers' motivations to engage in mathematics in professional develop-ment should be different from students' motivations in classrooms.* Professional develop-ment has an overarching goal of preparing teachers to teach, a goal not shared by students in the classroom. A student does not necessarily need to have command of the full range of solutions and their meanings. When engaging in mathemat-ics in professional development, teachers think about the mathematics, either explicitly or implicitly, in relationship to teaching. Often teachers work on tasks that they will be required to present to students. Engaging with mathematics tasks should enable teachers to develop the mathematical knowledge to teach students important mathematical ideas. This specialized knowledge of mathematics (see Ball, Thames, & Phelps, 2008) is detailed and different from what students need to know. For example, students need to have an understanding of what *subtrac-tion* means and have reliable and efficient ways to solve a subtraction problem. Teachers need this understanding and skill, but they also need to know much more about subtraction than do students. Because teachers need (a) to be able to predict the range of understandings and confusions that students may encounter while they make sense of subtraction situations and (b) to diagnose students' ideas in real time, they need to know the underlying mathematical reasoning involved in those procedures, understand the difference between removal and distance models of subtraction, and know how and when to evoke these models. They need not only to know the subtraction methods offered in their texts but also to be facile with a variety of methods that may be useful to students while they are learning what strategies are mathematically efficient. This clearer articulation for the ways a teacher needs to know mathematics has helped us better express the reasons for engaging in mathematics in professional development (for more dis-cussion of the specific mathematical demands of teaching, see also Adler & Davis, 2006; Ball et al., 2008; Lo, Grant, & Flowers, 2008; Stylianides & Stylianides, 2010; Suzuka et al., 2009).

Comparing the Work of Engaging in Mathematics With Students Versus With Teachers in Professional Development

After completing a mathematical task in professional development, a teacher may say, "This is just like doing math with my students." Whereas teachers may engage in the same task in professional development and with students and appear to have some similar experiences, for all the reasons above (and likely more), differences in these experiences should be recognized and discussed. We have found Ball and her colleagues' articulation of subject matter knowledge instrumental in this regard. They posited subject matter knowledge as being composed of at least two components: common content knowledge (CCK—the mathematical knowledge and skills teachers hold in common with other professionals using mathemat-ics) and specialized content knowledge (SCK—"mathematical knowledge and skills *unique* to teaching" (Ball et al., 2008, p. 400, emphasis added). CCK is the knowledge necessary to correctly complete a mathematics task posed to students. SCK is the disciplinary knowledge entailed in the mathematical work that teachers do.

Redesigning Our Professional Development on the Basis of Our Noticing

We recognized a need to identify more nuanced and detailed purposes for engaging in mathematics in professional development and to explicitly discuss these purposes with leaders to help them connect the work in RMLL seminars with the understandings they need to teach teachers. To support leaders' learning, we are refining our frameworks for leader practice. Our attention to and interpretation of leaders' thinking has changed our own view of the mathematical work visible in our videocases. We engage in mathematics with teachers in professional development to help them develop not just CCK but SCK as well. To develop SCK, teachers need to engage in explanations that make taken-for-granted ideas in mathematics explicit. Norms for explanation and representational use are vital. These norms are fostered through the orchestration of discussions. In redesigning seminars according to these ideas, we aim to have leaders select and design tasks that engage teachers more comprehensively with the mathematical knowledge they need to teach. Leaders need to know how to specify purposes for doing mathematics in ways that develop teachers' SCK and identify tasks and discussion prompts that immerse teachers in SCK. They need to know how to pursue this purpose when orchestrating discussions and support the development of sociomathematical norms in ways that unpack teachers' highly symbolic or incomplete reasoning. In short, we augmented our initial emphasis on sociomathematical norms with this new emphasis on SCK. We recognized that we were not attaining the quality of mathematical talk in our seminars by focusing only on sociomathematical norms. In the next section, we illustrate how this new emphasis could be reflected in redesigned professional development using the videocase of Janice's method.

Redesigning Professional Development Using the Videocase of Janice's Method

By understanding the distinctions between CCK and SCK, a leader might recognize that, whereas Janice was drawing on CCK to solve the subtraction problem, the discussion could have been extended to explicate how a removal or distance model of subtraction could be used to provide a justification. Consider two ways one could justify Janice's method:

1.   The expression *92 − 56* means "remove 56 from 92." We can make this computation a bit easier if we change the numbers first to 90 − 60. That

gives us 30. But we really began with 92. We therefore had 2 more to begin with (92 = 90 + 2). So we can add that 2 to 30 to give us 32. We removed 60 instead of 56, which is 4 too many. So we need to add 4 to 32 to give us 36.

2. The expression *92 − 56* means "find the distance between 56 and 92 on the number line or find how much more 92 is than 56." If we start at 60 instead of 56, then 60 is 30 away from 90. But we actually need to start at 56. The distance from 56 to 60 is +4. And we need to go beyond 90 to 92. The distance between 90 and 92 is +2. So we need to add 6 to 30 to get a total distance of 36.

Lo et al. (2008) suggested that teachers should include the meaning of the operation in explanations of computational methods to make explicit specialized knowledge for teaching. We have attempted to do that in the preceding justifications, employing first a removal model for subtraction and then a distance model. In the videocase of Janice's method, when the group considered paying the cashier $60, they were playing out a removal model for subtraction. When they represented the method on a number line (see Figure 12.1), the facilitator employed a distance model. Teachers could better understand Janice's method by considering how various contexts and representations are linked to each justification. How could one model the removal justification on the number line? What kinds of word-problem situations map onto a removal, versus distance, model? How do both justifications connect to a symbolic justification, such as the one in Figure 12.2?

We appreciate with new eyes the emphasis in some professional development materials to press for explicit justifications. For example, in the facilitator's guide for the professional development module *Developing Mathematical Ideas: Reasoning Algebraically About Operations* (Schifter, Bastable, Russell, & Monk, 2008) teachers are asked to generate representation-based proofs that must meet several criteria: (a) The meaning of the operation involved is represented in diagrams, manipulatives, or story contexts; (b) the representation can accommodate a class of instances (e.g., all whole numbers); and (c) the conclusion of the claim follows from the structure of the representation. To satisfy these criteria, teachers must make mathematical meanings explicit when they work to justify mathematical statements.

$$92 - 56 = (90 + 2) - (60 - 4)$$

$$92 - 56 = 90 + 2 - 60 - (-4)$$

$$92 - 56 = 90 - 60 + 2 - (-4)$$

$$92 - 56 = 30 + 2 + 4$$

$$92 - 56 = 36$$

FIGURE 12.2   A symbolic representation for 92−56

We propose to redesign tasks for use in professional development for leaders on the basis of what we have learned about the kinds of knowledge teachers need, for example by reimagining the task used with Janice's method. Instead of asking leaders to solve the subtraction problem, we may ask them to generate justifications that rely on the removal (versus distance) model and to compare how to model those justifications with representations such as cubes, the number line, or a hundreds chart; that is, we will encourage leaders to go beyond solving the problem. We believe that by using tasks designed to develop teachers' SCK, we can develop leaders' professional visions for attending to the quality and nature of teachers' explanations that arise from skillful use of the tasks, provide language for communicating with teachers the purposes for engaging in mathematics in professional development, and arm leaders with skills to orchestrate discussions so that teachers unpack and make explicit the important underlying mathematical ideas.

Conclusion

We reiterate that our work is focused on only one aspect of professional development for mathematics teachers: strengthening teachers' content knowledge. Our seminars will not prepare leaders to facilitate other components of mathematics professional development such as developing teachers' pedagogical knowledge and skills. We believe, however, that teachers need to employ specialized subject-matter knowledge for these pedagogical tasks. Because such knowledge is clearly connected with what teachers do in their classrooms, professional development focused on developing SCK is highly relevant for teachers. Through our noticing of leaders' thinking about videocases, we have reframed our work with leaders to focus on SCK rather than on only CCK or sociomathematical norms. By understanding how an SCK-oriented purpose for engaging in mathematics in professional development relates to classroom teaching and being able to articulate that understanding to teachers in accessible ways, leaders will be able to address the pressure to assure relevance in their professional development. Distinguishing between CCK and SCK is a relatively new idea in the field and not necessarily a part of how practitioners frame the work in professional development. In the next phase of our research and development efforts, we will test these ideas by following leaders while they work with teachers in professional development. Through this work, we will examine whether our revised framing will, more powerfully than the current program, develop the professional vision we propose leaders need to support teachers' subject-matter learning.

References

Adler, J., & Davis, Z. (2006). Opening another black box: Researching mathematics for teaching in mathematics teacher education. *Journal for Research in Mathematics Education, 37*, 270–296.

Ball, D. L., Thames, M. H., & Phelps, G. (2008). Content knowledge for teaching: What makes it special? *Journal of Teacher Education, 59*, 389–407.

Carroll, C., & Mumme, J. (2007). *Learning to lead mathematics professional development.* Thousand Oaks, CA: Corwin.

Elliott, R., Kazemi, E., Lesseig, K., Mumme, J., Carroll, C., & Kelley-Petersen, M. (2009). Conceptualizing the work of leading mathematical tasks in professional development. *Journal of Teacher Education, 60*, 364–379.

Erickson, F. (2007). Ways of seeing video: Toward a phenomenology of viewing minimally edited footage. In R. Goldman, R. Pea, B. Barron, & S. J. Denny (Eds.), *Video research in the learning sciences* (pp. 145–155). Mahwah, NJ: Erlbaum.

Even, R. (2008). Facing the challenge of educating educators to work with practicing mathematics teachers. In T. Wood, B. Jaworski, K. Krainer, P. Sullivan, & D. Tirosh (Eds.), *The international handbook of mathematics teacher education: Vol. 4. The mathematics teacher educator as a developing professional* (pp. 57–74). Rotterdam, The Netherlands: Sense.

Goodwin, C. (1994). Professional vision. *American Anthropologist, 96*, 606–633.

Jacobs, V., Lamb, L. C., Philipp, R., & Schappelle, B. (2009, April). *Professional noticing of children's mathematical thinking.* Paper presented at the American Educational Research Association, San Diego, CA.

Lo, J., Grant, T. J., & Flowers, J. (2008). Challenges in deepening prospective teachers' understandings of multiplication through justification. *Journal of Mathematics Teacher Education, 11*, 5–22.

Lord, B. (1994). Teachers' professional development: Critical colleagueship and the roles of professional communities. In N. Cobb (Ed.), *The future of education: Perspectives on national standards in America* (pp. 175–204). New York: The College Board.

Miller, K., & Zhou, X. (2007). Learning from classroom video: What makes it compelling and what makes it hard. In R. Goldman, R. Pea, B. Barron, & S. J. Derry (Eds.), *Video research in the learning sciences* (pp. 321–334). Mahwah, NJ: Erlbaum.

National Research Council (Eds.). (2000). *How people learn: Brain, mind, experience, and school.* Washington, DC: National Academy Press.

Remillard, J. T., & Rickard, C. (2001). *Teacher learning and the practice of inquiry.* Paper presented at the annual meeting of the American Educational Research Association, Seattle, WA.

Schifter, D., Bastable, V., Russell, S. J., & Monk, G. S. (2008). *Developing mathematical ideas: Reasoning algebraically about operations.* Parsippany, NJ: Dale Seymour.

Sherin, M. (2007). The development of teachers' professional vision in video clubs. In R. Goldman, R. Pea, B. Barron, & S. J. Derry (Eds.), *Video research in the learning sciences* (pp. 383–396). Mahwah, NJ: Erlbaum.

Star, J. R., & Strickland, S. K. (2007). Learning to observe: Using video to improve preservice teachers' ability to notice. *Journal of Mathematics Teacher Education, 11*, 107–125.

Stein, M. K., Engle, R. A., Smith, M. S., & Hughes, E. K. (2008). Orchestrating productive mathematical discussions: Five practices for helping teachers move beyond show and tell. *Mathematical Thinking and Learning, 10*, 314–340.

Stevens, R., & Hall, R. (1998). Disciplined perception: Learning to see in technoscience. In M. Lampert & M. L. Blunk (Eds.), *Talking mathematics in school: Studies of teaching and learning* (pp. 107–150). New York: Cambridge University Press.

Stylianides, G. J., & Stylianides, A. J. (2010). Mathematics for teaching: A form of applied mathematics. *Teaching and Teacher Education, 26*, 161–172.

Suzuka, K., Sleep, L., Ball, D. L., Bass, H., Lewis, J., & Thames, M. (2009). Designing and using tasks to teach mathematical knowledge for teaching. In D. S. Mewborn and H. S. Lee (Eds.), *Scholarly practices and inquiry in the preparation of mathematics teachers* (AMTE Monograph 6, pp. 7–23). San Diego, CA: Association of Mathematics Teacher Educators.

Wilson, S. M., & Berne, J. (1999). Teacher learning and the acquisition of professional knowledge: An examination of research on contemporary professional development. In A. Iran-Nejad & P. D. Pearson (Eds.), *Review of research in education* (Vol. 24, pp. 173–209). Washington, DC: American Educational Research Association.

Yackel, E., & Cobb, P. (1996). Sociomathematical norms, argumentation, and autonomy in mathematics. *Journal for Research in Mathematics Education, 27*, 458–477.

13

EXAMINING THE BEHAVIOR OF OPERATIONS

Noticing Early Algebraic Ideas[1]

Deborah Schifter

Third grade teacher Alice Kaye[2] presents events from her classroom:

> We were starting multiplication. Because of the range of learners I have this year, I decided to begin by extending the introduction to the unit to give more of an overview of how we will be thinking about the multiplication sign as "groups of" and "counts of" and "rows of" in order to help them visualize and attach meaning to the multiplication situations they will be encountering. They were so excited to wrap their heads around it, and the discussion was quite lively, leading to Fiona asking, "Is multiplication related to division in the same way that addition is related to subtraction?" Wow! Her question opened up a whole new opportunity to linger with the idea of the four operations and to speculate about how they might be related.
>
> Then, first thing this morning, Todd, a student who really loves math but often keeps his ideas in his head, walked in the door and marched right up to me. "Ms. Kaye, you know that thing you can do with addition when you keep one number whole and add the other one on in parts? Well, I was wondering. Can you do that same thing with multiplication?" I asked him to write his thoughts down. He also agreed to bring his question to the group.

In this message, Ms. Kaye described some of what she had noticed in her students' mathematical talk. She named the issues her students raised which, she realized, would take them into the heart of understanding multiplication—even though the discussion might lead them astray of the specific activities of the planned lesson.

What is it that Ms. Kaye heard in her students' questions? What framed Ms. Kaye's perspective that allows her to recognize the significance of their questions and the opportunities they afford the class? What has she established with her students that brought them to pose questions such as these?

In this chapter, I present episodes from Alice Kaye's class to identify what is essential in what she notices, examine how she follows up, and consider how her values and goals shape her own professional noticing. In particular, I consider the work of noticing in the context of early algebraic reasoning.

Background

Ms. Kaye had been participating in a professional development project focused on generalizations that arise from students' work in arithmetic. For an example of such a generalization, consider an observation made by many elementary school students: Already at first grade, children tend to notice that they can change the order of addends in an addition expression without changing the sum—3 + 4 gives the same answer as 4 + 3; if they determine the answer for 4 + 8, they know the answer for 8 + 4. Young students frequently name this phenomenon *turnarounds* or *switcharounds* or *backwards facts*. In later years, they may identify their observation as the commutative property of addition, represented as $a + b = b + a$, for any numbers a and b.

In the project, teachers learn to make such generalizations a subject of class-room discussion: Does this finding apply to other numbers or just to the numbers we have checked? Does it apply to *all* whole numbers, to fractions, to integers? How do we know? Does it apply to subtraction (to multiplication, to division)? When it does not apply, is there another pattern to be noticed? Such investigations—explicitly articulating generalizations about the behavior of the operations, justifying them, and considering the extent or limits of the generalization—are a central aspect of early algebraic reasoning (Carpenter, Franke, & Levi, 2003; Kaput, Carraher, & Blanton, 2007; Schifter, 1999; Schifter, Monk, Russell, & Bastable, 2007).

At monthly meetings of the project staff and participants, staff members presented to teachers mathematical challenges that involved noticing, articulating, and proving generalizations. For example, in one session, teachers were shown pairs of equivalent addition expressions—6 + 9 = 7 + 8; 12 + 13 = 10 + 15—and then were asked to state a claim: Of what are these equations examples? Although for many teachers it was a challenge to come up with general language—if you subtract some amount from one addend and add the same amount to the other, the total remains the same—some were familiar with this claim. Students frequently make this generalization, which can be justified using manipulatives. The union of two stacks of cubes represents the original expression; moving some cubes from one stack to the other transforms the representation to match the second expression. Because the total number of cubes remains unchanged, the expressions are equivalent. However, because the cubes necessarily represent whole numbers, the domain of justification is whole numbers. The question posed to the teachers in the professional development setting was whether the claim holds for integers, and, once they sorted out the idea and felt confident that it does, they were challenged to come up with a representation to justify the extended claim. Exercises like this were initially new endeavors to participating teachers; the activities required that they work with familiar content from a new perspective.

At the same time, project teachers investigated their own students' thinking about such generalizations. To this end, teachers set problems to their students and recorded the lessons that ensued. On a monthly basis, they selected a passage of classroom discussion to transcribe and wrote a narrative that was based on that dialogue.[3] The act of writing narratives and discussing them with colleagues contributed to teachers attuning their ears, bringing their attention to new facets of student thinking.

While project teachers and staff have pursued this work together, Ms. Kaye and her colleagues have come to see that noticing generalizations about addition, subtraction, multiplication, and division are events that occur frequently in a classroom when lessons are structured to elicit students' ideas. Furthermore, the group has found that investigating such generalizations takes students into the heart of their study of number and operations. At a recent project meeting in which the teachers were discussing what they had been learning in the project, they explained that they used to think of the focus of the K–6 arithmetic curriculum as understanding numbers and learning to compute efficiently. Now they had identified a third objective of equal weight—investigating the behavior of the operations.

Noticing on the part of the teacher—identifying opportunities for student learning—has a particular prominence in the content of early algebra, in which students learn to recognize, articulate, and prove generalizations. In this chapter I present three episodes from Alice Kaye's classroom to illustrate aspects of noticing: (a) noticing opportunities in the curriculum to investigate a generalization about an operation; (b) noticing student behaviors that are critical to establishing a classroom culture of discussing mathematics, in general, and the behavior of the operations, in particular; and (c) noticing students' mathematical observations that can be leveraged for the learning of the whole class.

Noticing Early Algebraic Content in the Curriculum

Late in the project, participating teachers described how, early on, when they were assigned to write a classroom case in which students were focused on a generalization, they had needed to set up a special task to create opportunities for students to generalize. At that time, when their attention was focused on helping their students develop computational proficiency, they had no sense of how all calculation is based on the behavior of the operations. Now they realized that generalizations were just below the surface in almost any lesson—they just had not noticed it before.

To illustrate what is entailed in noticing how generalizations about operations can arise and how easy it is not to notice, consider two third grade classes working on the same problem in early February:

> Oscar had 90 stickers and decided to share some with his friends. He gave 40 stickers away. Becky also had 90 stickers. She gave away 35 stickers. Who has more stickers now?[4]

Class 1[5]

When the teacher presented the problem, the students calculated the number of stickers each child had left and presented their computation strategies. To calculate $90 - 40$, students appreciated how much easier it is to think in terms of tens rather than counting back by ones. To calculate $90 - 35$, some students first subtracted 30 and then subtracted 5 ($90 - 30 = 60$; $60 - 5 = 55$). Others thought about what to add onto 35 to get to 90 ($35 + 5 = 40$; $40 + 50 = 90$; $5 + 50 = 55$). Still others thought of 90 in terms of 8 tens and 10 ones to subtract 3 tens and 5 ones (8 tens $-$ 3 tens $= 5$ tens; 10 ones $-$ 5 ones $= 5$ ones; 5 tens and 5 ones make 55). The class used number lines and interlocking cubes to demonstrate their strategies.

As soon as they had performed the calculations, the students knew that Oscar was left with 50 stickers and Becky, 55. In answer to the question posed in the problem, obviously, Becky has more.

Class 2

Ms. Kaye presented the same problem to her class, but the directions she gave differed from those given in Class 1. After the class determined that the context could be represented as $90 - 40$ and $90 - 35$, Ms. Kaye asked that they *not* perform the subtraction. Which child was left with more stickers?

Clarissa: I think Becky's going to have more left because she's giving away less.
Teacher: What do other people think of that? Paula?
Paula: Well, I think she's right, because it would make sense.
Teacher: Why does that make sense? I love that you're saying that! What sense are you making out of what Clarissa said?
Paula: If you start with the same number, if you take away less, then you'll have more.

The class continued to discuss the question, Ms. Kaye presenting variations of the problem, students using a hundreds chart and trying out language to explain how they knew which child would have more stickers. One student, Manuel, contrasted this context with what would happen if Becky and Oscar were *given* more stickers instead of *giving them away*.

Manuel: Yeah, Becky ends up more . . . and Oscar . . . since he gave away more, so he would end up with less. Like in plussing, he would end up with more, because he *got* more. But he *put away* more, so it's like reversing.

Teacher: Oh, that's interesting. . . . So Manuel's saying, if this was an addition problem and he started with 85 and *got* 27 more, he'd have more, and if she started with 85 and *got* 23 she'd end up with less.

At the end of the lesson, Ms. Kaye asked individual students to state the generalization about subtraction in their own words, curious to see what they understood and what they were still thinking through.

Consider what happened in the two classrooms. Both groups answered the question posed in the problem: Becky was left with more stickers. But the point of teaching is not merely to answer the question presented in the book. Rather, the mathematics problem is designed as a pretext for working on a skill, a concept, or a mathematical connection. Both classrooms did, indeed, work on important third grade content. However, they focused on very different issues.

Class 1 used the problem as a context for working on computation strategies for subtraction. Students were learning how decomposing numbers into tens and ones, rather than counting by ones, leads to more efficient calculation. They examined a variety of strategies based on such decomposition and demonstrated the strategies using different representations. This is important work that, on other days, also takes place in Class 2.

In Class 2, Ms. Kaye recognized that embedded in the problem about Oscar's and Becky's stickers was an idea about the behavior of subtraction, one that her students would profit by pondering and articulating. To have students focus on this idea, she asked them to answer the question *without* performing the calculation.

Clarissa began the discussion by answering the question in the terms of the problem context—"I think Becky's going to have more left because she's giving away less." Paula elaborated on Clarissa's idea by stating a principle about *taking away*, one interpretation of subtraction: "If you start with the same number, if you take away less, then you'll have more."

These students were learning to think about operations not only as instructions to do something with numbers but also as objects of reflection. The behavior of subtraction is different from that of addition—behavior that is consistent and can be noticed and described. The students were developing language for describing generalizations about the whole number system.

To notice the opportunity for early algebraic thinking on the basis of the stickers problem, Ms. Kaye had to recognize the value of students' thinking about the behavior of subtraction without performing the calculation. Her understanding of the task was embedded in a broader perspective that had developed while she learned about the importance of students engaging with generalizations about the operations. Over the previous few years, she had come to see her students' interest in such discussions, their developing sense of control over the number system, and how these investigations supported her students' understanding of and proficiency with more familiar elementary school content. At the beginning of this school year, Ms. Kaye articulated a focus of her class's mathematics work:

> This year, I am planning to examine more closely how my students develop understanding of the operations. I have been thinking about this a lot in the past several years, [especially] how students try to apply generalizations from addition to other operations. This difficulty first pops up when students attempt to decompose and recombine numbers in subtraction as they did with addition; and they run into all kinds of trouble. The confusion is very predictable, and very common for the full range of learners. . . . For example, a common strategy third graders use to solve 62 + 35 is to add by place. They break apart the tens and ones, deal with each separately, and then put them all back together. When they try to apply this same strategy to subtraction, they run into trouble. . . . They see the action of the strategy as something they do with numbers rather than something that is held by, related to, or controlled by the operations.

Teachers whose perspectives are focused on computational fluency but who have not had experiences that help them see how the study of generalizations supports it will not notice the opportunity provided by the stickers problem.

Noticing to Establish a Classroom Culture

Even though Ms. Kaye's third graders knew that they could perform the subtractions in the stickers problem, they understood that they were being asked to pay attention to something else. On the basis of class discussions that had been taking place throughout the year, they knew that the objective was to state a generalization about the mathematics of subtraction; the problem was a starting point, one that provided them with an image of subtraction that would support their thinking.

What were the experiences of Ms. Kaye's students prior to this lesson so that they could participate in this manner by early February? How did she initiate her class into the practice of engaging in discussions to explore the behavior of the operations? Let us visit her classroom early in the school year to gain insight into these questions. In her narrative, Ms. Kaye included observations and comments on her own actions, which are shown below in italics:

I began with a chart that posed the questions (Figure 13.1):

6 + 3 = 9	7 − 2 = 5
What does ADDITION mean?	What does SUBTRACTION mean?

FIGURE 13.1 Questions about addition and subtraction

Teacher: When you hear 6 + 3 = 9, what comes to mind? What picture do you get? What actions do you connect with it?

Clarissa: Addition is when you're going to add things on.

Teacher: And what's another word for *add*? Can you substitute another word for what you mean by *add*? Clarissa, call on someone who thinks she or he can pick up on the thread you started.

At the beginning of this year, as I am trying to establish with my class how we will work together as a learning community, I'm trying to have the people who want to share next actually tie their comments to what's just been said, in order to pick up on the thread of the conversation. I also like students to call on the next person so the interaction goes student to student without having to go through me, the teacher.

Helen: A different word for *add* could be . . . like *plussing on.*

Elizabeth: It's kind of like putting together. *[This is the first idea I heard that seemed to indicate an action rather than "symbol." At this point I started to record on the chart all of the ideas that had been offered thus far.]*

Teacher: Does anyone else have another idea for what *addition* means? Sierra, did you have another idea for what *addition* means?

Sierra: [After a long pause] It's like you have two numbers. . . . [Another long pause] I think I need a little more time.

At this point, I made a big deal of her being courageous and trusting enough to ask for what she needed. I talked about how good it felt to know that already this class was becoming the kind of place where people could do what they needed for themselves as learners and that we'd all be okay with it.

Helen: It's like putting one number on top of the other—like snap cubes.

Teacher: Were you thinking of a model or something you could show with the snap cubes?

Helen began to make two snap cube trains all of one color, but I asked if she could use a different color for each of the numbers up there. She did, and she literally "stuck" the train of three green snap cubes onto the end of the train of six yellow ones.

Teacher: Can anybody show us an action with your body? What does addition look like?

Sierra:	Oh. It's like painting, when you're putting colors together—like blue and red make purple.
Teacher:	So what does the action look like?
Sierra:	You mix them together.
Nancy:	It's like if you put two numbers together, you get a different number; and when you put two colors together, you get a different color, a new color.
Teacher:	Oh. It sounds like you're thinking about combining colors, combining numbers. [Ms. Kaye points to Sierra and then Nancy.] That idea bounced here and there. *[This is another strategy I use (pointing out that the idea "bounced" from one student to another) to help students recognize the power of building ideas together and being learning listeners who work to understand others' ideas and use them to think with.]*
Manuel:	[Gesturing with his hands elevated from varying heights off the floor] I was thinking about something this high plus this other part to make something this high. So it's kind of like you're adding. That's how you get the three numbers.
Teacher:	How does that action work for you?
Matt:	I was thinking, you've got this one, you've got this one, and then you've got this. [He is gesturing with his hands, as though he is holding something in his left hand, something in his right hand, and then he dumps what is in both hands into the middle.]
Teacher:	Is that an action we can use for addition? Here's some, here's some. These all seem like you're combining or bringing it together.

Throughout this lesson in which Ms. Kaye opened the discussion to students' observations, each of her comments, questions, and suggestions was targeted to bring students' attention to particular issues. She approached this lesson with two major goals in mind. First, she was looking for opportunities to help her students learn how to engage in mathematical discussion. But learning to engage in substantive discussion necessarily happens in the context of serious mathematics content. Thus her second goal was to begin the work of investigating the behavior of addition and subtraction. Because she was looking for opportunities to forward these two goals, they shaped what she noticed.

To address the first goal, Ms. Kaye looked for particular behaviors to which she could bring her students' attention to demonstrate *how* to participate. Without interrupting the flow of the discussion, she commented when one student's ideas were responses to those of another. She particularly praised Sierra, who started to speak and then asked to withdraw, emphasizing how important it is for the class to support an individual's learning needs.

At the same time, Ms. Kaye focused on her second goal, tracking the ideas that arose about the meanings of *addition* and *subtraction*. She noticed the language when students shifted from offering synonyms for *add* to describing actions that are modeled by addition. Keeping in mind the tools that would serve them throughout the year, she built on Helen's idea to demonstrate addition with stacks of cubes, offering the suggestion to use different colors to represent the two addends. Similarly, in response to thoughts offered by students, she introduced vocabulary (combining, bringing together) and emphasized actions that would help them relate symbol patterns to meanings of the operations.

Ms. Kaye's goals guided how she noticed opportunities to highlight behaviors, ideas, representations, and vocabulary in the moment of the discussion. She was also registering student thinking to inform future decisions. While the lesson proceeded, Ms. Kaye recorded students' ideas on a poster. At the end of the hour, it looked like the list shown in Figure 13.2:

In her narrative, Ms. Kaye concluded:

> I did learn a bit about how my students see these operations. I still have many questions, though:
>
> • When the parts get combined in addition, is it important to be able to still "see" the separate parts, or is the "paint mixing" analogy okay?
> • Students kept referring to two parts only. Were they just using this as a simplified case, or does it reveal something about the way they see addition?
> • Will this discussion form a basis for helping students see other forms of subtraction? Currently, they seem comfortable and familiar with subtraction as removal; but what will it take for them to see it differently, for example as comparison?
> • Currently, we are working on "How many more?" problems. Students are solving problems by using missing addends or by subtracting. I'm wondering how, and if, I should/could explicitly frame some of this in terms of looking at the relationship between addition and subtraction. In the curriculum, this comes later; but I'm wondering about "pushing" a bit on it at this time, just to see if students have thought about it as a different way of thinking about subtraction than we originally captured on our chart.

$6 + 3 = 9$ What does ADDITION mean?	$7 - 2 = 5$ What does SUBTRACTION mean?
* You're adding on * You're plussing on * You're putting together * You're putting one number on top of the other * You're combining the parts * You're bringing together the parts * You're heaping on the parts (to form the whole)	* You're going down * You're pulling it apart * You're separating the parts from the whole * You're taking away one part * You're pulling apart the part * You're tossing out the part * You're dropping one of the parts from the whole thing

FIGURE 13.2 Students' ideas about addition and subtraction

At the end of the lesson, Ms. Kaye reviewed her students' mathematical ideas with an eye toward how they connected to her mathematical goals. On the basis of this classroom discussion, she had more specific questions to guide her inquiry into their understanding of addition and subtraction and to inform her decisions about emphases of upcoming lessons. What she noticed in her students' thinking was shaped by her knowledge of the content of her curriculum, her understanding of the major concepts they needed to work through, and her commitment to build on the knowledge and ideas they currently expressed.

Noticing Opportunities in Students' Observations

In mid-February the class began a unit on multiplication. As mentioned at the beginning of the chapter, at the start of school the next morning Todd walked up to Ms. Kaye and said, "You know that thing you can do with addition when you keep one number whole and add the other one on in parts? Well, I was wondering. Can you do that same thing with multiplication?"

In Todd's question, Ms. Kaye noticed an opportunity for her class—noticing that was shaped by her values, her mathematical goals, and the history of mathematical discussions held among these students.

Among her values was that her students work together as a community of thinkers. They should be willing to offer their ideas and consider those of their classmates. In the area of mathematics, she particularly valued that they become curious about the structure of the number system. By bringing Todd's question to the class, she would be demonstrating the potential of students' questions and provide an opportunity for her students to investigate together their classmate's idea.

Todd's question arose just when the class was beginning a unit on multiplication. In her first lessons, Ms. Kaye emphasized various representations for multiplication and contexts in which multiplication is applied. Later the class would work on calculation strategies for multiplication, with particular emphasis on applying the distributive property. She was especially alert to students' tendencies to apply addition strategies in multiplicative situations and intended to highlight the different behaviors of these operations. In Todd's question, Ms. Kaye noticed the opportunity it would provide to move forward with these particular mathematical goals.

Furthermore, Ms. Kaye noticed that Todd's question was framed in the context of the discussions about addition and subtraction the class had been engaged in for the past few months. The students worked on strategies for computation and demonstrated their strategies with cubes, diagrams, and number lines. They identified generalizations that could be made about the behavior of addition and explained why addition behaves that way. When looking at subtraction, students often commented that they were surprised by the patterns that arose; they had been expecting patterns that looked more like those in addition. For example, when 1 was added to one addend and subtracted from the other, the sum remained the same. But when 1 was added to the first number in a subtraction expression (the minuend) and subtracted from the other (the subtrahend), the difference changed by 2. These discussions highlighted that the patterns they noticed when working on addition were about the operation of addition rather than about the nature of numbers under any operation. For each operation, they used representations and story contexts to make sense of why the operation behaved as it did.

Among the addition strategies that were discussed was that one can keep the first addend whole and add the second on in parts. For example, when adding 37 + 25, one can separate 25 into 20 and 5, add 37 + 20 = 57, and add 57 + 5 to get the final result of 62. In later years, students may notice that this is an application of the associative property of addition: 37 + (20 + 5) = (37 + 20) + 5.

After the many discussions in which the class had compared addition and subtraction, Ms. Kaye noted that Todd was now asking about comparing addition and multiplication. He had been thinking about *whether* or *how* this strategy for addition (decomposing the second addend) applies to multiplication. She decided that Todd should bring his question to the class later that afternoon:

Teacher: This morning, Todd came into school with a really interesting question that yesterday's discussion got him wondering about. Todd, could you say your question again?

Todd: I was wondering if you could do the same thing in multiplication that you could in addition. You know how you can add one number on in parts? Well, I tried it this morning [with multiplication], and it looked like you could.

Teacher: Can you give us an example of how this works in addition?

Todd: Like 53 + 38—you could add 7 from the 38 and get 60, and then plus 30 is 90 and then plus 1 is 91.

Helen: But that's just addition.

Teacher: Right. So, what *is* the thing that Todd is talking about here that we can do in addition? Don't worry yet about what he's asking about multiplication. Let's see if we can be sure we know what he's saying about addition first.

While the discussion unfolded, Ms. Kaye worked hard to separate out the two ideas Todd had brought together in his question: (a) Given two numbers to add, one can add the second number on in parts, and (b) one might be able to do something similar when multiplying two numbers. She wanted to ensure that all the students understood the first idea before moving to the second.

Hannah: I think he's trying to say . . . he knows that he can break stuff up in parts to get the answer.

Megan: So, I was just wondering . . . could you say your idea again? I don't really understand what you're asking.

Todd:	Yeah, like, can you start with one number whole, then add on the other number in parts in multiplication? [Megan and others say, "Oh!"]
Megan:	[restating his question] So, you're asking if you can break up one of the numbers and add it on in parts?
Todd:	Yeah.
Teacher:	So we're not really talking about multiplication yet. He knows he can do this thing in addition. What I want to make sure is that everybody knows what thing he's talking about in addition. Then his question about multiplication will be clearer.
Elizabeth:	I think it's kind of like trying to get to a more brain-friendly number, maybe? Breaking it up by brain-friendly numbers and then you add on the extras so you first can get to a 10, and then you add on all the other parts because you want to get to a brain-friendly number.

Even while Ms. Kaye was trying to focus on Todd's premise about addition, she diverged from that commitment to highlight Elizabeth's comment, which illuminated an important aspect of the larger idea:

Teacher:	Oh, so Elizabeth is pointing out here that there might be something behind Todd's question of, "Can I do this thing, that I know I can do in addition, with multiplication?" She's saying that the way that we do this in addition, and the reason we do it, is to end up with convenient numbers. I actually think, Elizabeth, that you raise a good point for Todd. You're thinking about why would you want to break the numbers apart in multiplication? Is it for the same reason as you would want to do it in addition?
Todd:	Yeah, that is what I was trying this morning.
Addison:	Well, I have a little bit different question. . . . How would you do that? Because, it's . . . I mean multiplication and addition. . . . Well, when we looked at those connections yesterday, [we talked about how] they are kind of both, in a way, adding; except multiplication . . . like . . . like if you were saying 53 + 38 and 53 × 38, it would just give you a whole different answer. How would you do that . . . to take it apart in multiplication? Because I was trying to do that, and it's hard.
Manuel:	Todd is saying, can you break multiplication into parts?
Teacher:	And Addison was saying, even though multiplication and addition seem related, they're different enough that, Todd's a little worried, that when you do that breaking apart, maybe it's going to go wacky.
Addison:	In a way, it is hard, because I tried it, and even after I did the multiplication I had to add it.

Addison had already been testing an idea similar to Todd's. However, before moving on to test Todd's idea on a multiplication problem, Ms. Kaye still wanted to be sure that everyone was clear about what he had claimed about addition:

Teacher: Todd, and classmates . . . are you okay with the first part of what Todd's question is, which is "You know that thing we can do in addition?" Is this okay for "the thing we can do in addition?" Are people all right with what this is referring to? Is there anybody who isn't sure what this is about?

After everyone in the class said that they understood the point about addition, Ms. Kaye was ready to move into a multiplication example:

Teacher: So, Todd, can you say it one more time for us?

Todd: We can keep one number whole and break up the other number in parts so we get to a brain-friendly number.

Teacher: Todd, now can you give us an example in multiplication that we can use to look at your question?

Todd: Five times four. *[This is one of the problems from the work the class had done earlier in the day.]*

Teacher: So, now, Todd's question would be "Can I break up 5 × 4 in a way that's going to help me make this more brain-friendly?" What do you think?

Todd: I think if you do 5 × 2 (and 5 two times is 10), and then you have two more; and then 10 × 2 is 20.

Teacher: So Todd is saying he thinks if he had five groups of 4 *[and, at this point, I began to write the equation as I said the words, 5 × 4 = (5 × 2) + (5 × 2)],* then he could do 5 two times and then another 5 two times, and he'd have 20. Would it be true that, if he had 5 groups of 2 and then another 5 groups of 2, he would have the same as 5 groups of 4?

Until now, exactly what Todd had meant by "break up the other number in parts" or what he would do with the parts was not clear. In his example of 5 × 4, he suggested doing 5 × 2 twice to get 10 × 2 = 20. Ms. Kaye chose to record his thoughts as 5 × 4 = (5 × 2) + (5 × 2), bringing the notation into a form that would be helpful to her students while they worked on other problems.[6]

Thus, Todd's question brought the class into its first investigation of the distributive property of multiplication over addition. In the coming weeks and months, the students would have numerous opportunities to view this property from a variety of perspectives. They would draw groups, create arrays, and write story problems for multiplication. They would work on two-digit multiplication problems and decide how to use smaller facts to find the products of larger numbers. They would contrast what happened when they added 1 to an addend with what happened when they added 1 to a factor.

However, at this time, not all students were convinced that the equation Ms. Kaye had written on the easel was true. Thinking about the number patterns, Sierra commented:

Sierra: But that would go over the amount. Wouldn't you have to change the first number too? How could you keep the 5?

Sierra had raised a question that reflected a common misunderstanding of the mathematics of multiplication. She expected that both factors needed to be decomposed to maintain equality. That is, just as 5 + 4 = (4 + 1) + (2 + 2) = (4 + 2) + (1 + 2), she expected that 5 × 4, which equals (4 + 1) × (2 + 2), must be equal to (4 × 2) + (1 × 2). This misunderstanding is one that bedevils many students throughout their educations. Students frequently but erroneously claim that, say, 16 × 28 is equal to (10 × 20) + (6 × 8) or, in the context of algebra classes, that (a + b)(c + d) = ac + bd.

Ms. Kaye chose to end the discussion at that point by acknowledging that Sierra's question is a very important one to consider. She rephrased the question for the class: "What do you have to pay attention to when you break up the numbers in multiplication that's different from what you have to consider when you're working with addition?"

Ms. Kaye concluded her narrative by writing:

> For this day, I felt we had gone as far as we could go until students had more experience with multiplication. I knew that students would be working a lot with multiplication problems that might cause them to think about how they could break the numbers apart in ways that could make the original problem easier to solve. For now, I was glad that Todd's question would continue to linger for the class.

When Todd had come to Ms. Kaye with his question, she realized that she could use it to frame a lesson for the whole class. Todd's observation would provide a mechanism for moving the class into questions at the heart of their investigations into the behavior of multiplication. While the conversation progressed, Ms. Kaye noticed when student comments provided occasions to highlight major ideas to which she wanted her students to attend. In particular, she used Sierra's confusion as an opportunity to pose a question that was a theme for the year: How are addition and multiplication different?

Conclusion

While children learn about the four basic operations—understanding the kinds of situations the operations can model, sorting out various means of representing them, and coming to understand how to compute efficiently—they observe and comment upon regularities in the number system. Several researchers (Carpenter et al., 2003; Schifter, Bastable, & Russell, 2008; Schifter, Bastable, Russell, Riddle, & Seyferth, 2008) have helped teachers make such observations the object of investigations in which students work to verbalize the generalizations they notice and then take on the questions "Does this hold for all numbers?" and "How do you know?"

Through such work with teachers, researchers have found evidence that students' engagement with early algebra can translate into greater computational fluency. Indeed, teacher collaborators have reported that these algebraic practices—stating generalizations about the number system and proving them—support *all* students: challenging those who tend to be ahead of their classmates even while helping struggling students gain access to basic arithmetic principles (Russell, 2008; Schifter, Russell, & Bastable, 2009).

As illustrated by Alice Kaye's example, noticing is a particularly prominent activity when one engages with early algebra in this way:

- Teachers notice that the behavior of the operations is important content to investigate. They notice where opportunities to engage in this content exist in their curricula.
- Teachers notice and comment on student behaviors that contribute to a culture of collaboration. In this way, the teacher brings students' attention to ways of working together to become a mathematics community.
- Teachers notice when students' comments provide opportunities to highlight ideas, introduce tools that support reasoning (representations, story contexts, vocabulary, forms of notation), or pose questions to ponder.
- Teachers notice and evaluate the ideas of individual students and the class as a whole to determine how to build on student thinking in future lessons.

More generally, when mathematics teaching is focused on students' conceptual understanding and when classroom discussion is a major mechanism for learning, what teachers notice in their students' communication is essential. It is what teachers notice and how they respond that guide students' attention to what they are to learn.

Professional development can provide the setting for developing teachers' noticing. In such a context, new mathematical domains can become visible to teachers, opening the potential for noticing that content in the curriculum and in students' ideas. Furthermore, the study of print and videocases and examination of student work (as illustrated in other chapters of this book) help to alert teachers to conceptual issues students work through and attune their listening for how students communicate their thinking.

However, the episodes from Alice Kaye's classroom illustrate additional dimensions of teacher noticing that are not captured in the professional development setting. In the moment of teaching, noticing is guided by what the teacher is trying to teach and is followed by an action. The teacher presents tasks designed to address particular mathematics content, which constrains her noticing. She notices with intentionality—listening for, attending to, and tracking student thinking about particular concepts. She watches for opportunities to build on students' thinking, bringing their attention to or emphasizing new ideas, representations, or questions. She gathers information about her students' understanding to inform her actions in the moment as well as decisions to be made for future lessons.

At the same time, a teacher can open her antennae wide, noticing her students' thinking about various issues throughout the day. While Ms. Kaye and her students were getting ready for the school day, Todd told her about what he had been thinking, and Ms. Kaye noticed that his idea could be framed to forward the learning of the class. Holding in mind the variety of goals a teacher holds for her students—goals in different content areas, goals for the classroom community, and goals for individuals—a teacher can notice which ideas or behaviors can be highlighted and molded to bring the class into her agenda.

On the last day of school, Ms. Kaye had one final conversation with her students about their work in mathematics throughout the year. They started to discuss a new generalization that applies to addition and then wondered whether it applies to other operations. They saw that it did not, and so Ms. Kaye presented her class with some equations that illustrate a different, analogous generalization that can be made about multiplication. The session ended with Addison's saying, "I just got this idea. I haven't completely developed it yet."

When Ms. Kaye wrote her narrative, she concluded with the following comments:

> What a perfect place to end the year! They are still wondering, still pursuing ideas related to the operations, still shifting between knowing and being uncertain; and yet they are so comfortable with it. There is so much more for them to explore, and they seem excited by the prospects that await them. Moving from numbers to operations has been a big shift in their work (and mine), and so I shouldn't be surprised by the way they move back and forth between knowing and not knowing. Through this work, students have become more confident as they use related problems to become more computationally fluent. I have seen how they activate their understandings about the operations as they compute, as if they know something, as insiders, about the nature of each operation. As Sierra said, "At first we were scared by numbers, but then, as we got all our ideas flowing [about the operations], we realized we could take over the numbers. We controlled the numbers."

Notes

1   The work on which this chapter is based was undertaken as part of the project Foundations of Algebra in the Elementary and Middle Grades, directed by Susan Jo Russell, Deborah Schifter, and Virginia Bastable, and funded in part by the National Science Foundation through Grant No. ESI0550176 to TERC. Any opinions, findings, conclusions, or recommendations expressed here are those of the authors and do not necessarily reflect the views of the National Science Foundation.

A great debt is owed to the teachers who met monthly to share what they were learning and how their practices were changing: Anne Marie O'Reilly, Lara Ramsey, Karen Schweitzer, Pam Szczesny, and Jan Szymaszek. Also thanks to the Professional Development Study Group for helpful feedback on earlier drafts of this chapter.
2 Alice Kaye and the names of her students in this chapter are pseudonyms.
3 The transcripts in this chapter, descriptions of classroom events, Ms. Kaye's commentary, and her reflections are all drawn from Ms. Kaye's classroom narratives.
4 *Investigations in Number, Data, and Space*, Grade 3, Unit 3, "Collections and Travel Stories," p. 170.
5 The story of Class 1 is a composite drawn from reports from mathematics coaches who described how several teachers treated the problem.
6 Another way to record Todd's idea would be $5 \times 4 = 5 \times (2 \times 2) = (5 \times 2) \times 2 = 10 \times 2$, illustrating the associative property of multiplication. Ms. Kaye has chosen to use his thinking to illustrate the distributive property instead.

References

Carpenter, T. P., Franke, M., & Levi, L. (2003). *Thinking mathematically*. Portsmouth, NH: Heinemann.

Kaput, J., Carraher, D., & Blanton, M. (Eds.) (2007). *Algebra in the early grades*. Mahwah, NJ: Erlbaum.

Russell, S. J. (2008). Computational fluency: Working with a struggling student. *Connect, 22*(1), 8–12.

Schifter, D. (1999). Reasoning about operations: Early algebraic thinking, grades K through 6. In L. V. Stiff & F. R. Curcio (Eds.), *Mathematical reasoning, K–12: 1999 yearbook of the National Council of Teachers of Mathematics* (pp. 62–81). Reston, VA: National Council of Teachers of Mathematics.

Schifter, D., Bastable, V., & Russell, S. J. (2008). *Developing mathematical ideas casebook, facilitator's guide, and videotape for reasoning algebraically about operations*. Parsippany, NJ: Pearson Learning Group.

Schifter, D., Bastable, V., Russell, S. J., Riddle, M., & Seyferth, L. (2008). Algebra in the K–5 classroom: Learning opportunities for students and teachers. In C. Greenes (Ed.), *Algebra and algebraic thinking in school mathematics: 2008 yearbook of the National Council of Teachers of Mathematics* (pp. 263–277). Reston, VA: National Council of Teachers of Mathematics.

Schifter, D., Monk, G. S., Russell, S. J., & Bastable, V. (2007). Early algebra: What does understanding the laws of arithmetic mean in the elementary grades? In J. Kaput, D. Carraher, & M. Blanton (Eds.), *Algebra in the early grades* (pp. 413–447). Mahwah, NJ: Erlbaum.

Schifter, D., Russell, S. J., & Bastable, V. (2009). Early algebra to reach the range of learners. *Teaching Children Mathematics, 16*, 230–237.

SECTION IV
Conclusion

14

NOTICING MATTERS. A LOT. NOW WHAT?

Alan H. Schoenfeld

The editors and authors of this volume have made a compelling case: Noticing matters. It is impossible to read this volume without coming to the conclusion that what teachers attend to as they teach is highly consequential. Given this, the next logical questions become: How and why does it matter, and what can be done about it?

I begin with two vignettes about noticing that suggest my answers to these questions. They both took place in the context of the National Research Council's Strategic Educational Research Partnership's (SERP's) collaboration with the San Francisco Unified School District (see http://www.serpinstitute.org/about/field-sites/san-francisco.php).

The SERP mathematics partnership in San Francisco includes a small number of teachers, researchers, and administrators who meet on a regular basis with the goal of collectively developing a deeper understanding of productive teaching practices in middle school mathematics. For multiple reasons our emphasis is on word problems in algebra: students have a hard time making the transition from arithmetic to algebra, word problems cause students (especially second language learners) significant difficulties, and performance on such tasks is a central component of California's high stakes testing system.

We decided at the beginning of the project that we would anchor our discussions in examples of student thinking. Thus we provided each of our collaborating teachers with a digital tape recorder and agreed upon the following. Each teacher would pick a student in whom he or she was interested and would interview the student while the student worked on a typical problem from that year's curriculum.

Vignette 1: Coming to Grips With Student Understandings

One seventh grade teacher chose to interview a particular student because of her feeling that the student was misplaced in her class. A recent district initiative had placed all seventh graders in pre-algebra. The district's goal, part of an attempt to undo the deleterious effects of tracking, was to ready all students for state-mandated eighth grade algebra. However, students with widely varying backgrounds were thus in seventh grade mathematics classes. This student's homework had never revealed more than "chicken scratches on the page," providing no evidence that the student was following the material.

The teacher decided to interview the student in order to get a better sense of what she knew and did not know. For the interview she chose a problem straight from the curriculum:

> A five-pound box of sugar costs $1.80 and contains 12 cups of sugar. Marella and Mark are making a batch of cookies. The recipe calls for 2 cups of sugar. Determine how much the sugar for the cookies costs.

This task is linguistically complex, especially for second language students. They must understand what a batch of cookies is and recognize that one recipe produces one batch; they must then sort through the verbiage in the problem to identify the underlying mathematical relationships involved. Many students had had difficulty with this problem, and the teacher expected this particular student to struggle. She asked the student to read through the problem and then to think out loud as she worked on its solution. By way of preface, the student's written work is shown in Figure 14.1. This is the kind of evidence the teacher typically has available, to judge what students understand.

Here is what occurred in the interview.

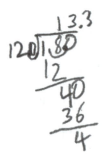

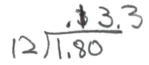

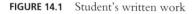

FIGURE 14.1 Student's written work

The student read the problem and immediately said, "So it'll be 1 dollar and 80 cents divided by 12." She then produced the computations given in Figure 14.1. Looked at by themselves, the figures are somewhat difficult to parse! (Why is 18 − 12 = 4? Just what is the number .13.3? Why is 13.3 + 13.3 = .26.6?)

The student stopped to look over what she had done. The teacher asked if she thought the answer was right, and the student said no. As the student began to redo the computation ("So 12 into 1.80 is . . .") the following dialogue took place:

T: So you like a dollar 80 divided by 12. Do you think that's right?
S: Yeah.
T: So how did you know to do that?
S: Because 12 is, the 12 cups of sugar is 1 dollar and 80 cents. It will cost 1 dollar 80 cents . . . so I got how much it will cost for one cup of sugar, so then add one cup to another cup to get this (pointing to the .26.6).
T: OK, good, I get that. So now what are you trying to figure out?
S: What I did wrong . . . the cup. [Points to the 13.3.]
T: And how do you know you did something wrong?
S: Because the answer's too much; it's like over the 1.80.
T: Oh, I see, so 2 cups of sugar couldn't cost more than 12 cups of sugar?
S: Yeah.
T: So that's how you know it's wrong. So what are you going to do to figure out what you did wrong?
S: Go back and check it.

The dialogue makes it clear that the student was right on target conceptually. She knew to divide $1.80 by 12 to get the cost of one cup of sugar, and to double it to get the cost of the sugar needed for the recipe. Moreover, and unlike many students, she checked the reasonableness of her answer. She knew she had done something wrong because the numerical value she had obtained did not fit the conditions of the problem.

When the teacher brought this tape to the SERP meeting, she was radiant. "I thought the student didn't belong in the class," she said. "All I'd seen were chicken scratches on the page. But now I see she totally gets it conceptually; she just has problems with the algorithms. She definitely belongs in the class. I can do remediation on the algorithms."

The teacher paused, shook her head, and then said, "I had a completely wrong impression of her. . . . Oh my God, I'm going to have to interview all my students!"

Vignette 2: Changing Instruction on the Basis of What Noticing Reveals

At about the same time, one of the SERP sixth grade teachers interviewed one of his students about the following problem:

> A dragonfly, the fastest insect in the world, can fly 50 feet in 2 seconds. How long does it take the dragonfly to fly 375 feet?

The student's first comment came immediately after reading the problem:

S: So, first I'll divide 375 with 50, and then—wait . . . [5-second pause] or I will multiply . . . like 50 . . . no, wait, now what? This is dividing . . . 5 times what can get 8?

T: So you're thinking divide . . .

S: I'm not understanding. Do you multiply 5 times the number first or is it the big number, this is 50, into it first?

T: Well, let's see, what are the quantities we're looking at here?

S: The numbers, like 375.

T: And what are you trying to find out?

S: Trying to find out how many seconds can the dragonfly . . . wait . . . [confused] in how many seconds can it fly in 375 feet. . . . Wait. How many seconds will it take it to fly 375 feet?

T: OK . . . why don't you draw a picture of what you think is going on? It might be helpful . . .

S: [Draws a picture of a road, a town, a little dragonfly.]

The teacher tries to use the student's picture as a way of focusing on the information given in the problem statement. They discuss what they know and what they want to find, and how to represent those quantities in the student's picture. Having co-constructed a representation with the information clearly labeled, the teacher continues:

T: So that looks good. So what are you gonna do next?

S: I have an idea, maybe 50 times 375 divided by 2? . . . [5-second pause] That won't work.

The student does the computation and sees that it goes nowhere. The teacher tries again:

T: What are we . . . once again, what are we trying to find out?

S: How many seconds will it take the dragonfly to fly 375 feet?

T: OK. And we know what? We know what so far?

S: It can fly 50 feet in 2 seconds.

T: All right. . . . What do you think? . . . Well, if it flew, it could go fly 50 feet . . .

S: In 4 seconds it would be 100 feet, in 6 it would be 200, 8 would be 300, so 9 would be 350, there's 25 missing, so 1/2 of it to get 375 so 9 1/2 seconds to get 375.

It was not until this exchange—6 minutes and 11 seconds into working the problem!—that the student's work was actually grounded in an understanding of the problem situation. Although he lost track of the units, inadvertently switching to a rate of 100 feet in 2 seconds and thus arriving at the wrong answer, the way he approached the problem showed that he finally understood both the given information and what he was supposed to find.

This exchange was catalytic for the group in two ways. First, everyone who heard the exchange recognized the student's behavior. The student rushed into combining the numbers without having made sense of the problem. Some of those present called this "the rush to compute," others called it "number mashing;" but, whatever you call it, all the teachers said that their students did it. This was a major problem. Second, this problem—once raised to the level of conscious awareness on the part of the group—was seen as sufficiently serious that it called for a solution. After brainstorming a number of different approaches, the group came up with a rather elegant way to address the issue. We call it "problem stems." We begin by giving the students some information, such as:

A dragonfly, the fastest insect in the world, can fly 50 feet in 2 seconds.

Then, rather than posing a problem and asking the students to solve it (thus providing an opportunity for number mashing), the idea is to compel the students to make sense of the given information. One way to do so is to ask the following:

Make up a meaningful mathematics problem that uses this information.

The problems that the students construct provide teachers with a chance to see what the students consider to be important in the situation and how they put the mathematics together—a wonderful opportunity for noticing!

This technique was adapted by eighth grade teachers for use with more complex problems. For example, the problem

Members of a senior class held a car wash to raise funds for their senior prom. They charged $3 to wash a car and $5 to wash a pickup truck or SUV. They earned a total of $275 by washing a total of 75 vehicles. How many cars did they wash? How many trucks or SUVs?

can be broken into a series of exercises, in which the relevant information is revealed one chunk of information at a time:

"Members of a senior class held a car wash to raise funds for their senior prom. They charged $3 to wash a car and $5 to wash a pickup truck or SUV. Make up a meaningful mathematics problem that uses this information."

. . .

"Now, suppose I tell you that they earned a total of $275. Make up a problem using all the information you have so far."

. . .

"What if I also told you they washed a total of 75 vehicles? What questions can you ask now? How would you think about solving them?"

. . .

"Here's the question the book asks. Given all the information you have, how many cars did they wash? How many trucks or SUVs?"

As in the case of the dragonfly "stem problem," framing the question in this way precludes the students' learned behavior of jumping into computations. In addition, the teachers expand on the use of stems by asking and discussing questions about the problems the students have crafted:

Can you draw a graph or diagram to interpret this situation? What method did you use to solve it?
Is the problem you made up easy or hard? What makes it easy or hard?
What is the (given) problem, in your own words?
What answer do you have, if any?
Does your answer make sense? Why or why not?

Pursuing these questions helps the students to build habits of mind that are focused on mathematical sense making.

Connections and Reflections

In what follows I build on the vignettes presented above and make explicit links to the chapters in this volume.

Noticing Is Consequential—What You See and Don't See Shapes What You Do and Don't Do

The consequential character of noticing in Vignette 1 is obvious—for the student (who remained in the class and received the help she needed), for the teacher (who began to develop a different perspective on her students and how to understand their understandings), and for her students (who, in general, began to experience a form of instruction that was more closely aligned to their understandings). Likewise, the noticing highlighted in Vignette 2 brought to light a major student problem. Once that problem was out in the open, it could be dealt with. The flip side of both vignettes is that, if the issues in each of them (the student's competency in Vignette 1 and the very common maladaptive practice in Vignette 2) had not come to light, they would not have been addressed. The consequences in both cases would have been serious.

The importance of noticing was made dramatically clear in Erickson's description of Ms. Wright's teaching, in Chapter 2. A group of veteran teachers was watching tapes of the first day of Ms. Wright's instruction. A large number of the first graders in Ms. Wright's kindergarten/first grade class had been students in the class she had taught the previous year:

> Mrs. Tobin, Mrs. Smith, and Mrs. Meijer were very skeptical that learning could be taking place [in Ms. Wright's classroom], because from their points of view "order" had not been firmly established first.
>   This conviction was so strong that, as the group watched a video clip of the first reading group held with first graders in September in Ms. Wright's room . . . [they] overlooked a crucial fact that was apparent [to others] in the clip. . . . *All the children in the reading group were reading aloud from their books, fluently, and with apparent understanding—and this was happening on the first day of the new school year!* (In the 1970s and 1980s it was still unusual for kindergartners to be taught to read.)
>
>   Erickson (this volume, chapter 2, p. 31)

The teachers were so focused on issues of order and discipline that they failed to notice that the students were amazingly competent! Consider what the consequences for Ms. Wright and her students might have been, had it not been for the fact that others in the project pointed out this seemingly obvious fact!

In one way or another, each of the book's foundational chapters highlights the consequential character of noticing. (Implications from the empirical chapters will be discussed below.) Mason notes that "*awareness* is what enables action" (this volume, chapter 3, p. 45). As Miller notes in his discussion of *situation awareness*, skilled teachers

> maintain attention to student understanding at the same time they are enacting a lesson, . . . show more systematic scanning patterns of students, whereas novices should be more likely to focus on a smaller sample of students while ignoring others

and are "quicker to identify situations (misbehavior, lack of understanding, disruptive activity) that require intervention" (this volume, chapter 4, p. 55). B. Sherin and Star's framing of "noticing as the selection of noticed-things from sense data" (this volume, chapter 5, p. 69) includes action as a natural consequence of noticing: After the teacher has attended to some element of sensory data in the classroom, the teacher "takes some action based on an NT [noticed-thing]." Of course, the teacher may or may not have the tools to deal successfully with what has been observed—but, if signs of potential progress or problems are not observed at all, there is far less hope of successful outcomes! For these reasons and more, M. Sherin, Russ, and Colestock emphasize the role of noticing as a significant component of expertise: "This book as a whole and the individual chapters within it are all predicated on the belief that this process—what has been called *noticing*—is a key component of teaching expertise and of mathematics teaching expertise in particular" (this volume, chapter 6, p. 79).

Noticing Is Important Because It Can Lead to Changed Practices

What makes noticing consequential, of course, is that people act on what they notice. That was the clear "moral" of the vignettes that began this chapter. The teacher's decision to keep the girl who produced "chicken scratches" in her class and to provide remediation for her made a big difference for the girl's future, and in the way the teacher looked at student work from that point on. The observation that students "rush to compute" or "mash numbers" without taking the time to understand the problems they are working on led the SERP team to create a series of instructional methods aimed at addressing that significant problem. Moreover, as Mason notes (this volume, chapter 3), the more sustained, systematic, and reflective the noticing process is, the more likely it is to produce beneficial change.

Each of the empirical chapters in this volume is either premised on or makes these assumptions. Jacobs, Lamb, Philipp, and Schappelle begin with a characterization of teaching as "a fluid process requiring extensive and critical decision making on the basis of reading a situation in a specific moment" (this volume, chapter 7, p. 97) and go on to document the relationship between emerging expertise and the development of enhanced noticing. Star, Lynch, and Perova (this volume, chapter 8) document the changes in the perceptions (and, presumably, the competencies) of preservice teachers as a result of having been enrolled in a semester long secondary mathematics methods course. The video clubs described by van Es are a form of professional development—and thus aimed at productive change, using noticing as a primary mechanism for achieving it. Van Es (this volume, chapter 9) posits and provides evidence in favor of a particular kind of developmental trajectory of noticing student thinking, and the impact of video clubs in helping to move teachers along that trajectory. Similarly, Santagata's chapter title announces her intentions (this volume, chapter 10). Her lesson analysis framework is aimed at improving classroom lessons, in that observations of student work are tied to discussions of how to react to it. Goldsmith and Seago (this volume, chapter 11), also in the context of professional development work, examine the ways in which teachers do or do not use evidence in forming their judgments about students and classrooms, and how teachers can be induced to make more and better use of the evidence potentially at their disposal.

With their focus on teacher leaders' mathematical knowledge, Kazemi, Elliott, Mumme, Carroll, Lesseig and Kelley-Petersen (this volume, chapter 12) add a necessary ingredient to this picture: After you notice something, you must have the mathematical and pedagogical wherewithal to deal with it! This point is echoed powerfully in the story that begins Schifter's chapter (this volume, chapter 13). Imagine the mathematical competence required to deal productively with the third grader's question, "Is multiplication related to division in the same way that addition is related to subtraction?" This is a decidedly nontrivial mathematical question on its own—and framing a productive conversation around it with third graders is a real challenge! And there is more.

In what follows, my goal is to provide a larger orienting frame for discussions of noticing, and to point to some potentially fertile arenas for investigation.

Teachers' Noticing Is Intimately Tied to Their Orientations (Including Beliefs) and Resources (Including Knowledge)

More broadly, teachers' decision making—of which noticing is a critical component—is a function of their resources, goals, and orientations.

One of my favorite videotapes is described on pages 239–247 of Malcolm Gladwell's (2008) book *Outliers*. Renee, who is at the center of the story, works for some time at a mathematical impossibility—she is trying to construct a vertical line using the slope-intercept form of an equation, $y = mx + b$—until, by dint of hard work and perseverance, she comes to realize both that it is impossible and why it is impossible.

The "back story" is that Renee had had bad experiences with mathematics. She had taken algebra four times, but remembered almost none of it. She had been invited into our lab to play with our newly developed graphing software and had, quite accidentally, set herself an impossible task. My programmer called me in, and I worked with Renee for about an hour. She had decided that $y = x$ made an angle of 45 degrees from the horizontal, so $y = 2x$ should make an angle of 90 degrees; when that did not work, she doubled again and then again, disturbed at the fact that the lines were not behaving as she thought they should. We began a long and slow exploration of the properties of lines. She dredged up the term "slope" from memory, thought about rise and run, and tried to use them. She tried a slope of 100, 100 up and 1 over. And then, after a lot of thinking, she got it.

> Oh, it's any number up, and zero over. It's any number divided by zero! A vertical line is anything divided by zero—and that's an undefined number. Oh. Okay. I see now. The slope of a vertical line is undefined. Ah. That means something now. I won't forget that!

For me, that moment was absolutely delicious. Renee had a history of difficulties with algebra, but here she had engaged in some real sense making. Now the math fit together for her. I was absolutely convinced that—for the first time—she would have and hold on to the notion of slope.

Proud of the tape, I showed it to a visiting colleague. As the tape progressed, she got more and more uncomfortable. She barely made it through to Renee's epiphany—and, once she did and I turned the tape off, she said, "You know, Alan, when we build our instruction we work with master teachers. A number of the teachers I work with could have explained the content to this student in much more straightforward ways." From my colleague's perspective, my teaching was terrible and a waste of time.

What I had attended to in my interaction with Renee was her nascent under-standings and the ways I could help her to build a solid knowledge structure with them. What my colleague had noticed was that Renee had a misconcep-tion—and that she could set Renee straight by telling her the right way to think about things.

In short, my orientations toward mathematical sense making and to what I have come to call "diagnostic teaching"—understanding and working with the knowledge students bring with them to any mathematical situation—led me to notice particular things in Renee's approach to the topic of slope, and to work with them. My colleague's orientation toward laying out content in clear ways and her orientation toward misconceptions as things to be undone or overridden resulted in her not noticing the parts of Renee's work that contained the seeds of sense making. In short, what you attend to—what you notice—is in large mea-sure a function of your orientations.

This, too, is consequential. The story I just told is hardly unique. Here is another example. I spent a year in the classroom of a well-liked and well-respected (by students and colleagues) teacher, who took a very didactic, step-by-step approach to instruction. One day I asked him if he had ever thought of just throwing a problem at his students and seeing what they would do with it. "Not these stu-dents," he said; "it would just confuse them. I might do that with my honors students, but not these." You can imagine what he was attuned to seeing and responding to in his students' work, and how that shaped his students' opportuni-ties to think mathematically.

These examples point to a fundamental point, that teachers' orientations to students, to mathematics, and to teaching have a fundamental impact on what they notice (and then do). So does teacher knowledge, in at least two ways. This was a main point of Kazemi et al.'s and Schifter's chapters (this volume, chapters 12 and 13). Consider any student comment with nascent mathematical potential, e.g., the third grader's question about whether multiplication and division are related in the ways that addition and subtraction are related. How much math-ematical knowledge does it take to be able to see the connection? How much mathematical and pedagogical knowledge does it take to help students see the connection? Absent these, some things will go unnoticed, and some things will not be acted on.

Let me make this point with another relatively elementary problem, discussed in a recent SERP meeting. The problem, drawn from Smith, Hughes, Engle, and Stein (2009), asks whether one is more likely to pick a blue marble at random from a bag that contains 75 red and 25 blue marbles, 40 red and 20 blue marbles, or 100 red and 25 blue marbles. The "standard" way to do this problem is to convert to percentages: the three bags have 25%, 33%, and 20% blue marbles, so the second bag is the best choice. But some students will focus on the ratio of red to blue marbles, some on the ratio of blue to red, some on the total number of marbles. Each of these *can* yield a solution, of different degrees of opaqueness to sixth graders. For example, the ratio of red to blue in the three bags is 3 to 1, 2 to 1, and 4 to 1 respectively; if you want the *largest* chance of getting a blue, you want the *smallest* ratio of red to blue. But what if the ratios do not work out nicely? You can scale up until all the bags have the same number of blues, and see which has the fewest reds. In the case of the given bags of marbles, 25, 20, and 25 all go into 100; the scaled-up bags would have 300 red and 100 blue, 200 red and 100 blue, and 400 red and 100 blue. The second bag is the best bet. This method generalizes: If the bags have A, B, and C blues, you can scale all of them up to have ABC blues, and then compare the reds. Similarly, you can equalize reds. The numbers 75, 40, and 100 all go into 600, so the three bags scaled up to have 600 reds would have 200 blue, 300 blue, and 150 blue respectively. Or you might scale up all three bags so that they have the same number of marbles. Under this condition, the bag with the most blues (again the second, of course) is the one that wins.

The point is that one has to know that such approaches can be productive if one is to recognize the seeds of a possible correct approach in a student comment; and one needs to be able to navigate the mathematical territory (at a level appropriate for the students!) if one decides to capitalize on what the students have said. Noticing is essential, but it does not suffice by itself. It takes place within the context of teachers' knowledge and orientations; and the decisions that teachers make regarding whether and how to follow up on what they notice are shaped by the teachers' knowledge (more broadly, resources) and orientations. Of course, what the teacher decides to do is also shaped by the teacher's goals. If the teacher is focused on helping students see mathematical connections, then pursuing the range of approaches to the probability problem described in the previous paragraph might be established as a goal. If the teacher's goal in introducing the problem is to provide students with practice using percentages to solve a certain class of probability problems, then pointers to alternative ways of thinking about the problem will not be noticed or, if they are noticed, will not be acted on.

In sum, teachers' decision making is shaped by what teachers notice. That is the raison d'être of this book. But what teachers notice, and how they act on it, is a function of the teachers' knowledge and resources, goals, and orientations. Hence the study of noticing must be situated within the larger picture of teacher decision making. An extensive treatment of teacher decision making is given in Schoenfeld (2010); some of the literature leading up to that volume can be found in Schoenfeld (1998, 1999).

And Next?

The editors have, themselves, provided a tentative answer to the question of what comes next. In the opening chapter of this book Sherin, Jacobs, and Philipp

> encourage readers to consider these questions while reading each chapter:
>
> 1. Is teacher noticing trainable? . . .
> 2. What trajectories of development related to noticing expertise exist for prospective and practicing teachers? . . .
> 3. How context specific is noticing expertise? . . .
> 4. How can researchers most productively study teacher noticing? . . .
> 5. Why do we (or should we) study teacher noticing?
>
> Sherin, Jacobs, & Philipp (this volume, chapter 1, p. 11)

This book as a whole stands in answer to Question 5. As noted above, the things that teachers notice (or fail to notice) shape what they act on. Noticing is thus a fundamental part of teachers' decision making—and highly consequential.

I think that Questions 1 through 4 (as elaborated by the editors in chapter 1) make for an excellent agenda for the field. Here I annotate those questions with a few additional remarks.

Is Teacher Noticing Trainable?

There is, to my mind, no question that the answer to this question is yes. That was in part the point of my opening vignettes; it is the underlying assumption of all the chapters in this book. But we will need a more refined set of questions to address what people can be trained to notice under what (personal) circumstances, and when teachers can be in a position to notice things and act profitably on them. As discussed in the previous section, noticing is very much a function of resources, goals, and orientations. Hence what is trainable, for whom, and when is not a simple matter. Sorting that out should be part of the research agenda.

What Trajectories of Development Related to Noticing Expertise Exist for Prospective and Practicing Teachers?

I would like to second the importance of this question and to reframe it slightly. There are no simple or uniform trajectories, as an individual's growth is always a function of experience, opportunity to reflect, and so on. (There *are* homogeneities, of course.) Rather than think of trajectories, I have been thinking recently in terms of *planes of activity and attention* on the part of teachers. My recent focus has been on the notion of *diagnostic teaching*, which is close enough to be useful for this discussion. The basic idea is that all teachers engage in multiple activities, among them classroom management, implementing engaging mathematical activities, and engaging in diagnostic teaching (listening to students, noticing important things, and building on those in the course of the lesson). Typically, a beginning teacher works hard at the first two, with a large percentage of his or her time devoted to the first. Thus a typical beginning profile might be represented as in Figure 14.2.

As teachers develop, they become more proficient at implementing engaging activities. One consequence of this is that they need to devote less overt time to issues of classroom management—when students are engaged doing mathematics, they do not need to be "managed." Thus, a time-and-attention profile of a typical accomplished teacher can be represented as in Figure 14.3.

Highly accomplished teachers—teachers who engage in noticing as a matter of practice, and use their observations to shape their instruction—are those who, in my framing, are largely engaged in diagnostic teaching. When the instruction builds on what students know and can do, it is much more likely to be engaging; and thus there is minimal need (once classroom norms have been established) for overt attention to classroom management. A time-and-attention profile of a highly accomplished teacher is represented in Figure 14.4.

I suspect that this form of representation (entirely consistent with the overarching perspective in this book) will be a useful way of tracing teacher trajectories.

A final note about trajectories and about change: *Change is slow.* It would be nice if one could get teachers to embrace the idea of noticing, and that changes in practice would follow. But, as explained above, noticing is intimately tied to orientations and resources—and these change very slowly. (David Cohen's

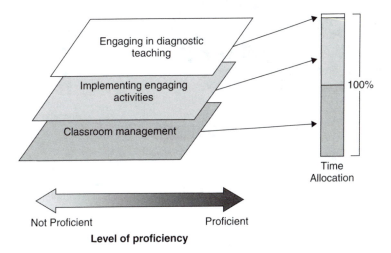

FIGURE 14.2   Levels of proficiency and time allocations of a typical beginning teacher

Note: The degree of shading in the planes represents the level of proficiency, and the arrows point to the percentage of time devoted to each plane of activity. Reprinted with permission from *How we think: A theory of human decision making with educational applications*, by A. H. Schoenfeld, 2010.

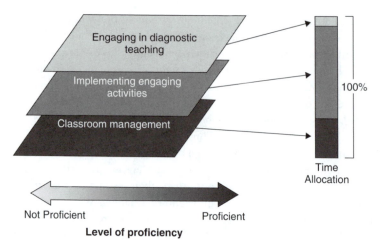

FIGURE 14.3   Levels of proficiency and time allocations of a typical accomplished teacher

Note: The degree of shading in the planes represents the level of proficiency, and the arrows point to the percentage of time devoted to each plane of activity. Reprinted with permission from *How we think: A theory of human decision making with educational applications*, by A. H. Schoenfeld, 2010.

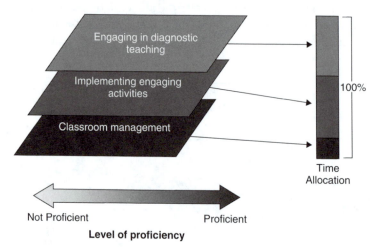

FIGURE 14.4   Levels of proficiency and time allocations of a highly accomplished teacher

Note: The degree of shading in the planes represents the level of proficiency, and the arrows point to the percentage of time devoted to each plane of activity. Reprinted with permission from *How we think: A theory of human decision making with educational applications*, by A. H. Schoenfeld, 2010.

1990 study "A Revolution in One Classroom: The Case of Mrs. Oublier" is a case in point. Mrs. Oublier adopted the rhetoric of reform, but her actions were grounded in her well-established classroom routines—and thus often contradicted her rhetorical stance. To act on what one notices, resources, goals, orientations, and the propensity to notice must all be somewhat in synch—and the growth of these takes time. Studies of teacher trajectories with regard to noticing must, therefore, look at more than "just" noticing. They must place noticing within the context of the teachers' growing knowledge (resources), goals, and orientations.

How Context Specific Is Noticing Expertise?

This is a lovely question, which will also require significant unpacking. Just what is a context? Is it the grade level? Is it the mathematics being studied? Is it the students' perceived ability? Is it the school and its socioeconomic characteristics? Is it some combination of these, and perhaps other things? It remains to be seen which of these will turn out to be analytically fruitful.

How Can Researchers Most Productively Study Teacher Noticing?

This, I hope, will be an ongoing issue as the field develops. This book makes a substantial contribution to that development.

References

Cohen, D. K. (1990). A revolution in one classroom: The case of Mrs. Oublier. *Educational Evaluation and Policy Analysis, 12*, 311–329.

Erickson, F. (this volume, chapter 2). *On noticing teacher noticing.*

Gladwell, M. (2008). *Outliers.* New York: Little, Brown.

Goldsmith, L. T., and Seago, N. (this volume, chapter 11). *Using classroom artifacts to focus teachers' noticing: Affordances and opportunities.*

Jacobs, V. R., Lamb, L. L. C., Philipp, R. A., & Schappelle, B. P. (this volume, chapter 7). *Deciding how to respond on the basis of children's understandings.*

Kazemi, E., Elliott, R., Mumme, J., Carroll, C., Lesseig, K., & Kelley-Petersen, M. (this volume, chapter 12). *Noticing leaders' thinking about videocases of teachers engaged in mathematics tasks in professional development.*

Mason, J. (this volume, chapter 3). *Noticing: Roots and branches.*

Miller, K. F. (this volume, chapter 4). *Situation awareness in teaching: What educators can learn from video-based research in other fields.*

Santagata, R. (this volume, chapter 10). *From teacher noticing to a framework for analyzing and improving classroom lessons.*

Schifter, D. (this volume, chapter 13). *Examining the behavior of operations: Noticing early algebraic ideas.*

Schoenfeld, A. H. (1998). Toward a theory of teaching-in-context. *Issues in Education, 4*(1), 1–94.

Schoenfeld, A. H. (Special Issue Ed.) (1999). *Examining the complexity of teaching.* Special issue of the *Journal of Mathematical Behavior, 18*(3).

Schoenfeld, A. H. (2010). *How we think: A theory of human decision making with educational applications.* New York: Routledge.

Sherin, B., & Star, J. R. (this volume, chapter 5). *Reflections on the study of teacher noticing.*

Sherin, M. G., Jacobs, V. R., & Philipp, R. A. (this volume, chapter 1). *Situating the study of teacher noticing.*

Sherin, M. G., Russ, R. S., & Colestock, A. A. (this volume, chapter 6). *Accessing mathematics teachers' in-the-moment noticing.*

Smith, M. S., Hughes, E. K., Engle, R. A., & Stein, M. K. (2009). Orchestrating discussions. *Mathematics Teaching in the Middle School, 14*(9), 549–556.

Star, J. R., Lynch, K., & Perova, N. (this volume, chapter 8). *Using video to improve preservice mathematics teachers' abilities to attend to classroom features: A replication study.*

van Es, E. A. (this volume, chapter 9). *A framework for learning to notice student thinking.*

AUTHOR INDEX

SUBJECT INDEX

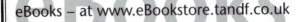

eBooks – at www.eBookstore.tandf.co.uk

A library at your fingertips!

eBooks are electronic versions of printed books. You can
store them on your PC/laptop or browse them online.

They have advantages for anyone needing rapid access
to a wide variety of published, copyright information.

eBooks can help your research by enabling you to
bookmark chapters, annotate text and use instant searches
to find specific words or phrases. Several eBook files would
fit on even a small laptop or PDA.

NEW: Save money by eSubscribing: cheap, online access
to any eBook for as long as you need it.

Annual subscription packages

We now offer special low-cost bulk subscriptions to
packages of eBooks in certain subject areas. These are
available to libraries or to individuals.

For more information please contact
webmaster.ebooks@tandf.co.uk

We're continually developing the eBook concept, so
keep up to date by visiting the website.

www.eBookstore.tandf.co.uk